Assessment and Correction of Language Arts Difficulties

Assessment and Correction of Language Arts Difficulties

PAUL C. BURNS

The University of Tennessee

Charles E. Merrill Publishing Company
A Bell & Howell Company
Columbus Toronto London Sydney

Published by
Charles E. Merrill Publishing Co.
A Bell & Howell Company
Columbus, Ohio 43216

This book was set in Oracle and Souvenir
Cover Design Coordination: Will Chenoweth
Production Coordination: Linda Hillis Bayma

COVER PHOTO: Dan Unkefer

Library of Congress Catalog Card Number: 79-89816
International Standard Book Number: 0-675-08198-X

1 2 3 4 5 6 7 8 9 10—85 84 83 82 81 80

Printed in the United States of America

Preface

Assessment and Correction of Language Arts Difficulties is designed to provide pre-service and in-service teachers with a complete view of concerns and issues in the area of corrective language arts instruction. In addition, the text presents practical techniques for helping students who exhibit language arts disabilities.

The text, providing major attention upon diagnostic/prescriptive procedures, may be used in conjunction with developmental language arts texts for college-level language arts methods courses. Classes designed specifically to focus upon language arts difficulties should find the text particularly useful. The book could also be used to good advantage by consultants and participants in conferences and workshops and other professional growth projects.

Assessment and Correction of Language Arts Difficulties is committed to the premise that learning can best be facilitated when the teacher takes a diagnostic view of the instructional process. Strategies and materials are suggested to help translate this principle into application and practice.

The text includes a number of special features, including:

1. The table of contents suggests the comprehensiveness of the text. For example, prior to discussion of specific areas of the language arts, attention is focused upon important general topics, such as factors that may be related to language arts difficulties, foundations for diagnostic teaching, tools for assessment, and some general resources. In these chapters, the reader is alerted to adjustments that may be made for disabled lan-

guage arts students; a diagnostic/prescriptive model; guidelines for diagnosis and remediation; a discussion of informal
and formal assessment instruments to probe readiness, basic
skills, affective dimensions, and aptitude; and numerous resources including activities and games, trade books, and multilevel materials, as well as classroom physical arrangements and
the role of parents and specialized personnel. Similarly, a
glance at the index suggests the scope and thoroughness of the
text: bibliotherapy, cloze, Fernald's VAKT, Gillingham's VAK,
language experience approach, modality testing, readability,
T-units.

2. Major areas of the language arts are examined in terms of disabilities and corrective suggestions: listening, oral communication, and written communication. Complete chapters are devoted to two facets of written expression: spelling and handwriting.

3. Each chapter dealing with a major area of the language arts
provides information relative to assessment, frequent disabilities, and explicit ideas for corrective instruction. Each of these
chapters also includes a separate section entitled Additional
Corrective Activities.

4. A case report is presented in the last chapter of the text. This
chapter pulls together much of the information presented in the
preceding chapters and so serves as a review of many important
ideas. Additionally, it associates the case study with the Individual Education Program (IEP) and various legal aspects inher-
ent in current mainstreaming endeavors.

5. All chapters conclude with Study Questions and Activities.
These are designed to help the reader determine and extend
his or her knowledge of important information presented in the
chapters.

6. At the conclusion of the book, the Selected References provide a listing of books and articles dealing with corrective/
remedial language arts for those who wish to supplement the
textbook material. The appendix provides sample scope and sequence charts for grammar, spelling, and handwriting.

7. Many examples of check lists, evaluation guides, inventories,
record-keeping devices, and sourcebooks are provided throughout the text.

8. Specific instructional activities to be used with corrective students are offered in abundance. These activities are presented
in a variety of forms: contract cards, grouping patterns, learning centers and packets, performance-oriented lessons, special

work sheets, teacher-made activities and games. Thus, this text should be a valuable reference book for a person who is currently teaching, as well as for a student in a methods class.

The author is indebted to many persons for their aid and support during the preparation of this book. Sincere thanks are expressed to reviewers who provided ideas and suggestions.

Finally, I wish to thank Linda Hillis Bayma, series editor at Charles E. Merrill, for her outstanding contribution to this text.

Contents

1
Causes of Language Arts Difficulties

Only rarely can one factor be specified as the cause of a child's difficulties with language; generally, there are several factors involved. Causal factors are not easy to pinpoint, but prescribing the uniquely appropriate treatment for each factor is even more difficult. By studying the various factors, teachers try to choose corrective materials and strategies most appropriate to the suspected causes. Each of the following factors that may cause disabilities will be discussed briefly in this chapter.

- Physical factors
- Intellectual factors
- Emotional factors
- Experiential and environmental factors
- Educational factors

PHYSICAL FACTORS

Vision

Vision is a factor because language learning begins with seeing. Certain vision problems are frequently found among disabled learners. Hyperopia (farsightedness) appears to be related to reading difficulties while myopia (nearsightedness) does not. Binocular difficulties, that is, problems connected with using the eyes together, occur more frequently in disabled learners than in average learners. Fusion problems, which are related to focusing the eyes in order to see a clear image, also occur more frequently in disabled learners.

Children with vision problems might exhibit symptoms such as these:

squinting
closing or covering one eye when reading
rubbing the eyes frequently
holding books too close or too far away when reading
red or inflamed eyes
frequent blinking
moving the head excessively when reading
frequent errors when copying board work

The teacher may find that a list such as the *Educator's Checklist: Observable Clues to Classroom Vision Problems* (Duncan, Oklahoma: Optometric Extension Program Foundation, 1968) will be useful in recording observations. Additional screening may be conducted using one of the following instruments:

Keystone Visual Survey Telebinocular, 2212 E. 12th Street, Davenport, Iowa 52803
Orthor-Rater, Bausch and Lomb Optical Co., Rochester, New York
Professional Vision Tester, Titmus Optical Co., Petersburg, Virginia
Titmus Biopter, Titmus Optical Co., Petersburg, Virginia

If several symptoms are evident, there is little doubt that the student should be referred for further examination. In the case of one or two symptoms, the teacher must use his or her judgment. Where there is any doubt about the seriousness of the problem, the child should be referred for further screening and examination. Any vision screening conducted by teachers should be considered preliminary to referral for examination by a specialist, an optometrist or an ophthalmologist.

The partially sighted or visually impaired child will require teaching and classroom adjustments, such as much instruction by touch, reading aloud and cassette tapes to build listening skills, seat close to chalkboard, large type books, keeping close work (such as writing) to a short period, adjusting shades so there will be no glare on the chalkboard, and minimizing the use of projectors that require a lighted screen. The child should wear properly fitted glasses.

Visual perception refers to the ability to correctly interpret visual symbols. Visual perception includes visual discrimination, which is the skill of seeing likenesses and differences in the physical characteristics of letters and words. Visual perception is a significant factor in language arts activities since many letters and words look very much alike in English; for example, the letters *b* and *d* or the words *was* and *saw*.

Hearing

Hearing influences language arts achievement because the learner often needs to make an association between the pronunciation of a word and the printed symbol. This is inhibited by hearing problems. Youngsters who are hard-of-hearing or hearing impaired show definite difficulty in acquiring some language arts skills and will need adjustments in teaching procedures, particularly reading and spelling instruction. The teacher will try to—

seat the child where he can read the teacher's lips.
allow the light to fall on the teacher's face.
speak slowly, clearly, and with adequate volume.
seat the child as far as possible from distracting sounds.
minimize the use of auditory channels in instruction.
provide materials that have clearly written instructions.

Auditory acuity refers to the physical ability to hear sounds. Research indicates that there are more cases of impaired auditory acuity among disabled learners than among average learners. Teachers can screen children for auditory acuity by noting the common symptoms, such as inattentiveness in class, turning the head so that the same ear always faces the speaker, asking the teacher to repeat directions, frowning when listening, and frequent rubbing of ears and earaches. If observations suggest the likelihood of a hearing problem, the child should have an audiometer test administered by trained personnel.

Auditory discrimination is a part of auditory perception—attaching meaning to the sounds heard. Auditory discrimination refers to the ability to hear likenesses and differences in the sounds of letters and of words. This is an important skill since many English language words have sounds in common—such as *run* and *fun*.

Perception

Some children who have no visual or hearing handicap have difficulty in processing visual or auditory sensations or stimuli correctly. Such perceptual difficulty may be exhibited in a significant discrepancy between the child's intellectual potential and his or her actual level of performance. The difficulty is often referred to as "learning disability." Perceptual difficulties may be of various types: *receptive perceptions, associational perceptions,* or *expressive perceptions.*

Receptive perceptions are those received by the brain through the visual or auditory senses (for example, identifying objects or situations described by the teacher). Associational perceptions call for the receiver to make connections in thought. The sensations that stimulate mental associations can be visual or auditory (for example, pairing objects by their use or function, as *needle* and *thread*). Expressive perceptions are those manifested vocally or using motor expression (for example, using a finger play).

Speech

Speech impairments exist when speech interferes with communication. While there are several categories of speech difficulties, the two that most frequently may interfere with learning in the classroom are articulation and stuttering. A child may exhibit articulatory disorders through continued use of substitutions, omissions, or distortions. Articulatory disorders that are the result of neuromuscular or structural deviations (such as cleft palate, cleft lip, cerebral palsy, or extreme malocclusion of the teeth) will require the attention of a specialist.

The most constructive steps the teacher can take are to help the child and his parents develop healthy attitudes toward a speech handicap, relieve anxieties and tensions, and enhance the classroom envirionment by improving the attitudes of the child's peers. Beyond this, classroom teachers help these children by attending to each child's particular speech needs.

General Health

Good general health is important to the learner. It enables him or her to be alert and to concentrate. Any physical condition which decreases the child's vitality creates fatigue and makes it difficult to be attentive. Poor health also may interfere with school attendance. Teachers may rely on observation, parent interviews, and permanent records for information regarding general health. Information should be sought from parents, other teachers, and the student regarding chronic and extended illnesses, allergies, stamina, medication, eating and sleeping habits, and school absences. Where justified, the child should be referred to a physician for a thorough physical examination.

INTELLECTUAL FACTORS

For many years intelligence tests have been used to predict academic potential. While intelligence is related to language at all levels, the correlation between intelligence and language arts success is closer in the higher grades of school.

Intelligence tests attempt to measure the abilities that have been developed by experiences. An important dimension of experience is language (oral and written). Much of the individual's experiences and store of information is processed through language and is blocked by lack of language ability, possibly causing many language disabled children to have low scores on intelligence tests. Intelligence tests also measure vocabulary in order to assess intelligence level. The vocabulary of the language disabled student may be limited by his lack of reading ability, and vice versa: reading proficiency is limited by a small vocabulary.

The outcome of intelligence tests may be influenced by the child's general health, emotional outlook, fear of the testing situation, and cultural factors. The cultural bias of intelligence tests is particularly apparent because the tests were designed for middle-class children. Such factors may work together to make children of other socio-economic levels appear to have lower intelligence.

Accepting test scores alone as the measure of intellectual potential is unwise. Teachers must not view intelligence test scores as static nor should they have higher expectations for students who make high intelligence scores and lower expectations for children with lower scores. Intelligence test scores may become a self-fulfilling prophecy for the child because children tend to achieve in accordance with teacher expectation.

Intelligence may be measured by group intelligence tests or individual intelligence tests; group tests are not recommended for the poor achieving reader, since they are primarily tests of reading skill. Individual intelligence tests should be administered by certified psychologists.

Slow learning children are ones who do not learn as readily as others of the same chronological age. They form 15 to 17 percent of the school population that cannot quite "keep up" and are usually doing the least successful work in the regular classroom. Children of low ability have special needs: an extended readiness program, introduction of formal instruction in the language arts at a later time than for children of higher ability. They will progress more slowly and it will be necessary for them to stay in each stage of learning longer than the average pupils.

Any evaluation of a child's intellectual level should include the teacher's observations of the child in a variety of situations with emphasis on such things as attention span, memory span, interpersonal relationships, following directions, problem solving, and the like.

EMOTIONAL FACTORS

There is no doubt that a child's emotions are a significant factor in learning. Since the language arts are highly valued in a literate society, failure to develop language facility has strong emotional impact on the child. The precise relationship between emotions and the language arts is difficult to ascertain, but it is apparent that emotional maladjustment may be a cause or result of language arts disability. Furthermore, the relationship between emotions and academic achievement is circular—each affects the other. Self-concept, which is one of the most important dimensions of emotional development, is very significant in language arts success or failure.

A large percentage of disabled language arts students manifest symptoms of emotional maladjustment that indicate poor personal and social adjustment, as well as failure to deal with the demands of school life. The symptoms may range from aggression to the opposite extreme of passive withdrawal.

Maladjusted children are frequently rejected by teachers who react negatively to their problems. Obviously, teacher rejection further complicates the problem. Unhappy relationships with teachers increase student anxiety—and anxiety has specific side effects in the language arts. It disorganizes behavior so the child cannot concentrate on the task at hand and decreases the ability to understand and to operate in new situations.

Teachers need to study the emotional reactions of children. Interviews with the child can aid in the diagnosis of emotional problems. Furthermore, teachers need to be sensitive to the emotional difficulties of children. When teachers understand the emotions exhibited by children (negative self-concept, anxiety, agression or withdrawal, negative feelings about home and school, extreme distaste for the language arts), they can better adapt instruction to meet the needs of pupils.

EXPERIENTIAL AND ENVIRONMENTAL FACTORS

The child's home life and his language experiences are important factors in language arts learning.

Home

Although it is difficult to establish a causal relationship between the home and language arts disability, many of the characteristics which are closely related to language arts success are influenced by the home environment. The home that provides love, understanding, and a feeling of security is the best possible preparation for learning.

Children who come from homes where the parents are able to provide good nutrition, opportunities for adequate rest, and a stable environment will have advantages in the learning situation. Children from homes where reading materials are available and language skills are valued by the parents have an advantage in school. So do children whose parents provide broad experiential backgrounds and encourage verbal interaction. Experiences are necessary for conceptual development; children who lack basic experiences also lack the basic concepts necessary for comprehension of language arts tasks.

Language

One source of language interference is dialect. The impact of a nonstandard dialect on the acquisition of language skills has not been fully resolved, but it is obvious that speakers of divergent dialects must experience some problems in speaking, reading, and writing standard English. Certainly speakers of divergent dialects have special needs: appreciation of their cultural backgrounds; a sense of personal worth; and concept and vocabulary development. Classroom practices will need to be examined to see if they provide a rich program in oral expression, an instructional program based on careful analysis of the child's language, and the like. Perhaps the most significant factor about dialect is the attitude and behavior of teachers toward children's oral language. In other words, while there may be little direct interference of dialect with language, there exists an enormous potential for indirect interference.

Observation of the child's language (vocabulary development, sentence structure, self-expression) is one of the best ways to diagnose the level of language development attained by individual children.

EDUCATIONAL FACTORS

There are a number of educational factors that may contribute to language arts difficulties: faulty early instruction, inappropriate materials, unbalanced language arts programs, and so forth. Any rigid curriculum or practice that prevents adjustments in instruction to meet individual needs will hinder pupil progress.

The consensus of language arts educators is that a large number of children with language difficulties have been handicapped through improper and inadequate classroom instruction. For this reason, some specific teaching weaknesses are stated below.

- Inadequate understanding of the language process and of the relationship of each major component (listening, speaking, reading, and writing) to the total process.
- Lack of a comprehensive language arts readiness or foundation program.
- Lack of a systematic program for the development of basic language arts skills.
- Inflexible use of one method or one set of instructional materials.
- Failure to adjust material to achievement levels and lack of adjustment to individual differences, particularly to those of faster and slower learners.
- Ineffective motivation of language arts interests.
- Failure to apply language arts skills in subjects such as social studies, mathematics, science.
- Failure to emphasize strengths as well as weaknesses. That is, providing children with practice in a weak area while they receive pleasure and status from doing something at which they are good. For example, a child can learn a great deal about spelling (weakness) while editing a poem (strength) for classroom display.

REVIEW QUESTIONS AND ACTIVITIES

1. What are some of the major causes of children's difficulties in learning language arts? Give some examples of language difficulties related to the causes. What may be done to alleviate the difficulty?
2. Develop a short paper on language arts for a child with one of the disabilities listed below. (See Selected References at end of this book for resource books.)

   mental deviation
   sensory handicap
   neurologic, orthopedic, or other health impairment
   behavioral (emotional) handicap
   communicative variation

3. Take one concept from the language, spelling, or handwriting charts in the Appendix and trace its scope and sequence through the grade levels.

2
Foundations
for
Diagnostic
Teaching

The Greek roots of the word "diagnostic" mean "to know thoroughly." Diagnostic teaching is knowing each child in the classroom: his capacities, his physiological condition, his emotional and social adjustments, his interests, attitudes, and drives, and his general level of language ability.

Diagnostic teaching is one way to provide for individual differences in children. Using this approach, the teacher can organize the classroom learning situation so that within reasonable limits each child can work at his own "next steps" in the ways which are most effective for him. It is *not* a panacea, but it does provide a way of working with children that is based on what is known about them and how they learn.

The "next step" idea reflects the view that learning takes place at the growing edge, and that all teaching efforts should be directed at this point. Teaching the child something he already knows will only bore him; trying to present materials the child does not have the previous experiences or competencies to deal with may make him feel that school is meaningless or that he does not have the ability to do what others expect of him. The teacher must search for the child's growing edge, or at least the range of his competencies, in order to select learnings appropriate for the child at a given time.

Continuous, functional assessment is an essential ingredient for the total instructional program as well as the language arts. Language arts diagnosis must not be solely a specialist function so that the techniques become divorced from the classroom teacher's concept of what his or her responsibility in the teaching of language arts must and does include. Diagnostic teaching, as described in this book, departs from the detailed, highly specialized, clinical analysis taught in many language arts clinics and focuses on the day-to-day decisions that have to be made to see that each pupil progresses in listening, speaking, and composition skills.

Most children with language difficulties can be located and treated successfully by the classroom teacher. All good teaching is diagnostic—and the classroom teacher can and must diagnose if language teaching is to become as effective, specific, and individualized as it needs to be.

This emphasis on the diagnostic point of view is not meant to imply that other evaluation devices are to be ignored. A broad spectrum of formal and informal procedures should be used, although, in practice, informal analysis, with its reliance upon intuitive judgments and observations, tends to take priority over such formal measures as standardized tests.

Diagnostic teaching is appropriate for all children: those who excel in language activities, those who sometimes have difficulty, and those who always have difficulty with language art skills. The diagnostic strategy enables the teacher to identify strong and weak areas in language skills for one child or the entire class, and to create teaching sequences which meet these specific needs.

The classroom teacher must also approach the language teaching process diagnostically. First, he must organize the various language art skills into some logical sequence, determining where each learner stands in the sequence. The teacher needs diagnostic tools and techniques to gather this information, but perhaps more than anything else, he needs an attitude that allows him to approach each classroom activity from a diagnostic point of view. Constantly on the alert for useful clues, the teacher watches for patterns of behavior that indicate an instructional need; he classifies information and relates it to language. Without such an approach, the task of teaching language arts can seem overwhelming. The myriad of necessary skills and the sea of children's faces can cause even a conscientious teacher to look for an easy way out—usually whole-class instruction with standard assignments and activities for everyone.

SOME DIAGNOSTIC PRINCIPLES OF LANGUAGE ARTS INSTRUCTION

The following principles should give some clues to the diagnostic approach to individualized instruction, classroom management, and use of materials.

Experience Background Is the Foundation for Language Study

While experiential background is important in all areas of the elementary school curriculum, it is particularly crucial in the language arts. The foundation for language study is the child's home experiences and community influences, and this fact is more fraught with implications for language instruction than, say, mathematics instruction.

The language ability of pupils entering school and in each succeeding year is likely to vary more than most other traits. For example, in a class of six-year-old pupils, one child might have a vocabulary of a 2,000 words; another, five or ten times that number. One child may speak in short, incomplete sentences while another uses long, complex sentences. To recognize this fact is not enough; the teacher must do something with the situation.

While the language of a child may differ from his classmate's and the teacher's—and *different* and *deficient* convey two separate ideas—the teacher must be willing to accept the child's modes of expression rather than condemning the child, his parents, or his culture. The teacher must accept each child as he is and use procedures that will provide for individual needs. A good rule is always to start at the concrete level, dealing with those things which a child knows, talks, and asks about; with material he can taste, touch, smell, manipulate, see, feel, and work. For example, caring for a gerbil in the classroom can generate considerable language learning. It provides an opportunity for children to talk and listen to each other, a focus for reading, telling, and writing stories, and a chance to grow in the vocabulary of common, everyday words.

The Language Arts Are Interrelated

While reading instruction is omitted from this book, the writer is aware that reading, writing, speaking, and listening are closely related. We write so someone else may read; what one reads can provide a "model" for one's own oral and written expression; and every act of speech is a listening act for someone else. While it is necessary to separate the language arts at times for instructional purposes, it must be kept in mind that they all share common elements and that an experience in one will reinforce another. Speaking and writing are both expressive skills, and listening and reading are especially related in that both are receptive. Spelling and reading are closely related since both involve the need for study of form and sounds of words. And, who could teach letter writing without giving attention to the skills of spelling, handwriting, and sentence structure—perhaps even listening and reading?

In a broader sense, language arts are an integral part of the entire daily curriculum since they are used in all other curriculum areas. Language learning increases a child's competency in all other areas of the curriculum; and, in turn, these areas provide use and content for the language activities.

Specific Skills Are Involved in the Language Program

The language arts must be taught through organized instruction. It cannot be assumed that the objectives of the language arts program will be automatically fulfilled. Incidental instruction will not provide the necessary understandings and learnings. Experiences, activities, and opportunities should be planned to incorporate the appropriate objectives.

The skills taught must be related to the life of the child, both present and future. This would suggest, for example, that words taught in spelling should be those which the child needs for his writing, not a long list of uncommon words.

Skills are acquired through imitation, direct instruction, and use in meaningful situations. Mechanics are most readily mastered in connection with a specific need at a specific time. For example, sometime during the year a business letter will be written in connection with the pupils' work. At that time, pupils can be taught the form of business letters. There is little or no need to make up topics for oral and written expression—these should be real and related to situations within the classroom.

Language learning must be used frequently if it is to be retained. The school tries to develop habits that cause pupils to be concerned about correct spelling, proofreading, and using specific procedures for learning to spell new words. The development of habits requires practice over a period of time. Pupils learn what they do, and if they are to speak and write well, they must be given practice in speaking and writing correctly.

Content and Teaching Procedures Are Strongly Aligned with the Language Arts

The content of the language arts program should be consistent with the findings of linguists concerning the nature of language—the history and development of English, dialect, speech intonation, different styles of usage, and grammar.

There are many aspects of teaching which are equally important for language arts and other subjects—one starts at the level of the child; individual differences and needs serve as the basis of instruction; and different styles of learning are respected and taken into consideration—but the following are aspects which are more or less unique to language instruction.

Oral language development is fundamental to the other language arts. Children who express themselves effectively in speech tend to succeed in other areas of language arts. For example, written expression is enhanced when it is the outgrowth of rich and frequent opportunities for speech activities.

Pupils should work with content in practical situations before the ideas are analyzed. In an introductory lesson in conversation, the initial experience might be to divide the class into groups and let each group converse. After this experience, the pupils may discuss the criteria for a good conversation. This procedure permits pupils to decide upon some basic standards without specifically criticizing individuals, and the evaluation of further conversations may be made from the group-evolved standards rather than "teacher standards." Inductive teaching is an especially productive technique. For example, the teacher writes sentences from pupil papers on the chalkboard—using *saw* and *seen*—and asks the pupils how the constructions are alike and different. Pupils would be encouraged to see a pattern for themselves, forming their own conclusion or generalization about the accepted use of words.

For fuller language development, the child must participate actively in the process of learning. Growth in any curriculum area requires action; growth in language skills requires greater action. The teacher who understands this will make every effort to see that each assignment has a purpose that is clear to the child and is related to his or her own concern. This can come about through well-planned instruction, the use of appropriate materials, and cooperatively established goals that will keep the pupil progressing steadily within his own level toward the next level.

All this implies the dynamic effect of interest on children's learning. Here "interest" should not be interpreted in a simplistic manner. Interest is a motivating force which leads to action and evokes effort. It gives the child a feeling of personal ownership of his learning tasks.

Because of the creative, intimate, personal nature of the relationship between language and the child, a feeling of regard and respect for the worth of each child must be maintained. This is important for successful learning in all areas; for language development it is essential. How can a pupil exhibit his thoughts and feelings in oral and written expression if he is made to feel inadequate? How can he have access to his sources of creative strength if he does not believe in himself? True respect creates a climate favorable to response; and acceptance by the teacher gives the pupil the courage to be himself. This is a frank plea for teachers to afford the acceptance, appreciation, empathy, encouragement, and support that provide an atmosphere for learning. Where that atmosphere is missing, it will be recognized by the child with detrimental effects to teaching and learning. It is missing where the teacher scolds, shames, or ridicules the pupil's efforts before others; where threats or sarcasm are used; where pupils are criticized for their best efforts; where undue pressure is exerted. When a child sees that his efforts count for something, he honestly tries. Tangible evidence of success will motivate him to keep on trying.

In summary, the personal development of the pupil is of paramount concern. The preceding four principles are only building blocks to achieve this goal. Language instruction must be varied to fit the different capabilities and needs of individual children. Numerous resources may be used to help provide for individual differences in learning and these are suggested in the following chapters.

INSTRUCTIONAL APPROACHES AND MATERIALS

As children discuss plans for a field trip, write letters requesting materials for a social studies project, or tell a story that they have read or heard, the opportunity is present for a language lesson. Such developmental lessons often include the following features:

Use of natural and meaningful experiences. It cannot be assumed that children's speaking and writing will improve through a discussion of the need for improvement and a program of practice exercises or activities.

Planning by teacher and pupils. What objectives are to be stressed and how they will be accomplished must be clear to both teacher and pupils.

Attention given by the receiver of the expression. Such attention motivates the child to make his expression as effective as possible.

Providing a model. If a teacher wants children to write neat letters, to give effective reports, and to tell stories well, he must present models for them to see and hear—the teacher himself, tape recordings, samples found in textbooks or composed by the class.

Standards established in the pupils' own words. These standards may be recorded in writing on the board or put on a chart where they can be seen and referred to as needed. Suggestions for standards may be obtained from the pupil's textbooks.

Self-correction. While a child can learn much in a school year about comparing his product with the standards, real skill in self- and group criticism is developed over several years.

Evaluation and diagnosis. By evaluating lessons, the teacher and pupils can identify specific errors, poor habits, and special weaknesses.

Diagnostic Teaching Procedures

It is in the process of evaluation that diagnostic teaching begins to differ considerably from traditional teaching. Flexibility will be the keynote. There will be times when the teacher and the total group work together (for example, on types of mistakes that are rather general). At other times, small groups may work by themselves (the same specific learning is needed, or additional practice is needed for retention and transfer); or individuals will work alone (errors that can be corrected individually). There may be combinations of small group and individual activities with the teacher working first with one and then another. Children who have mastered a concept may be directed to enrichment activities. Reteaching may be necessary for some children who have not profited from the instructional sequence and need a different set of learning experiences.

This flexible classroom structure requires records on each pupil. There are many ways to maintain such records; one is a loose-leaf notebook with each child's name on a tab so his pages can be found quickly. The purpose of the record is to note learnings the child has achieved and those he has yet to acquire. It provides the basis for teaching to meet an immediate need, either in groups or with individuals, and it helps to organize learners into useful and defensible teaching groups.

The flexible classroom model attempts to meet many learner needs. Each child is placed in a group or taught individually on the basis of specific demonstrated needs and interests. Intergroup mobility is made easy, and labeling which is characteristic of many plans using some type of homogeneous grouping is prevented. The whole-class activities help each child identify with the total peer group, providing interaction and interchange with the entire class. The use of clear-cut objectives helps in the defining of goals and evaluation of pupil progress. Finally, the child has continuous feedback from peers, teachers, and diagnostic evaluations concerning his success.

How can the proposed model be implemented? The first step is to define the instructional program in specific terms. Overviews of the scope and sequence of language, spelling, and handwriting skills appear in charts provided by the publishers of basal texts. (See examples in Appendix.)

Some of the major language skills and mechanics treated in elementary school language arts textbooks include the following:

    I. Language (its changes and development)
   II. Grammar
      A. Phonology
      B. Morphology
      C. Classes and structure of words
      D. Syntax
  III. Listening (informative, appreciative, critical)
  IV. Oral composition
      A. Conversation
      B.' Discussion
      C. Description, comparison, evaluation
      D. Reporting
      E. Storytelling
      F. Drama
      G. Other oral expression
         1. Making announcements
         2. Giving messages, directions, explanations
         3. Giving reviews of
            a. books
            b. movies
            c. television programs
         4. Using the telephone
         5. Making introductions and observing social courtesies
         6. Conducting interviews
         7. Conducting meetings
   V. Written composition
      A. Creative writing
         1. Prose
         2. Poetry
      B. Functional writing
         1. Letters (friendly and business)
         2. Reports
         3. Announcements and notices
         4. Records
         5. Forms
         6. Library, research skills

    C. Conventions
      1. Capitalization
      2. Punctuation
      3. Sentence sense
      4. Paragraph sense
 VI. Common elements of oral and written expression
    A. Vocabulary
    B. Semantics
    C. Lexicography and use of reference and information sources
    D. Usage
 VII. Literature
    A. Oral reading
    B. Prose and poetry
    C. Close silent reading
    D. Magazines and periodicals
    E. Visual arts
 VIII. Spelling
  IX. Handwriting

Having established the instructional program, the second step is to begin an informal preliminary evaluation. Simply by listening to children tell stories, make reports, and engage in discussions, and by examining compositions, the teacher can make some estimate of the general language ability of the class, identifying exceptional children, and possibly locating some specific areas of weakness.

The third step is to supplement this general evaluation with a more detailed, systematic analysis. Each pupil's level of performance on specific skills and subskills can be determined by using a device such as Chart 2–1.

CHART 2-1.   Punctuation skills: the period

Subskills	Pupil A	Pupil B	Pupil C
End of declarative sentence			
End of imperative sentence			
After abbreviations of titles before names			
After abbreviations in addresses			
After initials in a proper name			
After numerals in a list			
After Roman numeral in outlines			

More comprehensive charts may also be useful: for example, a check list for writing skills might cover capital letters, periods, commas, apostrophes, and quotation marks, and other major subskills—the particulars recorded will vary with the grade and ability levels of the children. Furthermore, since the same abilities and skills operate to some extent in many different language arts exercises—having something to say, sticking to the point, organizing logically, and using appropriate words and varied sentences apply to conversation, discussion, storytelling, and letter writing—a master check list of abilities and skills for all types of language experiences could be prepared. But for the beginning teacher's own information, and possibly for the use of pupils, it might be profitable to complete a separate check list for each major type of language experience.

The fourth step is to group children for instruction according to their individual needs, and provide them with appropriate instruction and practice materials.

Fifth, a test may be given to see whether difficulties are being corrected. Records of progress should be maintained by the teacher and by the pupil. This procedure provides a powerful incentive for corrective work.

Figure 2–1 summarizes in schematic form the procedure outlined in this section (see p. 20).

The flexible classroom format is not the only model which can be followed. Some teachers prefer to leave children in heterogeneous groupings where they can learn from each other and where subskills needed by some children can be practiced. For example, children needing practice in punctuation, in capitalization, or in sentence structure could all benefit when the class produces a newspaper. With the newspaper project, which is usually a powerful motivator, all children can continue to maintain skills they have mastered.

Supporting this point of view is the fact that real life situations involve many skills at once; by careful planning, teachers can manage to have children practicing skills on which they need to work. For example, using the newspaper idea, children needing practice in oral expression may serve as reporters or interviewers, while others needing practice in writing may be asked to prepare stories or columns.

A Systematic Lesson Plan

A sample lesson plan that involves a diagnostic and prescriptive approach is provided below. Figure 2–2 indicates the teaching sequence (see p. 21).

Performance Objectives
Given a set of data, the learner makes an oral announcement of an event, including five basic facts.

1. Establishment of scope and sequence of skills to be taught

2. Informal class evaluation

3. Determination of individual pupil's performance level

4. Application of appropriate strategies and materials, with flexible groupings for:

      a. reteaching

      b. presentation of specific skills

      c. additional practice

      d. enrichment activities

      e. meeting individual needs

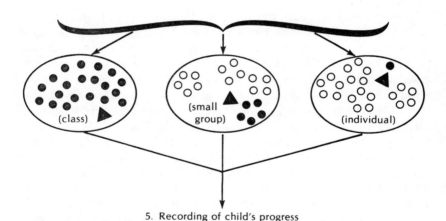

5. Recording of child's progress

FIGURE 2-1.   Flexible classroom

Pretest
Select an announcement that is appropriate to the learner and situation. For example, "Miss Brown's class invites you to our program about tools on Wednesday, November 23, at 2:00 p.m. in our classroom, Room 112. We hope you will be able to come." Read it aloud. Ask the student for the number of basic facts supplied. (These facts should be of the *who, what, why, when,* and *where.* Included would be (a) description of the event, (b) who is invited, (c) the date, (d) the time, and (e) the place—and price of

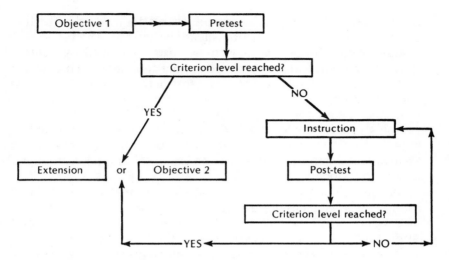

FIGURE 2-2. Flowchart of a teaching sequence (systematic)

admission if required.) Criterion for mastery is 80 percent. The purpose of this exercise is to be certain that the pupil attends to the basic facts needed in an oral announcement about an event.

Teaching Suggestions
Before reading a sample announcement, put the following formula on the chalkboard: Who? What? Why? When? Where?
Ask the learner to use this formula as a guide in making an announcement about a pet show to be held by his class.

Mastery or Posttest Suggestions
Assign a forthcoming event for an oral announcement. Ask the student to list the five facts contained in his statement.
The announcement provided in the pretest may be adapted and used in the posttest.

Reteaching Suggestions
Read a well-written announcement to the student. Ask him to find the basic facts.
From an announcement made by the student, ask him to list the key words which answer the five facts questions.

Basic Materials

Textbook. The teacher will want to make the best use possible of the textbook and teacher's edition. The text provides a basic program of work in language experiences; offers certain resources, such as samples of stories, reports, and outlines; and suggests reasonable goals or standards for particular language experiences. Within this framework, the teacher should feel free to modify by making use of

children's experiences in selecting subject matter for study. The textbook may be a ready source of evaluation material. The better texts
contain diagnostic pretests, inventory tests, self-checking devices,
spot reviews, chapter reviews, and similar features which can help
the teacher individualize language instruction. Many texts carry
enrichment and remedial suggestions in the form of optional chapters, special exercises, and the like.

Pretests enable the teacher to distinguish those pupils who are having difficulty with certain language skills from those who already use
them appropriately. The latter may be excused from the instructional
lessons to do independent work.

Teachers should prepare an analysis of the material in the text,
listing topics—such as the use of capitalization and pages on which
instruction, study examples, and practice exercises are provided.
Although the textbook may provide a detailed index, the teacher may
wish to cross-reference exercises and note single exercises in which
several skills are presented simultaneously. The complete index,
covering all essential abilities and skills, may be inserted in the
pupils' textbooks or placed in a language notebook for reference. The
teacher may prepare separate work sheets for each skill, listing
material from the class textbook along with other sources—supplementary textbooks, workbooks, and teacher-made exercises—as
illustrated in Chart 2–2. These can be passed out by the teacher in
making assignments, or filed where the children can get copies. It
would be very helpful, too, if the teacher duplicated and filed check-
out tests for each topic or each group of related topics. This may be
somewhat time-consuming, but the material is relatively permanent
and may be accumulated gradually.

Skills Box.   Boxes may be made for such skills as capitalization,
punctuation, spelling, outlining, use of the dictionary, vocabulary,
and handwriting. A primitive skills box is nothing more than pages
torn from various grade-level skills books and filed sequentially by skill
and grade level. When a teacher discovers that a pupil needs additional practice in capitalizing names of special places, he can pull
one or more skills sheets from the file and assign them to the pupil.
With a skills box or file, the teacher has materials at his fingertips.

Many exercises can be adapted for use in the skills box. Commercial
and teacher-made skills sheets, mounted on poster board and covered with acetate or laminated with a drymount press, can be used
repeatedly if the children use grease pencils to write their answers.
Such sheets can be labeled or color-coded by level, skill, or work
sheet number, and they can be made self-checking. They lend them-

CHART 2-2. Text analysis: capitalization of names of special places

Item	Text pages (Book 4)			Supplementary text pages (Books 3 and 5)	Workbook pages	Teacher-made pages
	Instruction (I)	Examples (E)	Practice exercises (P)			
Streets				Bk 3:83-84 (I)		Cap # 1-6A
Cities				Bk 3:126 (I)		Cap # 7-12A
States				Bk 3:126 (I)		Cap # 13-18A
Local geograph-ical names				Bk 3:134-135 (I)		
Countries						Cap # 9-24A
Oceans				Bk 5:112-114 (I)		Cap # 25-30A
Several skills presented simultaneously	115-117	115-117	115-117	Bk 3:104 (P); 140-141 (P); 150-151 (P); 198-199 (P); 265 (P) Bk 5:78-81 (P) 88-89 (P)	48, 50 114-115	Cap # 31-36A

selves to expansion—teacher aides can readily mount and label pages, make answer sheets, and the like. Games, transparencies, even filmstrips and audio tapes can be included in a file. A group of teachers can cooperate to establish a central file for common use.

These files, like all materials, can be abused. Overuse or inappropriate use should be avoided. They are not intended as ways to keep children quietly sitting in neat rows. Nor are they substitutes for direct teacher instruction or pupil-pupil interaction, or for engaging in activities requiring genuine use of langauge skills. Used properly, they can be a major step toward making diagnostic instruction a reality.[1]

Picture File. Pictures may be secured from magazines, discarded books, calendars, book jackets, posters, travel pamphlets, picture maps, commercial publications, and art reproductions. They can be used to initiate a new topic of discussion or catch the interest of children as they look at and talk about them. They may be used by individual children to illustrate a poem, story, or article.

Poetry File. Five-by-eight-inch cards or looseleaf notebooks are convenient for filing poetry. The poems may be filed by different classifications for varying purposes. They may be labeled as suitable for dramatizing, choral reading, memorizing, or simply reading for enjoyment.

Story File. A story file card should contain the name of the story, the author, the publisher, and the age level for which the material is most suitable, plus a brief summary of the plot and characters. Stories may be categorized as suitable for telling, dramatizing, puppetry, making up other endings, or reading for enjoyment.

Word File. A word file might contain lists of twelve to fifteen words related to a single topic ("Circus") with an appropriate picture. For durability, the lists should be mounted on poster board or oak tag. Of value to intermediate level pupils would be a word origin file. A file of phrases might be useful in creative writing, and story beginnings and endings could be prepared as motivational aids for writing.

Independent Activity Cards. Language arts activities often seem less like assignments if made available to children on individual cards, filed according to category. The child has a choice of concentrating on language, vocabulary, writing, or speaking. A sample activity card is shown in Chart 2–3.

---

[1]For help in preparing a skills box, see *Reading Activities for Pupil Involvement* by Evelyn Spache (Boston: Allyn and Bacon, Inc., 1971).

Interest Centers. A creative writing center might include table, chairs, writing materials, word lists, story starters, and a dictionary. A listening center would be composed of audio equipment, head phones, jack boxes, recordings, and tapes. The records and tapes might include music, story records, teacher-recorded books, and teacher-recorded individual study activities. A creative drama center would contain props useful for dramatizing—hats, coats, dresses, shoes, canes, gloves, scarfs, and aprons. A games or puzzles center would include a variety of language activities suitable for the range of abilities and interests of the children.

CHART 2-3. Sample activity card

Language: Geography of language
1 . There are geographic differences in the use of names for the same thing: *griddle cakes, batter cakes, flapjacks, hot cakes,* and *pancakes.* Circle the term commonly used where you live.
2. The same applies to *spigot,* a device that turns water on and off. Find other names for it.
3. What other words do you know or can you discover for
   a. bag
   b. pail
   c. salt pork
   d. snap beans
   e. peanuts

Language Arts Contract Cards. Some teachers negotiate assignments and tasks with individual pupils. The agreement may be in the form of a contract that is signed by the teacher and the child. The contract states what the pupil is to do and when the task is to be completed. Once agreed upon, the contract should be completed as specified. A sample of a pupil's contract form appears in Chart 2–4.

Instructional Bulletin Board or Chart. Chart 2–5 shows a sample of an idea to help children with slanting cursive letters.

Special Work Sheet. Many examples are given in this book.

Listening Center Material. See Chapter 5 "Listening."

GUIDELINES FOR DIAGNOSIS AND REMEDIATION

Most of the principles which apply to diagnosis and remediation of language problems for remedial pupils are also applicable to developmental language arts instruction.

CHART 2-4.   Sample pupil contract

To learn more about "why" and "how" things got to be the way they are, read one of the following:

A. 1. "The Doughnuts" in *Homer Price* by Robert McCloskey
    2. "How the Leopard Got His Spots" in *Just So Stories* by Rudyard Kipling
    3. "Why the Bear is Stumpy-Tailed" in *Popular Tales from the Norse* by George W. Dasent
    4. *Lion* by William DuBois
    5. *The Amazing Adventures of Archie and the First Hot Dog* by LeGrand

Share your reading one of these ways:

B. 1. Illustrate one incident in the story
    2. Write your own "why" or "how" story on something you read about
    3. Prepare an oral presentation of a "why" or "how" story to give to a younger group of children
    4. Write a "why" or "how" story on a topic of your choice
    5. Make a series of pictures to explain a "why" or "how" story

Choose one topic from A and one method from B for your contract

I plan to do A _____ and B _____
I will have this contract completed by _____
Student's signature _____   Teacher's signature _____

CHART 2-5.

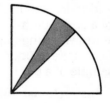

The slant of your letters should fall in
the shaded zone. Evaluate your handwriting
papers in terms of how well the letters are
slanted toward the shaded zone.

Both diagnosis and remedial instruction are most effective when there is good rapport established between the teacher and the pupil before the testing or teaching is begun. Students do not perform well in testing situations if they feel uncomfortable with the examiner. Actual conflict between the student and the examiner or tension can cause test scores to be lower than the student's capabilities. The resulting test information can be misleading.

Rapport between teacher and pupil is vital for cooperation. Pupils achieve more from language arts sessions when teachers take the time to build genuine cooperation, because the pupils work more readily with these teachers.

A relaxed, comfortable atmosphere needs to be maintained in testing and instruction sessions. This can be provided by being pleasant and friendly to the student, showing interest in helping the student overcome the current language arts difficulties, and being optimistic about his prospects for success.

The teacher should only administer tests which are useful to the diagnosis and the discovery of the cause or causes of the problem. The same tests will not be applicable to every pupil or situation. Care should be taken in analyzing tests to see if the same abilities are being measured. Avoid retesting the same abilities unless there is a reason to doubt the results of a previous test. An overabundance of tests can discourage the pupil regarding the benefits of corrective/ remedial language arts activities. Because a student should be enthusiastic about the learning process, the student's self-image should be protected and also strengthened throughout diagnosis.

A good diagnosis includes results of observations, interviews, and informal and standardized tests. Single test results may be misleading due to an assortment of emotional and environmental factors such as those cited earlier in this volume. Measurements and observations of physical abilities such as vision, hearing, speech, and general health should be used along with mental and language arts evaluations.

A pattern of causes is generally found to be responsible for a language arts problem. The possibility of other contributing causes should not be overlooked even though one apparent cause is discovered.

Whenever feasible, the teacher should encourage self-appraisal by the children. The teacher must remember to look for student strengths, as well as weaknesses, in order to build self-confidence. Strengths should be capitalized upon during the remedial instructional periods.

Diagnosis should always be followed by a plan of remediation and should continue after instruction has begun. The time spent in testing is wasted if no corrective action follows. Unless the findings are used to help correct discovered weaknesses, diagnosis will not accomplish much in correcting language arts difficulties. A continuous process of diagnosis is needed because the child's performance will change during corrective instruction.

Realistic goals should be set so that the remedial learner has an opportunity to experience success and progress in corrective sessions. Pupils must be aware of the goals of corrective instruction and the reasons for them. The cooperation of pupils will be secured more easily if the results of the diagnosis are shared with them, along with an explanation of techniques to be used to overcome difficulties. They will try harder if they see a reason for each instructional session and if short-term goals permit them to take successful steps.

To insure success, the teacher should start at the appropriate instructional level and take small steps. Too much material should not be undertaken in a short period of time. It is much better to teach thoroughly what is undertaken and provide experiences and topics which will interest and motivate.

Corrective and remedial programs must be carefully organized and systematically carried out. All of the pupil's problems should not be attacked at once. Other skill needs can be tackled once a few of the most crucial skills are mastered.

Disabled learners show better retention through the use of frequent short sessions, generous praise for success, and tangible evidences of accomplishments.

A variety of teaching methods and materials are required. Instructional procedures that are different from those previously used with a child can remove the fear of failure often associated with the earlier techniques. The choice of materials should take into consideration the interests as well as the current level of achievement of the child and the skills needed.

The main difference between remedial instruction and developmental language arts instruction is in the higher degree of individualization and personalization used in the former.

Remedial techniques are good, sound teaching methods applied in a more individual, personal, and intensive manner. While methods which failed for a language arts student in the past should not generally be used in the remedial sessions, the strategies that are used do not have to be unique to a remedial class. A few different procedures and materials may be seen in corrective classes, but this is frequently because a regular classroom teacher does not have the necessary time to use them as a part of developmental instruction.

"Good, sound teaching methods" mentioned in the above paragraph suggests that the teacher is aware of children's intellectual and emotional growth, such as explicated in *The Language and Thought of the Child* by Jean Piaget (Cleveland: World Publishing Co., 1955). Certainly a deep knowledge of all aspects of development of the young child is a necessity; for example, see Evelyn Goodenough Pitcher et al., *Helping Young Children Learn,* 2nd edition (Columbus, Ohio: Charles E. Merrill, 1974). In a like manner, teachers should have a firm grasp of language development such as provided in Philip Dale's *Language Development: Structure and Function,* 2nd edition (New York: Holt, Rinehart and Winston, 1976) and language itself, such as described in Ronald Langacker's *Language and Its Structure: Some Fundamental Linguistic Concepts,* 2nd edition (New York: Harcourt Brace Jovanovich, 1973). In brief, all teachers need a thorough grounding in and application of developmental knowledge — motor, cognitive, linguistic, aesthetic, and affective.

For example, let's take the teaching of one of the above-mentioned authors and see how it may be applied in the language arts program. Piaget labels the age range of 4-7 as the stage of intuitive thought. Children of this age level are imaginative, imitative, and egocentric in speech; they work or play for themselves. Taking advantage of these findings of Piaget, kindergarten and first grade teachers must serve as models of good listeners and play simple listening games with children, such as "Simon Says." To help with oral language development, mood music could be played and then each child could provide one or two words describing how the music makes him feel. To encourage working together while still permitting each child to express himself, group storytelling or composing may be encouraged. Many children entering the first grade are in the last part of this stage and may be showing some of the characteristics of the next stage; on the other hand, there are some first and second graders who remain at the intuitive thought level for some time.

The age range of 7-11 (grades 2-5) is labeled the stage of concrete operations. Children at that age are less egocentric and are able to see that language provides a system of concepts, ideas, and classifications. They develop concepts of relationships, make predictions, and give "natural" explanations when asked for reasons. Socially, they desire to be with peers, forming groups and clubs. Certain expectations, therefore, may be anticipated and provided for. When a selection is read aloud, children may be asked to predict endings, or to relate one character's actions to another's, or to list happenings in order of occurrence. Children in this stage enjoy broadening their vocabularies by classifying words in many different ways, as well as by contributing as many words as possible to describe an old house or the way a kitten plays. Interest groups may be formed and library research on a topic assigned. Each child would later share his findings with the others, and together they could prepare a composition.

The age range of approximately 11–15 years of age (grade 6 and above) is labeled the stage of formal operations. While many sixth grade children are at the beginning of this new period, for others the characteristics of this stage will be mingled with those of the preceding periods for some time. In this stage, language is used for abstract thought; thought turns to the speculative as well as the actual; and social behavior centers upon human relationships. Keeping these ideas in mind, the teacher may attempt to developmentally match language arts activities. For example, children in this new stage will enjoy listening to a wider variety of literature—biographies, historical stories, poetry, essays. To develop their oral expression, schedule debates on subjects from their everyday lives. Take advantage of the growth in their ability to mentally investigate possibilities; spark their creative writing by assigning provocative situations such as "If it were possible to live under water, what would life be like?"

An understanding of child development has an important bearing on the teacher's expectations for children at various stages of development and provides a rationale for selecting particular methods of instruction. With knowledge of the various components of the language arts, a teacher can then provide for maximum integration of language skills and their use within other subject content areas.

Superior teachers—in initial instruction or remedial instruction—do not neglect opportunities to show children how to use language skills for real purposes. Children who are in control of the basic language skills are those who most commonly make fullest use of them.

REVIEW QUESTIONS AND ACTIVITIES

1. What are four aspects of teaching procedures that are more or less unique to language arts instruction?
2. Prepare a developmental lesson plan for one language arts concept, following the seven features cited on pages 15–16.
3. Take one language arts concept. Analyze it into specific skills and subskills.

4. Develop a systematic lesson plan to teach a specific language arts skill, following the model provided on pages 19–21.
5. What do you consider to be the five most important guidelines for general diagnosis and remediation?
6. From the basic materials described on pages 20–22, 24–25, prepare one type of material that you think would be most helpful to you in working with a child who is having difficulty with language arts.

3
Tools
for
Assessment

There are two basic types of tools used by teachers to assess language arts progress: nonstandardized (informal) and standardized (formal).

NONSTANDARDIZED (INFORMAL) ASSESSMENT TOOLS

Importance of Informal Assessment

The classroom teacher cannot rely solely upon standardized measures for continuous information concerning the progress of the students for several reasons:

- Standardized tests are somewhat expensive and for financial reasons cannot always be obtained when the teacher needs a test.
- There are a limited number of equivalent forms available for a given standardized test, limiting the number of times a teacher can retest on the same skills without repeating identical items.
- Some standardized tests are relatively narrow in scope and may not cover some of the skills that the teacher wishes to evaluate.
- There are certain types of information teachers need about their pupils' language arts behaviors which cannot easily be detected from a standardized test (attitudes toward language arts, for example).

- Standardized tests would rarely be specific enough to test for the objectives of a particular teacher during a specified instructional period. They would more likely cover things not being stressed by the teacher at this time in addition to those actually being stressed currently.
- Standardized testing procedures may be difficult to administer by a person who has not had special training.

A teacher can make use of informal assessment procedures more easily than standardized assessments. The assessment procedure can be tailor-made to fit the class and the teacher's instructional procedures. Any skill that has been taught can be covered effectively with such tests. The teacher can construct informal assessment instruments whether there is money in the budget for testing purposes or not. Teachers understand the purposes and structures of the tests they construct themselves. An unlimited number of test forms covering a particular skill or group of skills can be produced, allowing frequent retesting without repeating items used previously. The teacher can also make informal tests that closely approximate actual language arts situations.

Both observation and informal testing procedures provide classroom teachers with continuous diagnostic feedback on the progress of their students. Where students are found to have difficulties, instructional adjustments can be made and further testing done to check the results of these adjusted procedures. If a child is far behind and having serious difficulties, the classroom teacher may use the informal assessment results as a basis for referral of the child to a specialist for further testing, or the teacher may obtain appropriate diagnostic instruments and proceed with further diagnosis.

Informal assessment results are useful in conjunction with formal assessment measures in constructing a complete picture of a particular child's needs. There are gaps in the information that may be obtained from standardized tests, and the informal tests and procedures can help to fill these gaps.

Readiness Inventories

An important aid to teacher observation is the language inventory test, which can be administered in the kindergarten or first year of school. (It also is applicable to children in the other primary years [grades 2 and 3] who are suspected of being below grade level in their language performance.) The results of this inventory should clearly show the proficiency of each child. Some items of the inventory can be administered to the class as a whole; some parts must be given to each child individually; still other parts can be checked during informal group activities or during small-group conversational periods. The test, or some variation of it, can be readministered during the second and third school years to note improvements and skills yet to be mastered. Dialect differences should be taken into account in marking parts of the inventory, especially number 1. The inventory and procedures are explained in Chart 3–1.

Five other abilities that usually contribute to success in learning to read and write can be rated as noted:

Auditory perception (Ask the child to recognize words that rhyme and words that have the same initial sounds after making sure the children understand the directions.)

Oral alphabet sequence (Ask the child to repeat the alphabet in sequence)

Alphabet reading (Ask the child to identify the letters as they are exposed to him on individual cards—both capital and lower-case letters)

Writing one's name (Ask the child to write his first and last names)

Reading signs (Ask the child to read word cards containing safety words)

The classroom teacher should not overlook other sources of information which can serve as a beginning point with the class or individual child. One such source is the child's cumulative folder, which contains records which previous teachers have made on each pupil. Scores earned on previous standardized and nonstandardized language tests may be perused for bits of evidence (but the teacher must avoid developing preconceptions on test scores alone.) Personal and family information (the type of language environment in the home, emotional or personality problems), health information (last date of eye and ear examinations) and other types of pertinent information can help the teacher begin to round out a picture of the individual child.

But remember—and this will be said more than once in this book—that information in and of itself has never particularly helped a pupil. It is the adjustment of instruction in the light of the information that makes the difference.

CHART 3-1. Inventory of language skills

1. Can he speak so others can understand him?
   Procedure: Check each child according to the speech analysis chart that
              follows:

	Positive		Negative	
GENERAL	Direct	☐	Indirect	☐
SPEECH	Relaxed	☐	Tense	☐
ATTITUDES	Easily erect	☐	Poor posture	☐
	Converses easily	☐	Talks too much	☐
			Timid	☐

	Positive		Negative	
	Volume	☐	Speaks too softly	☐
	appropriate		Speaks too loudly	☐
	Pitch quality	☐	Pitch too high	☐
	pleasant		Monotonous pitch	☐
			Nasal voice	☐
VOICE			Denasal voice	☐
AND			Husky or hoarse	☐
SPEECH	Speech rate good	☐	Speaks too fast	☐
CHARACTERISTICS			Speaks too slowly	☐
	Easily understood	☐	Speaks indistinctly	☐
			Has a foreign accent	☐
			Omits sounds	☐
			Substitutes sounds	☐
			Transposes sounds	☐
			Lisps	☐
	Speech rhythm	☐	Hesitates	☐
	appropriate		Stutters	☐

CONSONANTS
   Directions: show the child a picture representing a word below and ask him
to name or tell about the picture. If a word cannot be pictured, ask the child to
repeat a sentence containing the word. If the sound being checked is in-
distinct, draw a line through the word; if a substitution is made, write the
substituted form above the word; if the sound is omitted, circle the word.

NOTE. From *Manual for the Pre-Primers* of *The Ginn Basic Readers, 100 Edition* by David
H. Russell and others, pgs. 32, 63. © Copyright 1967, 1957, 1948, by Ginn and Company
(Xerox Corporation). Used with permission.

Items 2-14 adapted from *Language Arts in Childhood Education,* by Paul C. Burns and
Alberta L. Lowe, pp. 44-46. Copyright © 1966 by Rand McNally and Company, Chicago.

CHART 3-1 (cont)

	Initial	Medial	Final		Initial	Medial	Final
b	boat	cabbage	tub	sh	ship	machine	dish
d	dog	puddle	hand	ch	chicken	teacher	match
f	father	muffin	knife	t	tie	mitten	gate
g	girl	wagon	frog	th	thumb	nothing	tooth
h	house	behind		th	them	mother	with
k	key	turkey	book	v	vine	river	stove
l	lamb	collar	ball	w	wood	twins	
m	mouse	hammer	farm	wh	white		
n	nose	pencil	barn	y	yellow	barnyard	
ng		singer	ring	z	zoo	magazine	rose
p	pig	apple	cap	zh		treasure	garage
r	rabbit	shirt	car	j	jacket	engine	page
s	sun	postman	horse				

VOWELS

Directions: Note words in which the child makes vowel substitutions, nasalizes, or flattens vowel sounds. Typical examples are listed below.

Substitutes—*jist* for *just, kin* for *can, becuz* for *because*

Nasalizes—*dinner, fence, flame, man, light*

Flattens—*house, round, town*

Suggestions for Improvement
Notes on Progress

2. Does he use appropriate usage?

    Procedure: Check each child according to a usage chart similar to the one which follows. Use a check mark to indicate nonstandard usage.

come	went	did	ran	give	he	she	I
came	gone	done	run	gave	him	her	me

3. Is his vocabulary adequate?

    Procedure: Vocabulary proficiency can be checked by asking the individual child questions similar to those suggested below. Use a check mark to indicate lack of ability to give a satisfactory reply. (Vocabulary proficiency can also be observed through informal conversation with the child or a picture-naming test.) Can you give another word for big, good, pretty, little, under, skip?
    Can you give a word that means the opposite of bad, hot, work, dark, asleep, beautiful? (Give examples such as stop-go; day-night.)
    What is the softest thing you can think of?

CHART 3-1   (cont)

What is the quietest thing you can think of?

Check relationship words (in, under, on, beside, bottom, front, back) with manipulative objects.

4. Can he express himself orally in telling about creative art?

Procedure: Ask each child to draw pictures of —

What I Like to Do Best

Something I Did This Summer

A Picture of My Family and Me

Have each child tell about his picture.

5. Can he express himself in complete sentences?

Procedure: This item can be checked for each child through close obser-vation during sharing, storytelling, and conversational periods. (Sentence length can be noted also.)

Use a check mark to indicate unsatisfactory ability.

6. Can he reconstruct the sequence of events of a story, and can he understand and appreciate the final point of the story?

Procedure: Read a stimulating and interesting story to the children. In a private or semiprivate interview, ask each child to tell the story to you. Use a check mark to indicate unsatisfactory ability. Snipp, Snapp and the Red Shoes and The Three Billy Goats Gruff are ideally suited to this type of activity because in each story there are several characters, each of whom is in-volved in a different part of the adventure.

7. Does he understand the basic principles of courteous conversation?

Procedure: Observe the child's behavior during conversation.

8. Can he answer simple questions in a clear, concise way?

Procedure: Observe the child during the sharing period when others are given the opportunity to ask him questions. Use the period to record the names of children showing a need for improve-ment.

9. Can he follow clearly stated directions?

Procedure: Ask each child to do the following tasks or a similar task, "Go to the bookshelf, get a book, take it to your desk and then place it on the reading table." (Be careful to not overload cognitive capacity.)

Give each child a piece of paper and the following direc-tions, "Draw three boxes on your paper. Color the first box on your left blue; put an x on the box in middle; draw a line under the box on the right."

Record the names of children showing a need for improve-ment.

10. Does he listen politely?

Procedure: This can be checked during the sharing period or during a period of informal conversation.

CHART 3-1   (cont)

11. Can he copy geometric figures, letters, numerals, and words?
> Procedure: Give each child a piece of paper with the following figures, letters, numerals and words on it. Provide space for him to reproduce each one. Record the names of children who are unable to complete the visual and motor task satisfactorily.

□	b	7
	q	3
	s	6
	n	8
	and	5
A	see	4
p	one	9
d	red	2

For the more advanced pupils, the following items may be included:

12. Can he give a satisfactory introduction?
> Procedure: Ask the child to pretend to make the following introductions.
> A. Introduce your mother to the class.
> B. Introduce a classmate to your mother.
> C. Introduce your teacher to your parents. Check the following pertinent to the above introduction. A check mark indicates need for improvement. Is he poised and at ease? Does he use proper names? Does he identify persons being introduced? (For example: "This is Mrs. Brown, my mother.")

13. Can he participate in a telephone conversation satisfactorily?
> Procedure: With the use of toy telephones have the child pretend to make the following telephone calls—
> A. Invite a friend to come to his house to play.
> B. Ask a storekeeper the price of some article, or the hours his store is open.
> C. Relay some specific information for his mother to his father or to one of his mother's friends.
> Check the following items in relation to the above telephone conversations. A check mark would indicate need for improvement.
> Does he speak clearly?
> Is he courteous?
> Is the volume of his voice appropriate?
> Does he speak in complete sentences?
> Does he ask clearly stated questions?
> Does he identify himself?
> Does he give needed information?

14. Can he make simple announcements or convey a message?
> Procedure: Have each child announce to the class that there will be no

CHART 3-1   (cont)

music class today because the music teacher is ill; convey a specific message from the school nurse, principal, or the custodian. Record the names of children showing a need for improvement.

A teacher-made test for language arts readiness is shown in Chart 3–2.

CHART 3-2.   Teacher-made test for readiness

Part I. Auditory Discrimination.
Directions: Show a card with a pair of pictures. Say the words for the objects. Ask the child to tell you if the words for the objects are the same or different.

1. fox-box
2. jet-met
3. cheese-chick
4. boat-coat
5. house-mouse
6. rain-came
7. hen-pen
8. tree-truck
9. lake-cake
10. nurse-nest

Part II. Listening Comprehension.
Directions: Read the following story. Ask questions as suggested. Record the answers.

I have a kitten who says, "Meow, Meow." My kitten's name is Fluffy. One day my kitten was crying, "Meow, Meow." I ran outside to my yard. I found Fluffy in the tree. That is why she was crying, "Meow, Meow."
1. What does my kitten say?
2. What is my kitten's name?
3. What did I hear one day?
4. Where did I find Fluffy?
5. Why was she crying?

Part III. Vocabulary.
Directions: Use cards with pictures of the suggested words. Show a card. Ask the child to name the object. (Caution: Interpretations of pictures may vary according to the child's background.)

1. dog
2. shoes
3. horse
4. rabbit
5. apple
6. cat
7. boat
8. cake
9. bread
10. coat
11. truck
12. kite
13. star
14. airplane
15. balloon

CHART 3-2   (cont)

16. clock	23. leaf
17. key	24. bug
18. fish	25. train
19. letter	26. cow
20. bathtub	27. flag
21. eggs	28. lion
22. soap	29. chair
	30. red light

Part IV. Relationship Words.
Directions: Remove the lid from a small box and place to one side for the first eight items. Replace lid on the box for Items 9 and 10. Identify each object for the child before giving the directions.

1. Put the balloon in the box.
2. Put the nail under the box.
3. Put the button beneath the box.
4. Put the rubber band behind the box.
5. Put the white bean in back of the box.
6. Put the metal ring in front of the box.
7. Put the wooden peg beside the box.
8. Put the key next to the box.
   (Replace the lid on the box)
9. Put the paper clip on the box.
10. Hold the pencil over the box.

Part V. Sequence.
Directions: Read the following story aloud to the child. Then ask suggested questions.

Last week I saw a pet bird. It was in a tree with some wild birds. I asked my mother to help me. I asked my mother to catch the pet bird.

Mother got our old bird cage. She put some bird seed in the cage. Then she put the cage down on the ground. She put the cage near the tree.

Soon the pet bird came down from the tree. He hopped into the cage. He began to eat the seed. Then mother closed the cage door.

1. What happened first in this story?
2. What happened next in the story?
3. What was the last thing that happened in the story?

Part VI. Oral Language Development.
Directions: Choose a large size picture. Ask the child to tell you a story about the picture. Record exactly what is said. If possible, tape record. (See Chapter 6 for analysis procedures)

CHART 3-2 (cont)

Part VII. Following Directions.
Directions: Ask the child to do exactly what you say. Record what is done.

1. Hit the table with a pencil.
2. Show me your teeth.
3. Please go to the door and open it.
4. Stand up and point to a window.
5. Stand up, point to a window, and walk over to it.
   (Alternates: Stand up, hit the table with the pencil, and point to a window. Show me your teeth, hit the table with a pencil, and point to a window. Walk to the door, open it, and come sit down.)

Part VIII. Oral Context.
Directions: Read sentences with omitted words. Accept reasonable answers such as those listed.

1. Mother went to the _____. (store, neighbors)
2. The grape jelly is _____. (sweet, purple, lumpy, thick)
3. My dog likes to chew on _____ and then hides them. (bones, shoes)
4. We gave the cat some _____ to drink. (milk, water)
5. He has a little _____ wagon. (red or any color word, toy)
6. She threw the _____ to Daddy. (ball, some object with meaning)
7. I like _____ and ice cream. (cake, pie, candy)
8. We need _____ for our doll. (clothes, dress, a coat, other article of clothing or footwear)
9. Dad caught a _____ with a worm. (fish)
10. The _____ has four tires and a horn. (car, truck, bus)

Overall Summary

Student name _____   Date _____

   I. Auditory Discrimination: _____/10
Comments:

   II. Listening Comprehension: _____/5
Comments:

   III. Vocabulary: _____/30
Comments:

CHART 3-2   (cont)
_____

  IV. Relationship Words: _____/10
Comments:

  V. Sequence: _____/3
Comments:

  VI. Oral Language Development:
Comments:

  VII. Following Directions: _____/5
Comments:

  VIII. Oral Context: _____/10
Comments:

The summary analysis sheet of the results should provide some valuable data about the basic instructional needs of the child. While there is no separate chapter in this book on readiness or foundations of language arts, the probes cited in this section suggest the types of activities needed for children at this stage of development.

Basic Skills Inventories

A basic skills inventory of punctuation can be developed in the following manner. Chart 2–1 in Chapter 2 is the beginning point, that is, taking one particular language arts concept and analyzing it into specific skills and subskills. Then a pencil and paper test to check the items may be prepared. An example is shown in Chart 3–3:

CHART 3-3.   Sample basic skill inventory
_____

Concept:	Writing Conversation
Skill:	Using Quotation Marks
Subskills:	1. Placing quotation marks around actual speech
	"I saw him," said Bill.

CHART 3-3 (cont)

2. Beginning first word of a quotation with a capital letter
   Bill said, "*I* saw him."

3. Using a comma to separate the quotations from the rest of the sentence
   Bill said, "I saw him." "I saw him," said Bill.

4. Using question marks and exclamation points in quotations
   "Did you see him?" asked Bill. "I saw!" shouted Bill.

5. Placing the period at ends of sentences within the quotation marks
   He replied, "I saw him earlier today."

6. Using commas in a broken quotation
   "All right," he said , "I'll do it."

Test
Directions: Each sentence has something wrong. Use what you know about writing conversation to correct each one.

1. Tim is feeling much better this morning, mother said at breakfast.

2. Father said, "the car needs washing today, Bill."

3. The salesman inquired "Is your mother at home now?" "Yes" she replied.

4. "Where are you going, Mary" asked mother. "Away from here" Mary yelled.

5. Sue smiled and said, "It's fun to watch him race his toy sailboat"

6. "Yes" said Derek "I'll go with you."

Obviously, a number of similar skill inventories may be used throughout the school year as new language arts concepts are introduced. Inventories may be more comprehensive than the sample.

Skill inventories are often called criterion-referenced tests. A criterion-referenced test (CRT) is designed to yield scores that can be interpreted in terms of specific performance standards. For example, a CRT score might indicate that a pupil can use appropriate punctuation marks in direct quotations 90% of the time. Such tests do not tell the teacher anything about how a child compares with other children. A norm-referenced test (NRT), on the other hand, might indicate that the child can appropriately use punctuation marks better than 60% of the children his age. (See pages 52–67 for discussion of NRT.)

The results of criterion-referenced tests are intended to be used as instructional prescriptions (for example, if a child cannot perform the task of writing the contraction for *will not*, the need for instruction in that area is apparent). These tests are more useful in day-to-day decisions about instruction than are norm-referenced tests.

Criterion-referenced diagnostic tests are commercially available. One such instrument is the *Brigance Diagnostic Inventory of Basic Skills* by Albert H. Brigance (Newton, Massachusetts: Curriculum Associates, Inc., 1976). It covers kindergarten to sixth-grade levels and provides tests of basic skills in readiness, reading, language arts, and mathematics. The language arts section is composed of these parts:

A. Handwriting
    1. Writing Cursive Letters (lower case)
    2. Writing Cursive Letters (upper case)
    3. Personal Data in Writing
B. Grammar Mechanics
    1. Capitalization
    2. Punctuation
    3. Parts of Speech
C. Spelling
    1. Spelling Dictation
    2. Spelling Initial Consonants
    3. Spelling Initial Clusters
    4. Spelling Suffixes
    5. Spelling Prefixes
D. Reference Skills
    1. Alphabetical Order
    2. Dictionary Use
    3. Reference Books—Index
    4. Reference Skills—Encyclopedia
    5. Parts of a Book—Location
    6. Parts of a Book—Purpose
    7. Outlining
    8. Graphs
    9. Maps

Several curriculum guides also have been developed on this criterion-referenced concept; an example is *Developmental Sequences in Language: A Non-Graded Program for Ages Birth—Ten Years* (Los Angeles, California, Unified School District, 1972).

Analytical and Follow-up Checks

These are more intensive probing tests that can be administered after completing a general survey test or a basic skills inventory on a specific topic. An analytical test is limited to a few skills and provides corrective exercises. (See chapter 7 for a sample analytical test and follow-up materials.)

Error Patterns

Close study and analysis of a child's writings can reveal patterns of responses that will be helpful in follow-up instruction. For example, study the following writings and then respond to the questions.

> Jim's story: I have a sale boat. It is blew. Tom has too boats. Bill has one witch is red. There boats are not as big as mine.

What is the spelling error?
What spelling generalization is related to the errors?
What diagnosis and prescription would you make?

Mary's handwriting:

What are the major handwriting faults?
What pattern of errors is evident?
What diagnosis and prescription would you make?

Affective Probes

The affective domain is a term used to refer to interests, attitudes, and self-concept.

Interests. The teacher should know the specific interests of each child and how these interests can be used in the language arts program to encourage reading, promote ideas for oral presentations, and stimulate writing.

To do this, teachers must concern themselves with how a pupil spends his spare time, the clubs he belongs to, games he plays, his favorite radio and television programs, his travel experiences, and the like. In addition, teachers need to know the types of materials the child likes to read. A teacher-made interest inventory (see Chart 3–4) can provide valuable information.

CHART 3-4. Sample interest inventory

Name: _____

1. Circle your current interests:

animals	games/sports	famous people
pets	comic books	science
hobby	mystery stories	other (write in)_____

2. What do you like to do in your free time?
3. What are your favorite TV shows?
4. What are your favorite hobbies?
5. What games or sports do you like best?
6. What clubs or other groups do you belong to?
7. Do you have any pets? If yes, what?
8. What is your favorite type of movies?
9. What is your favorite school subject?
10. What is your most disliked school subject?
11. What things do you like to read about?
12. Which magazines or newspapers do you read? What part of them?

Specific language arts interests may be explored by asking such questions as:

1. Do you like to read books about language (history of our language, printing, alphabet, word origins, dictionary, word plays, etc.)?
2. What topics do you like for oral expression activities?
3. What topics do you like for written expression activities (writing about yourself, about your family, your friends, hobbies, feelings, places you've been)?
4. What type of writing do you like best (make believe stories, poems, letters, tall tales, plays, TV commercials, etc.)?
5. What types of language arts games do you enjoy (listening games, vocabulary, spelling, etc.)?

Attitudes. Classroom teachers should be sensitive to the probable causes for a child's like or dislike of the language arts. There is a relationship between attitude and achievement; that is, good attitudes or feelings about the language arts enhance achievement, and, in turn, achievement usually leads to better feelings about the language arts.

There are several ways to measure the affective domain. One way is to encourage the pupil to talk or write about his feelings regarding the language arts.

The primary means of gathering data about a child's attitude is by observing his responses to language arts in a variety of situations.

- Does he want to identify what he does not understand in the language arts? Does he listen carefully?
- Does he complete his language arts homework? Does he appear to derive pleasure from language arts activities?
- Does he actively participate in voluntary language arts projects? Does he eagerly await certain language arts activities?

A rating scale that can help answer such questions is shown in Chart 3–5.

CHART 3-5. Observation rating scale

Directions: Use this key and place A, B, C, D, or E before each statement.

A	Always occurs	C	Occasionally occurs
B	Often occurs	D	Seldom occurs
		E	Never occurs

The student—
_____ 1. listens attentively throughout the language arts class.
_____ 2. participates enthusiastically in language arts activities.
_____ 3. buys books dealing with language concepts.
_____ 4. selects and reads library books that deal with concepts studied in language arts.
_____ 5. vistis the language arts table regularly.
_____ 6. assists peers with language arts activities and shares activities with them.
_____ 7. constructs language games.
_____ 8. works aggressively on language arts assignments.
_____ 9. prefers language arts activities during free time.
_____ 10. volunteers to do additional language arts work.

, It is recognized that several variables play a part in influencing the child's feelings about the language arts such as (a) content (listening, reading, oral expression, written expression); (b) self-image (ability and achievement); (c) materials (textbooks, supplementary materials); (d) others (teachers, parents, peers); and (e) method (teaching strategy, classroom organization, homework, type of assignments). A diagnostic instrument for language arts attitude takes these variables into consideration in order to answer the questions: Does the child enjoy language arts? Why or why not? At this time there is no such instrument, but the scales in Chart 3–6 and Chart 3–7 provide a way of looking at attitudes.

CHART 3-6.   Attitude scale—primary level

Directions: Check the face that shows how you feel about these language experiences.

☺ ☺ ☹   Working at listening center

☺ ☺ ☹   Listening to stories and poems read by teacher

☺ ☺ ☹   Storytelling

☺ ☺ ☹   Acting out stories

☺ ☺ ☹   Learning when to say "saw" and "seen"

☺ ☺ ☹   Writing friendly letters

☺ ☺ ☹   Using the picture dictionary

☺ ☺ ☹   Practicing with periods, commas, and question marks

☺ ☺ ☹   Practicing manuscript writing

☺ ☺ ☹   Learning spelling words

A sample instrument that is appropriate for intermediate grade children is shown in Chart 3–7.

CHART 3-7. English attitude scale

Directions: Use this key and place A, B, C, or D before each statement.

A Strongly agree   C Disagree
B Agree   D Strongly disagree

_____ 1. If I had my way, everybody would study English.
_____ 2. English is one of the most useful subjects I know.
_____ 3. All people should be good at English.
_____ 4. English will help us in our daily lives.
_____ 5. English has its faults, but I still like it.
_____ 6. English is very interesting.
_____ 7. Nobody in our room likes English.
_____ 8. English might be worthwhile if it were taught right.
_____ 9. English is dull and boring.
_____10. I wouldn't take English if I didn't have to.
_____11. I don't even try to do my best in English.
_____12. I can't see how English will help me.
_____13. I really enjoy English.
_____14. I wish we'd miss English more often.
_____15. I like to work hard in English.
_____16. I've found English useful at home.
_____17. I sometimes do extra work in English just for fun.
_____18. English is just too hard for me to understand.
_____19. We get too much English.
_____20. I can't see how English will be useful to me out of school.
_____21. English teaches me to be accurate.
_____22. English is a waste of time.
_____23. English is the best subject in school.
_____24. English is okay.
_____25. I wish we had English more often.

To secure a numerical score from the scale, the following values may be assigned for each item. The more positive attitudes are reflected by the higher numerical scores (100 possible points).

	A	B	C	D
Items (*positive*)				
1, 2, 3, 4, 5, 6,				
13, 15, 16, 17, 21,				
23, 24, 25	4	3	2	1
Items (*negative*)				
7, 8, 9, 10, 11, 12,				
14, 18, 19, 20, 22	1	2	3	4

Various components of the language arts could be checked by replacing the word "English" with "spelling" or "handwriting." Subareas within English, such as listening, oral composition, written composition, and usage, could be checked by rewriting some of the items. The attitude scale should indicate which parts of the program pupils find appealing and which features might be incorporated in other types of language activities.

Specific topics may be explored in depth, as illustrated in Chart 3–8, to report feelings about oral composition.

CHART 3-8. Feelings about oral composition

Topic: Oral Composition	Dislike very much	Dislike	Like	Like very much
Conversation				
Discussion				
Reporting				
Storytelling				
Pantomime, creative drama, choral reading				
Making announcements				
Giving messages, directions, explanations				
Giving reviews of books movies, television programs				
Using the telephone				
Making introductions and conducting interviews				
Conducting meetings				

Another instrument is called the semantic differential technique. (See Chart 3–9.) This instrument is made up of a list of bipolar adjectives, that is, opposite qualities such as good-bad weighted on a seven-point scale. The name of the concept is written at the top of the set of scales. The child is asked to place a check in proper relation to the word that best tells his feeling. The scale may be weighted in the following manner for bipolar adjectives that are marked with an asterisk:

$$-3 \quad -2 \quad -1 \quad 0 \quad 1 \quad 2 \quad 3$$

The scale would be reversed, however, for all other sets:

$$3 \quad 2 \quad 1 \quad 0 \quad -1 \quad -2 \quad -3$$

Add the plus scores and subtract the sum of the minus scores. A high positive score indicates a positive attitude.

CHART 3-9. Semantic differential scale—handwriting

1. Good	— — — — — — —	Bad
*2. Distasteful	— — — — — — —	Agreeable
3. Pleasurable	— — — — — — —	Painful
*4. Hazy	— — — — — — —	Clear
5. Important	— — — — — — —	Unimportant
6. Sweet	— — — — — — —	Sour
7. Valuable	— — — — — — —	Worthless
*8. Negative	— — — — — — —	Positive
*9. Unpleasant	— — — — — — —	Pleasant
10. Nice	— — — — — — —	Awful
*11. Meaningless	— — — — — — —	Meaningful
12. Wise	— — — — — — —	Foolish
13. High	— — — — — — —	Low
*14. Unsuccessful	— — — — — — —	Successful
*15. Tense	— — — — — — —	Relaxed

Determining attitudes is difficult and there is no one best approach to the task. Some other approaches and sample items are:

a. Multiple choice questionnaire

I find the subject of language arts
(1) exciting
(2) interesting
(3) uninteresting
(4) dull

b. Completion test

I find language arts _____ because
_____

c. Adjective check list

Circle each of the words that tells your opinion of language arts.
    fun   easy   worthless
    hard   boring

d. Written statement

Write a paragraph about how you feel about language arts.

e. Nonverbal behavior

Does the child listen attentively throughout the English class? Does he prefer language arts activities during his free time?

Self-Concept. The teacher must meet several needs for each class member in terms of developing a positive self-concept: helping the child feel accepted; providing for feelings of success with activities that guarantee satisfactory completion; avoiding comparisons of pupils; and preserving the child's feeling of self-worth regardless of his language arts scores.

Information concerning a child's self-esteem can be obtained from several sources. The best single source is the teacher's observation of the child and his classroom behavior. Other sources include parents, former teachers, and tests of self-concept. One such instrument is called "How I See Myself, Elementary Form." It is found in Ira Gordon's *Studying the Child in School* (New York: John Wiley and Sons, 1966). Another instrument is the *Piers-Harris Self-Concept Scale for Grades 3–12* (Nashville: Counselor Recordings and Tests). One other instrument is *Inferred Self-Concept,* (Los Angeles: Western Psychological Service, 1974). A form such as the one below provides opportunities for self-appraisal:

Directions: Put an "x" in one box on each line to show whether you think you are that way most of the time or about half the time or hardly ever.

I think I am:	Like Me	Sometimes Like Me	Not Like Me
1. smart in school	☐	☐	☐
2. a hard worker	☐	☐	☐
3. lazy	☐	☐	☐
4. going to do well	☐	☐	☐

Again, the teacher can help the child's self-concept by using materials so he will achieve successfully, aligning activities and materials with his interests, and supporting him by encouraging his parents to react positively toward the child's efforts to work and learn.

STANDARDIZED (FORMAL) ASSESSMENT TOOLS

Standardized language arts tests yield objective information about language arts performance. Ideally, each response to a test item is subject to only one interpretation. Authors of standardized tests sample large populations of students to determine the appropriateness of items, and they seek to verify the validity and reliability of test results so that schools can be confident that the tests measure what they are supposed to measure and do so consistently.

A valid standardized language arts test represents a balanced and adequate sampling of the instructional outcomes (knowledges, skills) that it is intended to cover. Validity is best judged by comparing the test content with the related courses of study, instructional materials, and educational goals of the class. Evidence about validity is nearly always given in the test manual of directions; such information may be checked against the opinions of educational professionals. The teacher should also read the test carefully to make sure it measures what he wants it to measure.

Four Types of Test Validity

There are four types of validity: content validity, concurrent validity, construct validity, and predictive validity.

Content, or face validity, is one of the more important types of validity. The teacher must determine whether the items on the test are similar to the materials used to teach language arts. If there is not a close relationship between the material and the types of questions asked, the content of the test is likely inappropriate.

If a test possesses *concurrent validity,* the results will be consistent with those of other instruments that purport to measure the same skill or skills. If a high correlation does not exist, the instrument lacks concurrent validity.

A test possesses *construct validity* to the extent that the ideas on which it is predicated exist. For example, is there such a thing as "creative writing"? In other words, is the construct a test seeks to measure identifiable? Has its existence been verified by research or other instruments outside the field of language arts? A test has construct validity if the existence of such can be confirmed.

Predictive validity refers to the ability of an instrument to predict language performance. If an instrument indicates that a student is deficient in certain auditory discrimination skills, for example, the student should have difficulty with tasks that require the use of that skill.

Validity is generally established through a statistical process that yields a coefficient that can range from .00 to 1.00. For a test to be considered valid, the coefficient should be at least .80 or above. At the .80 level, 64 percent of the variation in one's measurements is caused by real differences between the individuals being measured, and only 36 percent is due to random error in the measurement process. A coefficient below .80 level should be considered questionable.

Test Reliability

The reliability of a test refers to the degree to which the test gives consistent results. There are three common ways to establish reliability. One way of establishing reliability is by giving the same test twice to a large group of pupils. If each student makes practically the same score in both testing situations, the test is highly consistent and reliable. If many students make higher scores in one testing situation than in the other, the test has a low reliability. Another method of measuring reliability is to compare students' scores on the odd-numbered items with their scores on the even-numbered items; if they are the same rank order, or if they have a high correlation, the test is reliable. A third method of measuring reliability is to compare one form of a test to an equivalent form of the test. Most tests have two or more forms to be used for test and retest purposes.

A test used to compare the average scores of different classes does not have to be highly reliable, as low reliability is unlikely to affect the comparisons. However, when measuring the level of achievement of an individual student, only a test of high reliability should be used as it is necessary to find his or her specific, not comparative, level of achievement. While a test of low reliability cannot be very valid, high reliability does not guarantee that a test is valid.

Another term that needs explanation is "standard error of measurement." Reliability estimates the overall accuracy of a test while the standard error of measurement refers to the accuracy of each individual score. The standard error of measurement is the difference between the true score and the obtained score. Since scores tend to vary when a test is repeated, the true range of a score must be established. If a standard error of 2 exists between the true score and the obtained score of 35, the true score ranges from 33 to 37. In some cases the range in a score can be extremely important, because a standard error of 2 may change an individual grade equivalency score, percentile rank, or other normative data. Without the standard error of measurement, the true range of an individual's performance cannot be determined. Test manuals report the standard error of measurement.

Test Results

The most common ways in which results of standardized tests are expressed are (a) grade scores or grade equivalents, (b) percentile ranks, and (c) stanines.

Grade equivalent indicates the grade level, in years and months, for which a given score was the average score in the standardization sample. For example, if a score of 25 has the grade equivalent of 5.1, 25 was the average score of pupils in the norm group who were in the first month of the fifth grade. If a pupil (not in the norm group) who is in the first month of the fifth grade scored 25 correct, his or her performance would be at "grade level," or average for his or her grade placement. If that pupil scored 30 correct, or a grade equivalent of 6.1, he or she did as well as the typical sixth grader in the first month. Similarly, a 3.3 grade equivalent for a fifth grader would mean that he or she is performing the way the average pupil in the third month of the third grade would perform on that test.

Percentile rank expresses a score in terms of its position within a set of 100 scores. The percentile rank indicates the percent of scores of the norm group that are equal to or lower than the given score. Thus a score ranked in the 35th percentile is regarded as equivalent to or surpassing the results of 35 percent of the persons in the norm group. A student who scores in the 84th percentile as compared with the local school norms may only score in the 54th percentile if his or her score is based on national norms.

A stanine ranks a test score in relation to other scores on that test. (The term is derived from the words *standard* and *nine*.) A stanine is expressed as a value from one to nine on a nine-point scale. Thus, the mean score of the standard population has a stanine value of 5. Descriptions often assigned to stanines are:

    stanine 9—highest performance—top 4 percent
    stanines 7 and 8—above average—next 19 percent
    stanines 4, 5, and 6—average—next 54 percent
    stanines 2 and 3—below average—next 19 percent
    stanine 1—lowest performance—bottom 4 percent

Through the use of test norms, one student's score may be compared to the scores of other students of similar age and educational experience. It can be useful to determine how a student's performance on one test compares with his performance on other tests in a battery and to compare the results of one test administered at different times. However, scores from two different kinds of standardized language arts tests cannot be easily compared since the tests probably differ in purpose, length, and difficulty. Even the results of the same test administered on successive days may vary, depending on the reliability of the test and factors related to the student.

Survey Achievement Tests

Uses of Standardized Language Tests. The results of langauge arts tests show in a general way how well children are performing. By examining a pupil's grade placement score, the teacher obtains a general impression of his language achievement. Grouping these scores gives an indication of the range of language arts achievement in the class.

The distribution shown below approximates the range of language arts scores for a fourth grade class:

Grade Score [1]	Number of Children
7.0-7.9	1
6.0-6.9	2
5.0-5.9	4
4.0-4.9	17
3.0-3.9	3
2.0-2.9	1
	N = 28

A cursory examination of this distribution shows that four children are performing below grade level, 17 at grade level, and seven are performing above grade level. A teacher who has this information at the beginning of the school year knows that he must make provisions for individual differences. It will help him to group children for instruction, placing children of comparable achievement together. Teachers can form initial groups on the basis of these achievement levels and make necessary adjustments as they work with the pupils. The number of groups will vary with the teacher's ability to provide meaningful instruction for each.

The results of standardized tests frequently are expressed as total scores. However, these scores do not reveal how children perform on specific language tasks unless there are subscores for test components. Many language tests designed for elementary children consist of separate sections dealing with capitalization, punctuation, usage, and spelling. Such tests yield separate grade placement scores for each section. A wise teacher will not merely be concerned with the total score but will want to know how it was obtained. Thus he can determine if a pupil is equally strong in all areas tested or if he is stronger in one area than another. Two children may have the same total language grade score but obtain it in different ways:

---

[1] A grade score of 4.6 represents the average achievement of the population used to standardize the test (children in the sixth month of the fourth grade). Raw scores are converted to grade scores by tables that accompany the test. A raw score of 30 may be equivalent to 4.6, a raw score of 34 to 4.9, and so on.

	Child A	Child B
Capitalization	3.0	3.7
Punctuation	2.5	4.5
Usage	3.9	2.2
Spelling	4.6	2.7
	3.5	3.5

This first analysis indicates general areas in which pupils may need more help. A careful examination of the composition of the test items and the children's responses provides the teacher with specific information about their language arts needs. Some tests identify subskills so teachers can categorize the children's responses, but most tests are not sufficiently refined to enable teachers to make this analysis easily. One way to learn more from the testing is go over the test items with the children. Perhaps they can explain how they made their responses. It is possible that even correct responses were reached in inappropriate ways, or that children guessed many of the answers. Teachers may be able to discern patterns of error by comparing similar test items and responses. Standardized tests suffer from real weaknesses, but the weaknesses would be lessened if teachers used the tests with more understanding.

The survey test provides general information about language ability and an estimate of performance level. It also helps to identify children who require further diagnostic assessment. Chart 3–10 lists such tests.

The survey tests cited in Chart 3–10 are achievement tests, evaluating students' language performance in terms of language content presented in the classroom. Currently, there is an emphasis on detecting a child's language competence and language habits, particularly for bilingual children. Some such tests include:

- *Bilingual Syntax Measure* (BSM)—Designed to measure the child's acquisition of grammatical structures in English and Spanish (Grades K–3). New York: Harcourt Brace Jovanovich, 1975.
- *Short Test of Linguistic Skills* (STLS)—Assesses the language dominance and the general achievement level of bilingual children in listening, speaking, reading, and writing. (Grades 2-8.) Parallel forms are available in a number of languages. Chicago: Department of Research and Evaluation, 1975.
- *Dos Amigos Verbal Language Scales*—Assesses the language dominance in children for both English and Spanish and defines the developmental levels for each child in both languages.

CHART 3-10. A list of survey tests

ENGLISH

Test and Publisher	Grade or Age Level	Content
American School Achievement Tests: *Part 3, Language and Spelling.* Indianapolis, Ind.: The Bobbs-Merrill Co., 1941-63.	Grades 4-9	Tests language and spelling.
Berry-Talbott Language Test: *Comprehension of Grammar.* Rockford, Il.: Berry Language Tests, 1966.	Ages 5-8	Test explores child's ability to make up and use rules of grammar and syntax using nonsense words.
Bristol Achievement Tests: *English Language.* London, England: Thomas Nelson and Sons, 1969.	Ages 8-13	Tests word meaning, paragraph meaning, sentence organization, organization of ideas, spelling, and punctuation.
California Achievement Tests: *Language.* Hightstown, N.J.: McGraw-Hill Book Co., 1970.	Grades 1.5-12	Tests mechanics of English, spelling, usage, and structure.
Comprehensive Tests of Basic Skills: *Language.* Hightstown, N.J.: McGraw-Hill Book Co., 1968-71.	Grades kindergarten-12	Tests mechanics, expression, spelling.
Cooperative Primary Tests: *Writing Skills.* Princeton, N.J.: Educational Testing Service, 1965-67.	Grades 1.5-3	Tests spelling, capitalization, punctuation, usage.

Cotswold Junior English Ability Test. Glasglow, Scotland: Robert Gibson and Sons, 1970.	Ages 8.5-10.5	Test junior English levels.
English Progress Tests. London, England: Ginn and Co., 1951-72.	Ages 7-3 to 15-6	Tests progress in English.
English Tests: National Achievement Test. Munster, Ind.: Psychometric Affiliates, 1936-57.	Grades 3-8	Tests capitalization, punctuation, language usage (sentence), language usage (words), expressing ideas, letter writing.
Hoyum-Sanders English Tests. Emporia, Kans.: Bureau of Educational Measurements, 1962-64.	Grades 2-8	Tests knowledge of rules in writing and ability to apply rules to sentences.
Language Arts Diagnostic Probes. Fort Lauderdale, Fla.: American Testing Co., 1970.	Grades 3-10	Tests capitalization and punctuation.
Metropolitan Achievement Test: Language. New York: Psychological Corporation, 1978	Grades K-10	Tests listening, punctuation and capitalization, usage, grammar, study skills, and spelling
Picture Story Language Test. New York: Grune and Stratton, 1965.	Ages 7-17	Tests productivity (total words, total sentences, words per sentence), syntax.
SRA Achievement Series: Language Arts. Palo Alto, Calif.: Science Research Associates, 1969.	Grades 2-9	Tests capitalization, punctuation, grammatical usage, and spelling.

CHART 3-10 (cont)

ENGLISH Test and Publisher	Grade or Age Level	Content
Sequential Tests of Educational Progress: English Expression. Princeton, N.J.: Educational Testing Services, 1972.	Grades 4-14	Tests spelling, capitalization, punctuation.
Sequential Tests of Educational Progress: Writing. Princeton, N.J.: Educational Testing Service, 1972.	Grades 4-14	Tests writing and mechanics of writing.
Stanford Achievement Tests: Spelling and Language Tests. New York: Harcourt Brace Jovanovich, 1940-68.	Grades 4-9	Tests spelling and language.
Tests of Basic Experiences: Language. Hightstown, N.J.: McGraw-Hill Book Co., 1970-72.	Grades kindergarten -1	Tests language abilities.
LISTENING COMPREHENSION		
Assessment of Children's Language Comprehension. Palo Alto, Calif.: Consulting Psychologists Press, 1969-73.	Ages 2-6	Tests child's comprehension and perception of language.
Cooperative Primary Tests: Listening. Princeton, N.J.: Education Testing Service, 1965-67.	Grades 1.5-3	Tests child's listening ability and the degree of comprehension on several levels.

Test	Level	Description
Sequential Tests of Educational Progress: Listening. Princeton, N.J.: Educational Testing Service, 1972.	Grades 4-14	Tests listening ability.
Tests for Auditory Comprehension of Language. Austin, Tex.: Learning Concepts, 1973.	Ages 3-7	Tests auditive capability of the child as to how much the child is able to comprehend.

LITERATURE

Test	Level	Description
A Look at Literature: The NCTE Cooperative Tests of Critical Reading and Appreciation. Princeton, N.J.: Educational Testing Service, 1968-69.	Grades 4-6	Test ability to respond critically to literature.

SPELLING

Test	Level	Description
Buckingham Extension of the Ayres Spelling Scale. Indianapolis, Ind.: The Bobbs-Merrill Co., 1918.	Grades 2-9	Tests spelling abilities.
The Iowa Spelling Scales. Iowa City, Iowa: Bureau of Educational Research and Service, 1945.	Grades 2-8	Tests spelling abilities.
Kansas Spelling Tests. Emporia, Kans.: Bureau of Educational Measurements, 1962-63.	Grades 3-8	Tests spelling abilities on different levels.
Lincoln Diagnostic Spelling Tests. Princeton, N.J.: Educational Records Bureau, 1941-62.	Grades 2-12	Tests students in pronunciation, enunciation, and the use of spelling rules.

CHART 3-10 (cont)

SPELLING Test and Publisher	Grade or Age Level	Content
The New Iowa Spelling Scale. Iowa City, Iowa: Bureau of Educational Research and Service, 1954.	Grades 2-8	Tests master word list with difficulty values by grades from which teacher may compile tests.
Spelling Test: National Achievement Tests. Munster, Ind.: Psychometric Affiliates, 1939.	Grades 3-12	Tests pupil's progress in spelling.
VOCABULARY		
Survey Test of Vocabulary. Lake Alfred, Fla.: O'Rourke Publications, 1931-65.	Grades 3-12	Tests the status of the vocabulary.
Vocabulary Survey Test. Chicago, Ill.: Scott, Foresman and Co., 1971.	Grades Kindergarten -1	Tests the status of vocabulary.
Vocabulary Test: National Achievement Test. Munster, Ind.: Psychometric Affiliates, 1939-57.	Grades 3-12	Tests vocabulary and word discrimination.
Wide Range Vocabulary Test. New York: Psychological Corporation, 1937-45.	Ages 8 and over	Tests vocabulary in ranges of degrees of difficulty.

(Grades K–10.) San Rafael, Calif.: Academic Therapy Publications, 1974.

- *Test for Auditory Comprehension of Language,* English/Spanish (TACL)—Designed to assign a developmental level of comprehension and to diagnose specific areas of linguistic difficulties faced by monolingual as well as bilingual children. (Ages 3-7.) Austin, Tex.: Learning Concepts, Inc., 1977.
- *Oral Language Evaluation* (OLE)—Designed in English and Spanish to identify children who need training in a second language, to assess individual oral language production, and to diagnose children needing second-language training. (Grades 1–4.) Clinton, Md.: Lewis Associates, Inc., 1975.

The content of language arts survey tests indicates that several areas of the language arts—those not lending themselves readily to pencil and paper responses such as oral composition, written composition (creative and practical), and literature—are usually not included. So it must not be assumed by the user that the all important learnings are necessarily treated by standardized language arts tests.

Many language arts tests use similar techniques for assessing the various language skills. Procedures generally used by the *California Language Test* will be provided as examples. For capitalization, pupils are instructed to mark each word in a sentence that should start with a capital letter (for example, Bill saw jim). For punctuation, the pupil is to provide the periods, commas, and question marks that have been left out of series of sentences or a story. Usage is measured by selecting the correct word in a sentence, such as "He (is, are) my friend." For spelling, a list of words is dictated to the child. (In intermediate level spelling tests, the student may be asked to proofread to find any misspelled word.) For sentence sense, the instructions frequently are "For each statement below that is a complete sentence, write *Yes.* For each that is not, write *No.*"

A few language tests provide an analysis of test items in table form. This analysis aids the teacher in classifying types of language skills with which children are having difficulty. (A teacher can obtain this information if the test doesn't provide it by studying each section and its parts and identifying the skill areas covered by them.)

Limitations of Standardized Language Tests.   If standardized tests are understood and their results properly interpreted, they can be of help in assisting teachers to plan for language instruction. But their limitations should be clearly understood.

Which test should be used? A test is inappropriate if the sample population used to standardize the test is significantly different from the children being tested. The test manuals should contain information about the way in which the sample population was selected and its character, that is, from what geographical areas and socioeconomic groups it was drawn.

What about the content? How many different skills do the test items sample? Children who have participated in a comprehensive program will be penalized if the language arts test is narrow in scope, and many of them are. Most tests require only a short period of time to complete. Tests of such short duration cannot possibly sample many different skills, nor can they include more than a few items covering any one skill. Thus, results of some test instruments must be viewed as rough estimates at best.

How accurate are the scores? It is doubtful if the results of standardized tests can be accepted with great confidence. Teachers should not assume that a grade score earned on a test is comparable to the performance level of the child. Some children perform much better in language arts tasks than is indicated by their test score. Others perform less well. Furthermore, grade scores at the lower and upper ends of the range of possible scores are not as valid as those which fall in the middle.

Teachers who use standardized language tests should understand their limitations and be able to interpret their results. The tests results, at best, permit the teacher to speak with some objectivity about the language achievement of groups of children as well as provide him with some language goals that specialists believe should be part of the program.

Intelligence Tests

Intelligence may be measured by individual or group intelligence tests. Group tests are not recommended for the poor language arts student. The best instruments for measuring the intelligence of students are individual tests such as the *Wechsler Intelligence Scale for Children, Revised* (WISC-R). This test should be used with children up to the age of 16—after the age of 17, the *Wechsler Adult Intelligence Scale* (WAIS) should be used. Both of these tests are available from the Psychological Corporation, 304 East 45th. Street, New York, New York. The *Stanford-Binet Intelligence Scale* is a widely used individual test. This test is available from Houghton-Mifflin Company, 110 Tremont Street, Boston, Massachusetts. The WISC-R, the WAIS, and the Stanford-Binet must be administered by psychologists.

The WISC and the WAIS give a verbal score, a performance score, and a total score. The Stanford-Binet gives only a mental age.

These are the subtests (and some indication of what they measure and the type of tasks required) which evaluate the verbal IQ on the WISC-R:

1. *Information*—background of information the student has gained (questions to be answered)
2. *Comprehension*—student's ability to use good judgment (situations to be resolved)
3. *Arithmetic*—student's ability to solve non-pencil-and-paper word problems (timed)
4. *Similarities*—student's ability to generalize, abstract, conceptualize (likenesses of items to be discerned)
5. *Vocabulary*—processes used in vocabulary development (words to be defined)
6. *Digit span* (supplement or alternate)—student's ability to concentrate, attention span, and auditory memory (unrelated digits to be repeated forward and backward).

These are the subtests on the WISC-R which evaluate the performance IQ. All are timed.

7. *Picture completion*—student's visual perception and ability to note details (missing elements to be identified)
8. *Picture arrangment*—ability to place events in sequence (pictures to be put in logical order)
9. *Block design*—student's hand-eye coordination and ability to synthesize (a design to be copied)
10. *Object assembly*—student's ability to analyze and synthesize (puzzles to be assembled)
11. *Coding*—student's ability to copy a number of symbols
12. *Mazes* (supplement or alternate)—student's planning and foresight (maze to be traced).

The full scale IQ is probably the least valuable score for the regular or special classroom teacher. The chief value of the verbal and performance scale IQs lies in the magnitude of difference between them. A large difference—15 or more points—may indicate deficiencies in processing information (auditory vs. visual/motor), in modes of expression (verbal vs. nonverbal), or in working under timed conditions. The subtest scales can help teachers generate hypotheses as to strengths and weaknesses.

The WAIS is almost identical in organization, administration, and scoring to the WISC-R. The principal difference is that on the WAIS the digit span is required and mazes are omitted.

The WPPSI (Wechsler Preschool and Primary Scale of Intelligence, designed for ages 4 to 6½)also is divided into verbal and performance scales.

The subtests on the Stanford-Binet are as follows: information and past learning, verbal ability, memory perception, and reasoning ability.

Though an individual intelligence test is administered by a psychologist who reports the data to the classroom or language arts teacher, teachers need to be familiar with such tests and their contents in order to sense whether results are heavily dependent upon achievement, background experiences, or language abilities. More important to the language arts teacher is knowing how to use test results to improve student performance: What type of language arts program is needed? What strategies should be used with children who perform in a certain manner? (See, for example, Evelyn Searls, *How to Use WISC Scores in Reading Diagnosis* [Newark, Delaware: International Reading Association, 1975]).

While the merits of all types of standardized tests are being increasingly questioned, "intelligence" tests have borne the most withering attacks. California, New York City, and Washington, D.C., have banned standardized group intelligence tests altogether because of doubts about their validity and reliability. The National Education Association has called for the abolition of all standardized intelligence and aptitude tests. Their major complaint is against the use of the tests for tracking the low-scoring students in classes. Minority groups also protest that the tests favor middle-class whites.

One attempt to make testing fairer to members of minority cultures has involved "renorming" data in traditional standardized tests to create separate statistical profiles for minority groups from which "adjusted" scores can be derived. The best known attempt at such cultural adjustment is Jane Mercer's "System of Multicultural Pluralistic Assessment," known as SOMPA (New York: Psychological Corporation, 1977). SOMPA (for children 5 to 11 years old) includes (a) a Wechsler IQ test, giving a measure of the child's mental ability within the "dominant" school culture (i.e., of his social intelligence and competence); (b) a complete health history and a "socio-cultural inventory" of the family's background; (c) an "adaptive behavior inventory" tapping the child's nonacademic performance in school, at home, and in the neighborhood; and (d) a complete medical examination giving details of the student's physical condition, manual dexterity, motor skills, and visual and auditory ability.

Though adopted by several states for determining student placement in special education programs, SOMPA is not without its detractors. Some psychologists reject it because it uses the Wechsler IQ test, which they consider too biased to be used as a baseline measure.

For the typical situation, the following tests are the most appropriate ones since they can be administered and interpreted by classroom teachers. The *Peabody Picture Vocabulary Test* may be used with children from 2½ years of age through 18 years. It is available from American Guidance Service. Publishers Building, Circle Pines, Minnesota. The examiner using this test presents a page containing four pictures, provides a stimulus word, and asks the child to indicate the appropriate picture. The test takes approximately 15 minutes and can be given by a teacher without special training in test administration. Raw scores can be converted into IQs, percentile scores, and mental age.

Another brief, individually administered test is the *Slosson Intelligence Test* (SIT) (East Aurora, N.Y.: Slosson Educational Publications).It provides an MA and an IQ.

Two of the best intelligence tests to use with young children (preschool and those who have hearing or language handicaps) are the *Harris Children's Drawing Test* (New York: Harcourt Brace Jovanovich) and the *Pintner-Cunningham Primary Mental Test* (New York: Harcourt Brace Jovanovich). No reading is required on either of these tests.

Several group aptitude (general academic ability) tests are:

- *California Short-Form Test of Mental Maturity* (K through college levels). Monterey, California: California Test Bureau.
- *Cognitive Abilities Test* (Grades K–3; 3–12). Boston: Houghton-Mifflin.
- *Otis-Lennon Mental Ability Tests* (Pri. I and II; Elem. I and II; Int.; Adv.). New York: Harcourt Brace Jovanovich.
- *SRA Primary Mental Abilities Tests,* (Grades K–1; 2–4;6–9; and 9–12). Chicago: Science Research Associates.

HOW TO IDENTIFY THE UNDERACHIEVER

Very seldom is it enough to look at a child's grade placement score on a standardized achievement test to decide whether or not he is an underachiever. Since all children do not have the same intellectual capacity, a grade placement score may mean one thing for one child and something entirely different for another. For this reason it is helpful to be able to determine the child's expected grade placement (XGP) based on his intellectual capacity.[2]

The steps for finding the expected grade placement score are:

1. Find the child's IQ (a nonverbal test is recommended)
2. Determine the child's age (CA, when the IQ test was administered)
3. Find the child's mental age (MA), using the formula

$$IQ = \frac{MA}{CA} \times 100$$

4. Identify the child's present age
5. Find the child's expected achievement age
6. Convert expected achievement age score to expected grade placement score.

Let us hypothesize that a 9-year-old child in fourth grade was found to have an IQ of 102. He was 8 years and 2 months old (8.2) at the time the IQ test was administered. This means his mental age was 8.4, as shown below

$$IQ = \frac{MA}{CA} \times 100$$

$$102 = \frac{MA}{8.2} \times 100 \qquad \frac{836.4}{100} = MA$$

$$102 \times 8.2 = MA \times 100 \qquad 8.364 = MA$$

$$836.4 = MA \times 100 \qquad 8.4 = MA$$

In order to find the child's expected achievement age, use one of the following formulas. CA refers to age at the time of IQ testing in the formula; use the child's present age to determine *which* formula to use.

---

[2]The formula was devised by Alice Horn in *Southern California Education Monographs*, No. 12 (Los Angeles: University of Southern California Press, 1941).

If present age is:	Use this formula:
6.0 - 8.5	$\dfrac{MA + CA}{2}$
8.6 - 9.11	$\dfrac{3MA + 2CA}{5}$
10.0 - 11.11	$\dfrac{2MA + CA}{3}$
12 and above	$\dfrac{3MA + CA}{4}$

Since this pupil is now 9.0 years of age, use the following formula to obtain his expected achievement age (XA):

$$XA = \frac{3MA + 2CA}{5}$$

$$= \frac{3(8.4) + 2(8.2)}{5}$$

$$= \frac{25.2 + 16.4}{5}$$

$$= \frac{41.6}{5}$$

Now convert the expected achievement age (8.3) to the expected grade equivalent. This is done by selecting the grade level at which the average 8 year old is placed. Normally, a child of 8.3 is in the third month of third grade.

$$XA = 8.3 = XGP \text{ of } 3.3$$

Suppose that a standardized language achievement test was administered to this 9-year-old child in the eighth month of fourth grade (or 4.8). His grade placement average on this language test is 3.6, a score which is one year and two months below his actual grade placement. However, his expected grade placement score was found to be only 3.3. Therefore, this child is not considered an underachiever. For a child to be considered an underachiever, his actual grade placement scores on tests should be significantly below his expected grade placement score, as below:

Grades 1-2   3–6 months
Grades 3-4   6–8 months
Grades 4-5   9 months-1 year
Junior High   1-1½ years

A number of people believe that the results of the Horn Formula become more reasonable when, instead of letting the CA be the child's age at the time of the IQ test, the child's *present age* is used in the formula

$$IQ = \frac{MA}{CA} \times 100$$

and also in the second step of the formula. This adaptation results in more reasonable expected achievement ages and expected grade placements. In all cases, the formula renders a more reliable result when the CA at the time of the IQ testing is near the student's present chronological age. The reader is cautioned that expectancy levels in estimating language arts potential are estimates only and not precise indicators of students' capacity for learning language arts.

Language Development Tests

Various tests of language development, particularly for younger children, are available:

- Phoneme (encoding and decoding): *Goldman-Fristoe Test of Articulation,* Circle Pines, Minn.: American Guidance Service.
- Semantic: *Peabody Picture Vocabulary Test,* Circle Pines, Minn.: American Guidance Service.
- Syntax: *Bilingual Syntax Measure* (BSM). New York: Harcourt Brace Jovanovich, Inc.

One rather complete language battery is:

- *Test of Language Development* (TOLD), by P.L. Newcomer and D.D. Hammill. (This test is for children ages 4–9. Five subtests are provided: picture vocabulary, oral vocabulary, grammatical understanding, sentence simulation, and grammatical completion. Two supplemental subtests include word discrimination and word articulation.) Austin, Tex.: Empiric Press, 1977.

Diagnostic Tests

At this writing, there are no truly diagnostic standardized language arts tests commercially available. However, diagnostic tests in spelling do exist (see Chapter 8) and a diagnostic chart is widely used in handwriting (see Chapter 9).

Selection of Standardized Tests

In addition to measuring the language arts skills it claims to measure (validity) and having subtests that are long enough to yield reasonably accurate scores, a test should not result in a chance score, with students obtaining a high score by luck, guessing, or other factors (reliability). The more reliable tests have a reliability coefficient of .90, with subtests above .75.

The following ideas on test selection and evaluation are proposed for consideration.

Determine the purpose for testing. Is it to compare class achievement with national or local norms or to determine the status of a class or individual to learn whether corrective steps should be taken? Is it to evaluate an on-going developmental language arts program or specific language arts skills?

Locate suitable tests. Probably the most useful single source of assistance in locating suitable tests is the *Seventh Mental Measurement Yearbook,* edited by Oscar K. Buros, (Highland Park, New Jersey: Gryphon Press, 1972) or *English Tests and Reviews* by the same author and publishers (1975).

Evaluate tests in terms of such items as these:

Age-grade level. Is it suitable for the students?
Reliability. Does it yield consistent results?
Validity. Does it actually measure what it is supposed to measure?
Adequacy of the manual. Is adequate information given regarding the reliability and validity of the test?
Relevance of the norms provided. Are the norms based on sound sampling procedures and are tables or profiles provided for their interpretation? Is the norming population comparable to the student?

Appropriateness of the content. Is it fair to minority groups and inner-city children?

Ease of administration. Are directions for administering the test clear and concise?

Time. Can the average student attempt at least half of the items within the time range?

Economy. What is the initial cost? Are test books reusable? Is scoring easy?

Availability of alternate, equivalent forms. Can the test be used for test-retest comparisons?

A good way to become familiar with a test is to take it yourself and then to administer it to a few students. Specimen sets of tests are available from publishers at a reasonable cost.

ADDITIONAL ASSESSMENT TOOLS

This chapter has dealt with the broader and more general tools of assessments, both informal and formal. Particular assessment instruments appropriate for specific components of the language arts (listening, speaking, written expression, spelling, and handwriting) are cited in the chapters dealing with these skills.

REVIEW QUESTIONS AND ACTIVITIES

1. From the language skills inventory for the younger child, what do you consider the most important diagnostic items for early identification of language arts difficulty?
2. Administer the language skills inventory (or teacher-made informal readiness test) to a child. Analyze the results and report your findings.
3. Prepare a basic skills inventory for one particular language arts skill.
4. Discuss strengths and weaknesses of criterion-referenced tests, norm-referenced tests.
5. What error patterns in spelling can you detect in the following passage? What generalizations are related to these errors? What would be your diagnosis and prescription?

Wensday
Febuary 19

Dear Uncle Jim:

Thank you for takeing me swiming. Mom is hopeing you will take me campping on my birthday. I want a nife. I am writeing you since Mom said i could not use the telefone.

Your friend,
David

6. What are the features of an analytical test with follow-up materials?

7. Administer an interest inventory to a child. Write an analysis of the results.

8. Administer an attitude scale to a child. Write an analysis of the results.

9. Administer a self-concept scale to a child. Write an analysis of the results.

10. Administer an intelligence test to a child. Write an analysis of the results.

11. Differentiate between the four types of validity.

12. Describe the three ways that reliability may be measured.

13. Explain what is meant by "standard error of measurement."

14. Explain the three common ways of reporting results on standardized tests.

15. Administer a language arts survey test to a child. Write an analysis of the results.

16. Write an analysis of a standardized test based on the features cited in "Selection of Standardized Tests."

17. Using the formula on page 69, determine if the child described here is an underachiever.

    Child—10 years of age

    Grade level—5

    IQ—102 (given when 9.2 years old)

    Language Achievement Test—4.6 (given in eighth month of fifth grade)

    MA _?_

    XA Age _?_

    XGP _?_

    Underachiever (yes or no) _?_

18. Discuss the intelligence testing controversy.

4

Some
General
Resources

This chapter focuses upon several resources that are helpful in all facets of the language arts. These include (a) activities and games (b) source books for activities, (c) library, or trade, books, (d) special multilevel materials, (e) parents, and (f) pupils. While each is important in any developmental language arts program, they are particularly invaluable in planning instructional strategies for those who are having difficulties with the language arts program. The chapter concludes with other special resources and suggestions for physical arrangements of the classroom.

ACTIVITIES AND GAMES AS INSTRUCTIONAL STRATEGY

Activities and games can be used to introduce new learnings and to practice previously learned concepts. They can be a valid means for developing and reinforcing language arts skills.

In selecting games and activities for instruction, the teacher should ask such questions as these:

- Do the activities or games develop or reinforce important language art objectives?
- Once the idea of the activity or game has been taught, can it be played by several children without teacher direction?
- Are there self-correction features that help to settle arguments? (While this is desirable, it is not always possible.)
- Is the format interesting? Does the activity look like a game rather than a language arts practice sheet?

- Will the children find it interesting as well as helpful?
- Does the activity or game produce measurable effects on those that participate?

Source Books for Activities

At the present time an ever-growing number of source books are available that can be useful in providing ideas for the teacher. A listing of such resource books appears at the end of this chapter.

Teacher-Made Activities

The development of activities or games for language arts instruction is one of the creative phases of teaching. For teachers wishing to develop such materials, the following suggestions may be helpful:

- First, decide what objective you wish your activity or game to accomplish.
- Carefully review the guidelines for activity or game selection listed on pages 74–75.
- Keep in mind the various types of games you might use. For example, there are race games, war games, games of position, card games, bingo and lotto games, board games, dice games, and others.
- Keep in mind the interests of the children. If a number of boys and girls are interested in hospitals, use a hospital activity, and so on.
- Make a mock-up of the activity and play it with several children to develop refinements.
- Write a set of instructions. Have a group of children try to use the activity or game using only the mock-up and the instructions. (If the children are at the prereading level, record the instructions on a cassette tape.)
- Refine the activity or game and the instructions on the basis of the trial.

Chart 4–1 (page 76) shows a teacher-made activity.
Often, activities or games are a part of learning centers. Some books about learning centers are listed at the end of this chapter.

LANGUAGE ARTS TRADE BOOKS

There are many nontext books, called "trade" books by publishers, that deal with language arts concepts. Usually thought of as library books, rather than instructional texts, they are really books for a child

CHART 4-1. Teacher-made activity

In Other Words (Intermediate—Grades 4-8)

Objective: By completing this activity, the student will be practicing the identification of certain synonyms and antonyms.

Materials: A 4 × 6 foot sheet of heavy plastic sectioned off into squares. Write one word per square using a magic marker. Provide a small bean bag.

IMME-DIATELY	LOOSE	CROWD	HALT	SCRAP	KNOW	PURE	ASSIST
GENEROUS	APPROVE	LOUD	GRASP	RUN	RELAXED	FANCY	TIGHT
AID	GOOD	CHEAP	TRIVIAL	GROW	FRIEND	QUIET	IM-PORTANT
CLEAR	NOW	RESTORE	ARGUE	CLASP	DEPART	STRANGE	SCURRY

Directions: This game is to be played with two students or two teams. One at a time, the players throw the bean bag on a word. The player is to supply a synonym or antonym on the chart for the word the bag lands on. If there is no synonym or antonym on the board, the player says "None." One point is scored for each correct answer. A third person serves as "judge" and is given an answer key. At the end of a specified time, the student or team with the most points wins.

to read to learn more about language arts. Lists of such books are found at the end of this chapter.

Bibliotherapy

Sometimes a library book is selected for a child because it may help him or her with a specific problem. The matching of a personal problem with a problem in literature is sometimes called bibliotherapy, that is, the use of reading material to fulfill the needs of a person. For example, a boy struggling with fear or with apparently unreasonable expectations of father or other adult to become a football player could find a kindred spirit in *Shadow of a Bull,* by Maia Wojciechowska, about a boy who is terrified of becoming a bullfighter.

Bibliotherapy produces its effect through identification, catharsis, and insight. The reader first identifies with a character or situation in literature. Living through the situation vicariously, the reader experiences catharsis—an emotional release. The overall result is insight into the problem, with the hope that such insight will transfer to the individual's own confrontation and solution of the problem.

Several cautions should be recognized: (a) serious problems (such as mental illness, physical abuse, or drug misuse) require help beyond the insight afforded by a literary work; (b) literary selections should not always be used to pinpoint a problem; and (c) the individual's possible response to reading about a similar situation must be considered.

Two references which deal with bibliotherapy are:

Moody, Mildred T. and Hilda K. Limper, ed. *Bibliotherapy: Methods and Materials.* Association of Hospital and Institution Libraries, American Literary Association, 1971.

Reid, Virginia M. *Reading Ladders for Human Relations.* 5th. edition, Urbana, Illinois: National Council of Teachers of English, 1972.

A few selected books for use in bibliotherapy are suggested below. The first book listed is appropriate for primary level, and the second for intermediate level.

Overcoming Handicaps
Orgel Doris, *Next Door to Zanadu.* New York: Harper, 1969 (overweight)

Davidson, Margaret. *Helen Keller.* Hastings House, 1969 (blind and deaf)

Family Situations
Keats, Exra Jack. *Peter's Chair,* New York: Harper, 1967 (new baby in family)

Blume, Judy, *It's Not the End of the World*. New York: Bradbury, 1972 (divorce)

Understanding Emotions
Welber, Robert. *The Train*. New York: Pantheon, 1972 (fears of every-day things)

Lee, Virginia. *The Magic Moth*. New York: Seabury Press, 1972 (death)

Social Concerns
Clifton, Lucille. *Good, Says Jerome*. New York: Dutton 1973 (making friends)

Konigsburg, E. L. *The Dragon in the Ghetto Caper*. New York: Athenium, 1974 (crime)

Estimating Readability

In using trade books and other supplementary materials with children having difficulty in the language arts, teachers often need to use readability formulas to judge the difficulty of printed material. There are several such formulas; the one presented in Figure 4–1 is a quick

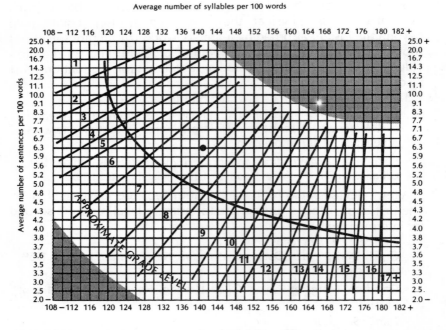

FIGURE 4-1. Graph for estimating readability—extended, by Edward Fry, Rutgers University Reading Center.

way to estimate readability. (Caution: readability formulas do not take several factors into consideration such as concept load, style, content, literary devices and other nonquantifiable factors which may affect readability.)

1. Randomly select three sample passages and count out exactly 100 words each, beginning with the beginning of a sentence. Do count proper nouns, initials and numerals.
2. Count the number of sentences in the hundred words, estimating length of the fraction of the last sentence to the nearest one-tenth.
3. Count the total number of syllables in the 100-word passage. If you don't have a hand counter available, an easy way is to simply put a mark above every syllable over one in each word, count the number of marks, and add 100. Small calculators can also be used as counters by pressing the numeral 1 and the + sign for each word or syllable when counting.
4. Enter graph with *average* sentence length and *average* number of syllables; plot dot where the two lines intersect. Area where dot is plotted will give you the approximate grade level.
5. If a great deal of variability is found in syllable count or sentence count, putting more samples into the average is desirable.
6. A word is defined as a group of symbols with a space on either side; thus, *Joe, IRA, 1945,* and & are each one word.
7. A syllable is defined as a phonetic syllable. Generally, there are as many syllables as vowel sounds. For example, *stopped* is one syllable and *wanted* is two syllables. When counting syllables for numerals and initials, count one syllable for each symbol. For example, *1945* is four syllables. *IRA* is three syllables, and & is one syllable.

SPECIAL MULTILEVEL MATERIALS

There are materials which can help a teacher provide for children's differences in the language arts. Materials of a multilevel nature (usable for children of varying levels of achievement) can be particularly helpful. The listing at the end of this chapter is suggestive of such materials.

Evaluating Instructional Materials

Teachers must evaluate instructional materials they use in their classrooms. Some criteria are—

- Is the basic theory on which the materials have been developed a sound one?

- Is the material designed to teach the skills the children need? Are these skills adequately and appropriately presented?
- Is the material appropriate to the maturity levels of the children?
- Is the material appropriate to the backgrounds and experiences of the children?
- Will the material be interesting to the children?
- Is the need to develop readiness for each instructional activity recognized? Are readiness activities available at all levels of instruction?
- Are the activities and materials designed to motivate children to learn?
- Are provisions made to encourage application of skills taught by the material to situations outside the class including the content areas?
- Is the material free from role stereotypes (of different nationalities, ethnic groups, sexes)?
- Does the material have a controlled vocabulary? If so, what kinds of controls have been used?
- Is the material up-to-date?
- Do all the components of the language arts program receive the proper emphasis?
- Does the material provide for continuous diagnosis of language arts difficulties? Are materials self-correcting?
- Does the material include an adequate teacher's manual?
- Is the format of the material suitable to the group that is to use it? Is the size of print, quality of paper, and so forth appropriate?
- Has research shown this material to be effective in teaching skills?
- Is the cost of the material reasonable in terms of (a) lifetime of the materials; (b) spectrum of skills taught; (c) replacement of lesson parts?

Teachers should be particularly aware of materials that are appropriate in terms of career, culture, race, and sex. The issues of representation, sexism, and stereotyping of ethnic or racial minorities are very serious. There are a number of reference guides to nonracist/nonsexist materials, such as:

Bresnahan, Mary. "Selecting Sensitive and Sensible Books About Blacks," *Reading Teacher* 30 (Oct. 1976): 16–20.

Feminists on Children's Media. *Little Miss Muffet Fights Back,* rev. ed. New York, 1974.

Interracial Books for Children Bulletin, vol. 7. New York: Council on Interracial Books for Children, 1976.

Mullins, Jane and Wolfe, Suzanne. *Special People Behind the Eight-Ball: An Annotated Bibliography of Literature Classified by Handicapping Conditions.* Johnstown, Pa.: Mafex Associates, 1975.

PARENTS

Research suggests that increased parental knowledge of classroom language arts activities results in higher pupil achievement. This certainly warrants giving some attention to the parent. Parents need to be aware of the purposes that the teacher is trying to achieve—regardless of the fact that they may not seek such awareness or that they may prefer to stand on the sidelines.

The teacher can suggest several ways that parents can help a child who is having difficulty with language arts. They can be encouraged to read and study the material he is using in the class so they can be better listeners and questioners of the child as he explains his work. They may be urged to encourage the child when they notice interest in any facet of the language arts (voluntary reading, composing, spelling, or handwriting). Certainly, a good study environment should be provided for the child (space, time, and tools needed for lessons).

Teachers must be prepared to answer questions asked by parents:

- How are the language arts taught at the school?
- Is my youngster at grade level in the language arts?
- What can I do to help my child like the language arts?
- Should I hire a tutor for my child?
- What can I do to help our child who is poor in the language arts?
- What special programs do you have for children who have difficulty with language arts?
- What are some suggestions for the language gifted child?

Many of the opportunities to reinforce the language arts program at home should be explored with parents: conversing with the child, being a good listener, providing first-hand and vicarious experiences for the development of concepts and vocabulary, reading aloud to the child, and discussing homework assignments. It is also helpful to point out language arts opportunities in ordinary daily activities such as cooking, tending the garden, or taking trips.

Teachers can send notes to parents along with homework assignments, such as "We have been learning about words to capitalize. This activity sheet gives your child an opportunity to share his skills with you." The activity sheet should be a practice sheet for the child who has learned and practiced the skill, but requires more practice for mastery. The activity sheets should be as interesting as possible. One example is provided.

Directions: Color the parts that contain words needing a capital letter. What is the hidden animal?

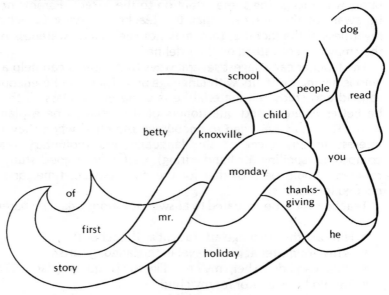

CHART 4-2. Sample homework activity

A complete and on-going way of reporting to the parents should be maintained: sharing of work samples, weekly test scores, standardized and nonstandardized testing results.

Further contact with the home can be maintained by sending bulletins and letters to parents about various aspects of the language arts program. Here is a list of topics suitable for bulletins and letters:

- How parents can help in building concepts and vocabulary.
- How new work is introduced in the classroom.

- Individual differences and levels of development in learning language arts.
- How to make "homemade" language arts games for children.
- Using media for enhancing language learning—library, television, and the like.

Specific resources may be cited for parents: language arts games, language arts trade books, and other helpful items that mãy be purchased rather inexpensively.

To further bridge the parent-teacher gap, the parent may be invited to serve as a volunteer in the language arts class; a typical language arts period may be demonstrated for the parent-teacher association; or parents may be employed as teacher-aides. At all times, they should be encouraged to offer suggestions and ideas which they feel may be helpful for their child.

The following ideas could be offered by the teacher who is asked to suggest ways parents can help in remedial situations.

- Help the child achieve the best physical health with respect to hearing, vision, and other physical and psychological factors. This may mean more sleep and rest; it may mean hearing and vision screening examinations.
- Help the child to feel secure and confident. Provide affection, confidence and cheerfulness, rather than becoming impatient with the child. Parents need to realize that a student's emotional health affects his growth in the language arts. Help develop constructive attitudes. Parents need to realize what the frustrated child experiences day after day in school and not put him through the same thing at home. This understanding can best be developed through a parent-teacher conference.
- Surround the child with conversation, listening, reading, and writing opportunities. Talking with children provides a backlog of information that is basic to the language arts program. As parents listen to children, they are conveying the idea that the child has something worthwhile to say. Special preparation is not necessary; rather, share everyday things, answer questions and explain, provide experiences. Make visits to libraries to supply books. Read to the child and encourage him to read aloud to others and talk about the reading. Share your writings with the child, so he can see the purpose for them.
- Visit the classroom to become aware of the methods of instruction used. An interested mother or father who can volunteer a

few hours a week in a classroom will have an opportunity to learn much about teaching methods.

- Seek an interview with the teacher concerning the child's language arts program. The parent and the teacher can discuss such items as
  a. Some likely causes of the child's difficulty
  b. Loss of confidence, if evidenced by the child
  c. Samples of the child's work
  d. Appraisal as indicated by test scores
  e. What the teacher is doing to alleviate the difficulty
  f. What the parent may do to assist

THE PUPIL

Stimulating children to identify their own needs is a basic procedure that will pay rich dividends. Children should be taught to observe their language progress by noting the listening they do, the talking, and the papers they write. By examining their own product, children will learn to recognize their own strengths and weaknesses—and search for means of improving.

Pupils may participate in the assessment procedure by (a) using a check list to record performance on a particular skill; (b) keeping a folder of samples and records of their work, with notes as to needs; (c) participating in class discussion of needs and their efforts or plans for improvement; (d) proofreading and editing many of their own papers; (e) plotting or recording their own test scores on spelling and other tests; (f) keeping a notebook of things they need to work on— new vocabulary words, spelling words, and the like.

Do not overlook the ideas of using *pupil pairs* or *partners* who have marginal mastery of a skill. They may work cooperatively on such activities as practice activities and games for spelling and crossword or hidden-word puzzles based on new vocabulary words. Partners work together best when they are at the same language arts level and when they are congenial. Setting a very specific task and a time limit for the partners to complete it can help a partnership remain task-oriented.

At times, class members can be allowed to work on a certain assignment in *friendship groups* (with friends of their own choice).

In situations where corrective/remedial help is needed by a large number of students and insufficient professional staff is available to offer help to all who need it, *peer tutoring* may be mobilized. The children who are to act as tutors are given training by the teacher in how to assist their peers who need help. Then the students provide one-to-one assistance to their classmates while the teacher is helping other children. Older children may move to lower grades to offer assistance. In some cases, tutors who have been remedial students themselves have been used effectively.

OTHER SPECIAL RESOURCES

In some school systems, special language arts services are provided beyond classroom instruction. While the arrangements differ from place to place, they often involve a language arts special teacher and a language arts consultant.

The language arts specialist provides instruction in all major phases of language arts to supplement the regular classroom program. The following tasks are among the responsibilities of the language arts specialist:

1. Assists in the implementation of a school-wide testing program.
2. Helps select those children who require more intensive and individualized diagnosis.
3. Plans programs for children who require special assistance.
4. Works directly with children who require small-group or individual instruction in addition to the regular classroom program.
5. Provides progress reports to classroom teachers for children in special programs.
6. Assists classroom teachers with choice of materials and instructional methods for children in special programs.
7. Consults with parents whose children are involved in special programs.
8. Evaluates student progress in special programs.
9. Assists in in-service education as a demonstration teacher or resource person.
10. Helps inform the community as to the purposes and progress of special programs.

In large school districts, a language arts specialist may direct a language arts program for severely handicapped children besides performing the usual functions of a language arts specialist.

A large number of schools have established summer programs for children who have not made adequate progress during the school year. The language arts specialist is often responsible for such programs and is particularly responsible for selecting the children who are to be assisted. In addition, the specialist may select the teachers who will be involved.

As noted above, diagnosis is a major obligation for most special language arts teachers. The specialist not only diagnoses but prepares recommendations for remedial work. Following a diagnosis, the language arts specialist may draw certain children from the classroom for the instruction needed. This calls for a language arts room with appropriate materials. Special language arts groups must be small, instruction must be individualized, and schedules flexible. Instruction may also be provided within the classroom setting, either by the language arts specialist or by the classroom teacher. (See Chapter 10 for a sample case study report from a language arts specialist to the classroom teacher.)

A language arts consultant is a person who works directly with teachers, administrators, and other school personnel to develop and coordinate a school-wide language arts program. The consultant is freed from classroom teaching, individual assignments, and the instruction of special language arts classes. Instead his attention is focused upon such activities as the following:

1. Provides for professional growth through demonstrations, inservice courses, workshops, and seminars.
2. Consults with classroom teachers on matters relating to language arts instruction.
3. Recommends materials to aid instruction.
4. Assists the building principal and other administrators in implementing the language arts program.
5. Assists in the evaluation of ongoing programs and makes recommendations for change.
6. Orients beginning teachers and school aides as to the philosophy, procedures, and materials for the school language arts program.
7. Works as a resource person with special cases, the difficulty or complexity of which requires a high degree of professional knowledge and skill.
8. Keeps the community informed as to the purposes and progress of the language arts program.
9. Keeps the school staff informed as to new developments in language arts.
10. Encourages the implementation of promising ideas and the development of research projects.

Other resources designed to help teachers with disabled language arts students include:

1. College or university language arts facilities. Some colleges and universities operate language arts centers. Children who are brought into these centers for assistance are generally diagnosed and tutored by students doing advanced work in the field of language arts. Some centers limit themselves to diagnosis, while others include remediation.
2. Privately operated facilities. A variety of privately operated language arts facilities is often available in larger population centers. The effectiveness of these facilities sometimes is limited by restrictions on the personnel and materials available for diagnosis and remediation. Referrals to this type of facility should be made only after the personnel and program of such a clinic have been carefully examined.
3. Private tutoring. The effectiveness of a program designed by a private tutor depends upon the proficiency of the tutor and the materials available for precise diagnosis and remediation. Private tutors are obligated to work closely with the school in which the child is enrolled.

PHYSICAL ARRANGEMENTS

Classroom

One possible example of classroom (or special language arts room) arrangement for more effective treatment of children with language arts difficulties is shown in Chart 4–3.

As can be seen in that chart, some individual problems can receive attention at a listening post. The teacher can tape an individual or small-group exercise, with specific directions for the children who listen through headphone sets and then respond to this tape. When the teacher realizes that a child or group of children are weak in a skill such as forming contractions, he can have that child or small group work at the center desks with a series of exercises taken from a supply of resources in the materials file. The audio-visual area, containing an overhead projector, filmstrip projector, and a screen is used for a variety of instructional and motivational purposes. The typewriter can be used by students for typing personal experiences and even stories. The reading corner can be used to encourage personal work, such as silent reading or working on individual language arts activities and games. There are two large tables at which small

groups of children can work on joint language arts projects and research projects. Although not shown, it is desirable to include a center for oral activities, including drama, as well as a few individual
carrels where students can participate in individual work with a minimum of distraction.

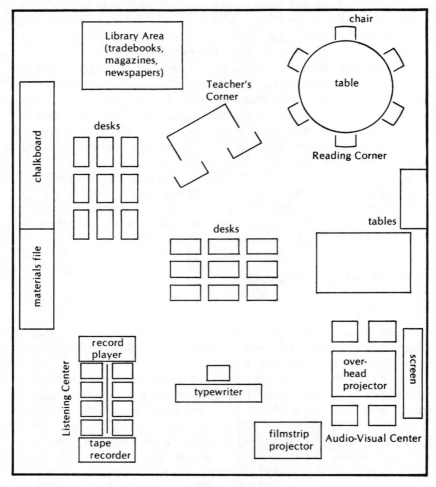

CHART 4-3. Sample classroom arrangement

Intraclass Grouping

Within the physical setting of the classroom, various ways of grouping to provide for individual differences can be successful.

Achievement grouping involves dividing children into language
arts groups within the classroom on the basis of language arts ability.

The teacher may divide the class into two, three, or more groups, providing appropriate time for teacher-directed activity and independent work. There will likely be a need for more teacher-directed activities for the slower learning groups.

The concept of achievement grouping does not preclude the use of some total-class language arts activities for class cohesion, motivation, and sharing purposes. Some examples of total class language arts activities may include certain dictionary activities, reviewing skills taught to each group earlier, sharing newspaper reports, choral reading, dramatization, and participating in library activities. Independent work may include completing practice exercises and playing games that reinforce language arts skills. As suggested above, assistance from student tutors can be helpful in providing time for greater attention to individual children who need help.

In any form of grouping, the teacher must give close attention to change in language arts ability by each child to see that he or she is appropriately placed in the group where the most progress is possible. Flexibility in grouping must remain a key concept.

Within any groups, special needs will exist, thus requiring *special skills* or *needs grouping*. Here children who need work on the same skill can be grouped together. For example, several children may need additional help with capitalization and punctuation in addressing an envelope. These children would be grouped together for one or more sessions until that need no longer exists. Such special needs groups will involve different children at different times. Again, a student tutor who has mastery in the area being studied by the group can be assigned to help them.

Interest grouping involves a group of students who have a common interest, such as creative writing or producing a class newspaper.

Other Group and Individual Arrangements

There are other useful arrangements which attempt to individualize instruction according to various learner's needs cited throughout this book, such as learning centers, contract cards, and special assignment sheets, to name but a few possibilities.

REVIEW QUESTIONS AND ACTIVITIES

1. What ideas should be kept in mind in developing activities and games for language arts instruction?
2. Prepare an activity or game to be used to develop or reinforce a language arts concept.

3. Study some of the source books available for language arts activities. Describe how they might be used with a class, a group, or individual.

4. Utilize a particular language arts trade (library) book designed as an instructional resource in introducing or reinforcing a language arts concept with a child.

5. Examine some multilevel instructional materials available for the language arts. Apply the evaluation critera.

6. Apply the Fry Readability Formula (see page 79) to a language arts trade book or other supplementary language arts materials. Report the results.

7. Prepare a bulletin or letter to a parent about some facet of the language arts program.

8. How may pupil involvement in the assessment and correction process be achieved?

9. Discuss the roles of the special teacher in language arts and of the language arts consultant.

10. Discuss physical arrangements and grouping for corrective/remedial students.

SOURCE BOOKS FOR ACTIVITIES

Anderson, P.S., & Groff, P.J. *Resource materials for teachers of spelling* (2nd. ed.). Minneapolis, Minn.: Burgess Publishing Co., 1968.

Ashley, R. *Successful techniques for teaching elementary language arts.* West Nyack, N.Y.: Parker Publishing Company, 1970.

Bergman, F. *The English teacher's activities handbook.* Boston: Allyn and Bacon, 1976.

Bureau of Curriculum Development. *Language arts games.* New York: Board of Education of the City of New York, 1971.

Carlson, R.K. *Speaking activities through the grades.* New York: Teachers College Press, 1975.

Carlson, R.K. *Writing aids through the grades.* Teachers College, Columbia University: Teachers College Press, 1970.

Chappel, Bernice M. *Listening and learning: Practical activities for developing listening skills,* Grades K–3. Belmont, Calif.: Fearon, 1973.

Cheney, A. *The writing corner.* Santa Monica, Calif.: Goodyear Publishing Co., 1978.

Clure, Beth. *Why didn't I think of that?* Glendale, Calif.: Bowmar, 1971.

Collier, M.J. et al. *Kid's stuff: Reading and spelling.* Nashville, Tenn.: Incentive Press, 1969.

Crawford, M. *Teaching study skills.* Dansville, N.Y.: Instructor Curriculum Materials, 1973.

Croft, D.J., & Hess, R.D. *An activities handbook for teachers of young children.* Boston: Houghton Mifflin, 1972.

Dean, J.E. *Games that make spelling fun.* Belmont, Calif.: Fearon, 1973.

Duffy, G.G. *Teaching linguistics.* Dansville, N.Y.: Instructor Curriculum Materials, 1975.

Farnette, C. et al. *Special kids' stuff: High interest, low vocabulary reading and language skills activities.* Nashville, Tenn.: Incentive Publications, 1976.

George, M.Y. *Language Arts: An idea book.* Scranton, Pa.: Chandler Publishing Company, 1970.

Gerbrandt, G.L. *An idea book for acting out and writing language, K–8.* Urbana, Ill.: National Council of Teachers of English, 1974.

Gigous, Goldie M. *Improving listening skills.* Dansville, N.Y.: Instructor Curriculum Materials, 1974.

Harnick, J. *Elementary creative bulletin boards.* New York: Citation Press, 1969.

Henning, D.G. *Smiles, nods, and pauses: Activities to enrich children's communciation skills.* New York: Citation Press, 1974.

Henning, D.G. *Words, sounds, and thoughts: More activities to enrich children's communications skills.* New York: Citation Press, 1977.

Holden, M.M. *Fun with language arts.* Dansville, N.Y.: Instructor Curriculum Materials, 1973.

Hucklesby, S. *Opening up the classroom: A walk around the school.* ERIC Clearinghouse on Early Childhood Education (University of Illinois at Urbana), 1971.

Hunt, S.D. *Language arts game handbook.* Jackson, Miss.: State Department of Education, Administrative Unit.

Hutson, N.B. *Stage: A handbook for teachers of creative dramatics.* Stevensville, Miss.: Educational Service, 1968.

Johnson, Ida Mae. *Developing the listening skills.* Freeport, N.Y.: Educational Activities, 1974.

Kaplan, P, Kohfeldy, J., & Sturla, K. *It's positively fun.* Denver, Colo.: Love Publishing Co., 1974.

Learning Magazine, Editors. *Mud puddles, rainbows and asparagus tips: Learning's best language arts ideas.* Palo Alto, Calif.: Education Today Co., 1979.

Lorton M.B. *Workjobs: Activity centered learning for early childhood education.* Reading, Mass.: Addison-Wesley, 1972.

Lutz, J. *Expanding spelling skills.* Dansville, N.Y.: Instructor Curriculum Materials, 1973.

Lyle, K. *Creative writing.* Memphis City Schools, Reading Center, 1975.

Moore A. & Pate, J.E. *Handbook of kindergarten activities.* New York: Teachers Publishing Corp., 1971.

Peck, M.J., & Schultz, M.J. *Teaching ideas that make learning fun.* West Nyack, N.Y.: Parker Publishing Co., Inc., 1969.

Perkins, T.W. *Understanding the news.* New York: Scholastic Book Service, 1970.

Phillips, W.H., & O'Lague, J.H. *Successful bulletin boards.* Dansville, N.Y.: Instructor Curriculum Materials, 1973.

Platts, M.E. *Spice.* Stevensville, Mich.: Educational Service, Inc., 1973.

Polon, L., & Cantwell, A. *Making kids click: Reading and language arts activities.* Santa Monica, Calif.: Goodyear Publishing Co., 1978.

Reeke, A., & Laffey, J. *Pathways to imagination: Language arts learning centers and activities.* Santa Monica, Calif.: Goodyear Publishing Co., 1979.

Rockwitz, M. *Arrow book of word games.* New York: Scholastic Book Services, 1964.

Russell, D.H., & Russel, E. *Listening aids through the grades,* 2nd ed. New York: Teachers College Press, Columbia, University, 1979.

Saludis, A.J. *Language arts activities* (2nd ed.). Dubuque, Iowa: Kendall/Hunt Publishing Company, 1977.

Schaff, J. *The language arts idea book: Classroom activities for children.* Pacific Palisades, Calif.: Goodyear Publishing Co., 1976.

Scott, L.B., May, M.E., & Shaw, M.S. *Puppets for all grades.* Dansville, N.Y.: Instructor Curriculum Materials, 1972.

Silverblatt, I.M. *Creative activities.* Cincinnati, Ohio: Creative, 1964.

Smith, C.W. *The listening activity book: Teaching literal, evaluative, and critical listening in the elementary school.* Belmont, Calif.: Fearon Publishers, 1975.

Spencer, Z.A. *Flair: A handbook of creative writing techniques for the elementary school teacher.* Stevensville, Mich.: Educational Service, 1972.

Thompson, R. *Treasure of teaching activities for elementary language arts.* Englewood Cliffs, N.J.: Prentice-Hall, 1975.

Tiedt, S., & Tiedt, I.M. *Language arts activities for the classroom.* Boston Mass.: Allyn and Bacon, Inc., 1978.

Wade, P.W., & Short, V. *Who says an old lemon can't have a new twist?* Santa Monica, Calif.: Goodyear Publishing Co., 1979.

Wagner, G. *Listening games*. Darien, Conn.: Teachers Publishing Corporation, 1962.

LEARNING CENTER REFERENCES

Bennie, F. *Learning centers: Development and operations*. Englewood Cliffs, N.J.: Educational Technology Publications, Inc., 1977.

Blake, H.E. *Creating a learning-centered classroom*. New York: Hart, 1976.

Crabtree, J. *Learning center ideas*. Cincinnati, Ohio: Standard Publisher, 1977.

Davidson, T. *Learning center book*. Salt Lake City, Utah: Goodyear, 1976.

Dick. N. *Ideas for reading learning centers*. Sacramento. Calif.: Reading Association, 1973.

Fisk, L. *Learning centers*. Glen Ridge, N.J.: Exceptional Press, 1974.

Forte, I., & Forte, M. *Nooks, crannies, and corners*. Nashville, Tenn.: Incentive Publications, Inc., 1972.

Forte, I. et al. *Center stuff for nooks, crannies, and corners*. Nashville, Tenn.: Incentive Publications, Inc., 1972.

Glasser, J.F. *Elementary school learning center for independent study*. Englewood Cliffs, N.J.: Prentice-Hall, 1971.

Greff, K., & Askov, E.N. *Learning centers: An ideabook for reading and language arts*. Dubuque, Iowa: Kendall/Hunt Publishing Company, 1974.

Horton, L. *The learning center: Heart of the school*. Minneapolis, Minn.: Denison, 1973.

Kaplin, S. et al. *Change for children*. Pacific Palisades, Calif.: Goodyear Publishing Company, 1973.

Maxim, G.W. *Learning centers for young children*. New York: Hart, 1976.

Morlan, J.E. *Classroom learning centers*. Belmont, Calif.: Fearon, 1974.

Nations, J.E. *Learning centers in the classroom*. Washington, D.C.: National Education Association, 1975.

Peterson, G.T. *Learning center: A sphere for non-traditional approaches to education*. Hamden, Conn.: Shoestring, 1975.

Ptreshene, S.S. *A complete guide to learning centers*. Palo Alto, Calif.: Pendragon House, 1977.

Rapport, V. *Learning centers: Children on their own. Washington, D.C.: Association for Childhood Education International, 1970*.

Thomas, J.I. *Learning centers: Opening up the classroom*. Boston: Holbrook Press, 1975.

Waynant, L., & Wilson, R.M. *Learning centers: A guide for effective use*. Paoli, Pa.: McGraw-Hill, 1974.

LANGUAGE ARTS TRADE BOOKS

Burns, P.C. Elementary school language arts library—a selected bibliography. *Elementary English,* 1964, *41,* 879–884.

Delmare, M. Language books for the library. *Elementary English,* 1968, *45,* 55–66.

Noyce, R.M., & Wyatt, F.R. Children's books for language exploration. *Language Arts* 1978, *55,* 297–301, 357.

Tiedt, I.M., & Tiedt, S.W. A linguistic library for students. In *Contemporary English in the Elementary School* (2nd ed.). Englewood Cliffs, N.J.: Prentice Hall, 1975.

Following is a sample list of books to indicate the scope and variety of such trade books:

Alphabet: Dugan, W. *How our alphabet grew.* New York: Golden, 1972.

Antonyms: Hanson, J. *Still more antonyms,* New York: Lerner, 1976.

Cliches and Idioms: Funk, C. *Heavens to Betsy,* New York: Warner, 1972.

Codes/Ciphers: Yerian, C., & Yerian, M. *Fun time codes and mystery messages.* Chicago: Children's Press, 1975.

Concepts: Hoban, T. *Push, pull, empty, full: A book of opposites,* New York: MacMillan, 1976.

Content Area Words: Asimov, I. *Words of science.* Boston: Houghton Mifflin, 1961.

Dictionary: Rosenbloom, J. *Daffy dictionary.* New York: Sterling, 1977.

Early Developing of Writing: Cahn, W., & Cahn, R. *The story of writing from cave art to computer.* New York: Harvey House, 1963.

Foreign language: Feelings, M. *Swahili counting book.* New York: Dial, 1973.

History of the English Language: Sparke, W. *Story of the English language.* New York: Abelard-Schuman, 1965.

Homophones: Hanson, J. *Homographic homophones,* New York: Lerner, 1973.

Language sounds: Curtis, F. *The little book of big tongue twisters.* New York: Harvey, 1977.

Letter Writing: Jacobson, H., & Mischel, F. *The first book of letter writing.* New York: Watts, 1957.

Library: Bucheimer, N. *Let's go to the library.* New York: G.P. Putnam's Sons, 1957.

Listening: Rand, A., & Rand, P. *Listen! listen!* New York: Harcourt Brace Jovanovich, Inc., 1970.

Nonverbal: Rinhoff, B. *Red light says stop!* New York: Lothrop, Lee, and Shepard, 1974.

Printing: Epstein, S., & Epstein, B. *The first book of printing.* New York: Watts, 1973.

Reporting: Brandt, S.R., *The first book of how to write a report.* New York: Watts, 1968.

Spelling: Van Gelder, R. *Monkeys have tails.* New York: McKay, 1966.

Word Origins: Hudson, P. *Words to the wise.* New York: Scholastic Book Services, 1967.

Word Play: Nurnberg, M. *Fun with words.* Englewood Cliffs, N.J.: Prentice Hall, 1970.

SPECIAL MULTILEVEL MATERIALS

1. American Book Co.
   1582 Stoneridge Drive
   Stone Mountain, Ga. 30083
   Our Language Today — Level 1–8
   Patterns of Language — Level 1–8

2. American Guidance Service
   Circle Pines, Minn. 55014
   Peabody Language Development Kits

3. BFA Educational Media
   3470 Old Fairburn Road
   Atlanta, Ga. 30331
   Tell the Whole Story Series
   (Super 8 silent filmloops for primary-elementary)

4. Barnell Loft, Ltd.
   958 Church Street
   Baldwin, N.Y. 11510
   Capitalization and Punctuation — (Set A-I), Grades 1–9

5. Benefic Press
   10300 West Roosevelt Road
   Westchester, Ill. 60153
   Oral Reading and Linguistics — Grades 1–6

6. Bowmar Publishing Corp.
   622 Rodier Drive
   Glendale, Calif. 91201
   ABC Serendipity — Grades 2–6
   Language Stimulus Program — Grades 3–8

7. Churchill Films
   662 N. Robertson Blvd.
   Los Angeles, CA 90069
   Let's Write a Story (films)

8. Communicad
   Box 541
   Wilton, Conn. 06897
   Wordcraft (Vocabulary program)
   Grades 4–6 — Remedially 7–13

9. Coronet Instructional Media
   65 East South Water Street
   Chicago, Ill. 60601
   How to Prepare a Class Report (film)
   Improve Your Handwriting (film)
   Improve Your Pronunciation (film)
   Improve Your Spelling (film)
   Know Your Library (film)
   Listen Well, Learn Well (filmstrip)

10. Curriculum Associates
    94 Bridge Street
    Chapel Hill Park
    Newton, Mass. 02518
    A Child-Centered Language Arts Program — Grades 3–8
    Children Writing Research Reports — Intermediate/middle school
    Elaborative Thinking Sets — Primary/intermediate

10. Curriculum Associates (cont.)
    Letters in Words—Preprimary/
      primary
    Right is Write—Grades K–8
    Thirty Lessons in Outlining—
      Organization skills for ele-
      mentary grades
    Word Growth Programs (Spell-
      ing)—Grades 2–6

11. D. C. Heath and Co.
    2700 North Richardt Avenue
    Indianapolis, Ind. 46219
    Communicating—The   Heath
      English Series, Levels 1–6
    English is Our Language—
      Grades K–6
    Primary Listening Skills—Grades
      K–3
    On My Own in Spelling—Grades
      3–6
    Reading Caravan—Grades 1–6

12. Disneyland Records
    Walt Disney Educational Ma-
      terials
    Glendale, Calif. 91201
    *The Art of Learning Through
      Movement*—Grades K–6

13. Doubleday Multimedia
    Box 11607, 1371 Reynolds Ave-
      nue
    Santa Ana, Calif. 92705
    *Learning Language Through
      Songs and Symbols*—Sets I,
      II, and III (filmstrips, teaching
      guide)
    More Road to Meaning (film-
      strips, teacher's guide, dupli-
      cator master)

14. Ealing Films
    Chapel Bridge Park
    Newton, Mass. 02158
    Springboards to Writing—
      Grades 4–6 (film)
    Story Starters—Grades 1–3
      (film)

15. Economy Co.
    P. O. Box 25308
    1901 North Walnut
    Oklahoma City, Okla. 73125
    Continuous Progress in Spelling

16. Educational Developmental Lab-
      oratories, Inc.
    1221 Avenue of the Americas
    New York, N.Y. 10036
    EDL STudy Skills Library
    Listen-Think Tapes
    Listen and Read

17. Educational Progress
    P.O. Box 45663
    Tulsa, Okla. 74145
    Spelling Progress Laboratory—
      Grades 2–6

18. Educational Services, Inc.
    P. O. Box 219
    Stevensville, Mich. 49127
    Anchor (for intermediate lan-
      guage arts)
    Flair (suggestions for creative
      writing)
    Spice (games, ideas, activities
      for primary language arts)

19. Encyclopedia Britannica Educa-
      tional Corp.
    425 N. Michigan Avenue
    Chicago, Ill. 60611
    *Language Experiences In Early
      Childhood*
    *Language Experiences In Read-
      ing*—Levels 1, 2, 3, and 4
    Magic Moments (20   16mm
      sound films)

20. Follett Education Corp.
    1010 West Washington Blvd.
    Chicago, Ill. 60607
    Follett Spelling Program
    Spelling and Writing Patterns—
      Grades 1–8
    The World of Language—Grades
      1–6
    Sound, Order, and Sense—
      Grades 1 and 2

21. Ginn and Co.
9888 Monroe Drive
Dallas, Texas 75229
Ginn Individualized Spelling Program
Invitations to Speaking and Writing Creatively
Let's Listen
22. Harcourt Brace Jovanovich
757 Third Avenue
New York, N.Y. 10017
The Bookmark Reading Program by M. Early—Grades K–8
Durrell-Murphy Phonics Practice Program
Language for Daily Use—Eight Levels
The Palo Alto Reading Program —Sequential Steps in Reading
Plays for Echo Reading (books and records, primary level.)
Sound and Sense In Spelling— Grades 1–8
Speech-to-Print Phonics: A Phonics Foundation for Reading
The Story Plays: Self-directing Materials for Oral Reading
23. Holt, Rinehart and Winston, Inc.
383 Madison Avenue
New York, N.Y. 10017
Holt's Impact—Grades 7–9
The Owl Program
Snoopy's Phonics Program— Grades K–6
Sounds of Language Readers— K–8
Story Starter Film Loops— Grades 1–6
Writing Center (set of stimulus cards)
24. Houghton Mifflin
2 Park Street
Boston, Mass. 02107
Interaction—K–12
Listen and Do
Listen and Learning

25. Individualized Instruction Inc.
P. O. Box 25308
Oklahoma City, Okla. 73125
Continuous Spelling Kit—Intermediate
Continuous Spelling Kit—Primary
26. Instructional Fair
4158 Lake Michigan Drive
Grand Rapids, Mich. 49504
Creative Writing Masters— Grades 1–6
27. The Instructo Corporation
Cedar Hollow and Matthews Road
Paoli, Pa. 19301
Contracations Magic Show— Grades 2–5
Decoding Everyday Abbreviations—Grades 2–5
Homonyms—Grades 2–5
Learning When to Capitalize (and when NOT)—Grades 2–5
Letter Writing (series of 4 transparencies, intermediate)
Punctuation and Capitalization (series of 11 transparencies) primary-intermediate
Punctuation-Periods, Questions and Exclamation Marks— Grades 2–5
Word Usage (series of 10 transparencies—intermediate-junior high
28. Laidlaw Brothers
A Division of Random House, Inc.
30 Chatham Road
Summit, N.J. 09701
Laidlaw Language Experiences Program—Grades K–8
New Laidlaw Spelling Series— Levels One through Eight
29. Lewing Press
720 Adrian Way
San Rafael, Calif. 94903

29. Lewing Press (cont.)

    Developing Listening Skills— Grades K–6
    Oral Language Skills Series— Grades K–6

30. Lyon and Carnahan
    407 E. 25th Street
    Chicago, Ill. 60616
    Handwriting with Write and See

31. Macmillan Publishing Co., Inc.
    866 Third Avenue
    New York, N.Y. 10022
    Adventures in Handwriting (plus support materials)—Grades 1–8
    Composing Language—English and Language Arts, Grades 1–8
    English Composition—Books 3–8
    Spelling: Sound to Letter— Levels 1–8

32. McCormick-Mahers Publishing Co.
    450 West 33rd Street
    New York, N.Y. 10001
    Skills and Spelling—Levels 1–8

33. McGraw-Hill Book Co.
    1221 Avenue of the Americas
    New York, N.Y. 10036
    How to Use An Encyclopedia (filmstrip)

34. Charles E. Merrill Publishing Co.
    1300 Alum Creek Drive
    Columbus, Ohio 43216
    Building Reading Power
    Merrill Linguistic Readers—Primary grade
    The Productive Thinking Program: A Course in Learning to Think—Upper Elementary

35. Miller-Brody Productions Inc.
    342 Madison Avenue
    New York, N.Y. 10017
    Building Verbal Power I (five 12" 33 1/3 rpm records)

35. Miller-Brody Prod. Inc. (cont.)

    Newbery Award Winners (records)
    Sounds for Young Readers (six 12" 33 1/3 rpm records)

36. Noble and Noble Publishers, Inc.
    1 Dag Hammerskjold Plaza
    New York, N.Y. 10017
    Spell/Write—Grades 1–8
    Story-Go-Round—Grades K–3
    Try (reading readiness experiences program for young children)

37. Pacific Production
    414 Main Street
    San Francisco, Calif. 94102
    Learning to Use the Dictionary (filmstrip)

38. Pied Piper Productions
    Box 320
    Verdugo City, Calif. 91046
    English Composition for Children—Series 1, 2, and 3 (filmstrips, teacher guide, records or cassettes)

39. Popular Science Publishing Co.
    355 Lexington Avenue
    New York, N.Y. 10017
    Goals in Spelling Series (filmstrips)

40. Prentice-Hall
    Englewood Cliffs, N.J. 07632
    The Phoenix Reading Series— Grades 4–6
    Spelling Spree (filmstrips and cassettes)

41. Random House School Division
    201 East 50th Street
    New York, N.Y. 10022
    Aware—(A poetry learning unit)
    Enrichment Records
    The Writing Bug—Middle grades

42. Reader's Digest Services Inc.
    Education Division
    Pleasantville, N.Y. 10579

42. Reader's Digest Serv. Inc. (cont.)
   Advanced Reading Skills Library
   Reading Skill Builder Kits
   Reading Skills Library
   Reading Tutors
   Write to Communicate: The Language Arts in Process—Grades 3–6

43. Scholastic Magazine and Book Services
   50 West 44th Street
   New York, N.Y. 10036
   Creative Expression Series (a five-book writing skills series)—Grades 2–6
   Firebird Library (history and biography of minority Americans)—Grades 5–8
   Scholastic's K–6 Pleasure Reading Library
   Scholastic's K–3 Poetry Collection
   Scholastic's Listening Skill Program—Grades 1–6

44. Science Research Associates, Inc.
   259 East Erie Street
   Chicago, Ill. 60611
   Basic Composition Series II and III—Grades 5–8
   Penskill I—Grades 1–3
   Penskill II—Grades 4–6
   Spelling Word Power Laboratory
   Listening Skills Program
   Words and Patterns
   Writing Skills Laboratory

45. Scott, Foresman and Co.
   1900 East Lake Avenue
   Glenview, Ill. 60025
   Sounds I Can Hear (record)
   Sounds Around Us (record)
   Talkstarters

46. Society for Visual Education, Inc.
   1345 Diversey Parkway
   Chicago, Ill. 60614

46. Society for Vis. Ed., Inc. (cont.)
   The Comma Series (filmstrip)
   How to Listen (filmstrips)
   Making English Work for You (filmstrips, teacher's guide, records or cassettes)
   Use Your Library (filmstrip)

47. Steck-Vaughn Co.
   P. O. Box 2028
   Austin, Texas 78767
   The Experience Series
   The Human Values Series—Grades K–6
   Imaginary Line Handwriting Series—K–8

48. Teachers College Press
   Columbia University
   1234 Amsterdam Avenue
   New York, N.Y. 10027
   Composition: Guided-Free—Grades 1–5

49. Teachers Publishing Corp.
   A Division of MacMillan Publishing
   100 F Brown Street,
   Riverside, N.J. 08075
   Strengthening Language Skills with Instructional Games
   Listening Games

50. Troll Associates
   320 Rt. 17
   Mahwah, N.Y. 07430
   Listen and Think: A Cognitive Listening Skills Program—Intermediate
   New Goals in Listening—Grades 1–3
   New Goals in Listening—Grades 2–4

51. Webster Division
   McGraw-Hill Book Co.
   1221 Avenue of the Americas
   New York, N.Y. 10020
   English For Today—Grades 2–8
   Learning Language Skills: A Creative Approach—Ages 4–8

51. Webster Div. McGraw-Hill (cont.)
   Let's Speak English—Grades 1–6
   Listening Time (record album)
   —Grades 1–3
   Programmed Reading—Grades
   1–3
   Sullivan Storybooks—Grades
   1–3 (correlated with pro-
   grammed reading)

   Tell Again Story Cards—Pre-
   school- Grade 1 (Levels I
   and II)

52. Xerox Education Publications
   Education Center
   Columbus, Ohio 43216
   Listen! Imagine and Write (re-
   cords and books)—Grades 3–6

5
Listening

There are several reasons for the neglect of listening instruction in elementary schools. Some teachers falsely think that listening, like walking, is naturally developed; that listening is the same as hearing; and that listening is not as important as the other language arts. Many children's language arts books do not give much attention to listening, as may have been true of the language arts textbook studied by the teacher.

While listening can be correlated with activities in all subjects (children listen for unknown words in a social studies report, for example), and is certainly interrelated with the other language arts (choral reading can evoke appreciative listening), nevertheless listening cannot be fully developed in the content areas or even in the general language arts context. Listening must be the focus of special attention at times.

In order to provide listening instruction, teachers must provide conditions that are conducive to attentive listening. The following suggestions can aid in developing a positive environment toward listening:

- Provide comfortable physical conditions, such as proper temperatures, comfortable seats, quiet atmosphere free of distracting noise.
- Serve as a model of a good listener.
- Pace your speaking tone, pitch, volume, and speed to the chil-

dren's listening speed. (Normal speech rate for accurate comprehension is considered to be 150–175 words per minute.)
- Provide listening opportunities that are purposeful.
- Help children realize that varying degrees of attention are required for different kinds of listening.
- Praise the children for good listening.
- Hold discussions concerning practices that could encourage better listening.
- Avoid needless repetitions in providing directions and instructions.
- Help children develop rules for good listening habits.
- Help children eliminate poor listening habits.

LISTENING DISABILITIES

An analysis of listening difficulties should include diagnosis of hearing difficulties and a consideration of total adjustment, including personality.

Furness has made an analysis of learning disabilities and their possible causes. She also suggests teaching procedures to help in overcoming these disabilities. These are listed in Chart 5–1. (Caution should be exercised where an item may not account for dialect differences.)

EVALUATION OF LISTENING

In the evaluation of listening, both formal and informal tests may be used. Two standardized listening tests are *Sequential Tests of Educational Progress* (STEP) (grades 4–12) and *The Cooperative Primary Tests* which contain a listening test for primary level children. Both are published by the Educational Testing Service, Cooperative Test Division, Princeton, New Jersey.

Astute observation by the teacher in daily activities and occasional teacher-made listening tests are the important parts of the listening evaluation program.

Check Lists

Even at the early primary levels, children can formulate standards for listening and judge whether or not their performances meet their own standards. Self-evaluation check lists such as Chart 5–2 can help children become aware of the many factors involved in listening.

CHART 5-1. An analysis of listening disabilities, causes, and teaching procedures

Disabilities	Possible Causes	Suggested Teaching Procedures
Physiological Faulty auditory discrimination	Unable to hear sounds. Unable to distinguish between two sounds of differing frequencies (tones). Does not recognize similarities and differences in the sounds of words and word elements. Hears a certain range of pitches (vowels or consonants—low or high tones). Has such disabilities as: partial deafness, middle ear infection, partial blocking of Eustachian tube, diseased or enlarged tonsils and adenoid tissue, nerve involvement, improper development of auditory nerve relative to acuity at the time speech is learned. Poor auditory memory. Social factors: mispronunciations heard in home, foreign accent, sectional speech, tension.	1. Give individual tests with a pure tone audio-meter. 2. If an audiometer is not available, use a watch, or observe child's reactions to words spoken in a normal tone. 3. Urge delinquent listeners to improve overall personal health, to regulate diet and bodily comfort. 4. Place child in front of room with better ear toward teacher. 5. Encourage child to watch faces of those talking. 6. Train ear to hear differences in vowel sounds as well as similarities of voiced and voiceless consonant sounds. 7. Have pupils listen to low tones and high tones on piano.

NOTE. From "A Remedial and Developmental Program in Listening," by Edna Lue Furness. *Elementary English*, 1955, 32, 525-31. Copyright © 1955 by the National Council of Teachers of English. Reprinted by permission of the publisher and Edna Lue Furness.

CHART 5-1 (cont.)

Disabilities	Possible Causes	Suggested Teaching Procedures
		8. Sing two tones and ask pupils to tell whether tones are same or different, open, up, high or low.
		9. Have pupils speak their names and addresses on a record and then play back.
		10. Have pupils listen to passing vehicles, trucks, automobiles, street cars, and airplanes, and identify sound with source.
		11. Train pupil to recognize likenesses and differences in speech sounds in complete sentences or thought groups.
		12. Use songs and poems for dictating and repeating.
		13. Pronounce words which have same beginning sound: *cake, come.*

Poor motor coordination	Unevenness of growth. Result of hereditary factors.	1. Engage in rhythmic activities and games.
Speech problems (faulty enunciation, articulation, pronunciation, speech defects)	Lowered power of auditory discrimination. Substitution of one sound for another: *dough* for *go*. Poor speech habits. Inflexibility of tongue. Enlargement of tongue. Foreign language spoken in home.	1. Teach correct placement of tongue and lips. 2. Train pupil to hear distinctions between *where* and *wear*, *witch* and *which*. 3. Hear rhyming words. 4. Identify rhyming similarities. 5. Tell original stories, tall stories, fables. 6. Give oral reports, choral readings, dramatizations, debates. 7. Repeat tongue twisters. 8. Have child listen to a playback of his speech. 9. Listen to speech of associates. 10. Teacher should use a conversational tone in oral reading. 11. Refer child to a clinic or speech correctionist.

CHART 5-1 (cont)

Disabilities	Possible Causes	Suggested Teaching Procedures
Fatigue	Poor physical condition. Inadequate diet. Poor eating habits. Inadequate rest or poor habits of sleep. Too much close work. A too heavy schedule. Too many outside acitivities. Excessive homework or home duties.	1. Check child's general physical condition. 2. Confer with parents about physical diagnosis, in carrying out remedial treatments, in giving child adequate rest and relief from tensions or distracting outside duties and disturbances. 3. Recognize signs of fatigue or boredom as a signal for closing the listening period.
Physical discomfort	Room is too warm, humid, or chilly. Noises distract. Speaker uses ungainly gestures, speaks in guttural or loud voice, looks over the heads of his audience.	1. Provide classroom conditions and environment conducive to easy and uninterrupted listening: proper temperature, comfortable seats, proper lights. 2. Adjust acoustic conditions of classrooms. 3. Avoid strong draft, a hot, sticky atmosphere, a cramped position, loud talking. 4. Avoid unseemly gestures, lack of poise, a grating or shrill voice. 5. Help pupil acquire a pleasing manner of presentation.

Psychological
Lack of listening readiness

Poor health. Poor hearing. Muscular incoordination. Low mentality. Lack of general language facility. Deficiency in oral language. Mental and physical immaturity. Lack of experiences which provide a meaningful background and earlier learning activities. Lack of an adequate and pertinent listening vocabulary. Lack of good speaking and comprehension vocabularies. Lack of purpose for listening. Failure to see relationship between listening and his other activities. Lack of independence and desire to learn.

1. Increase child's background of experience.

2. Present concrete materials.

3. Give special oral directions.

4. Give pupils meaningful activity along with opportunity to execute specific directions.

5. Arouse pupil's interest, by relating subject matter to interests and past experiences.

6. Have child envision the actions, feel the emotions, admire characters portrayed in graphic oral reading.

7. Have younger children sense time sequence.

8. Have older children determine main points in a discourse, and make a mental outline of what they hear.

9. Provide speech activities such as conversation, discussion, storytelling, and dramatizations.

10. Have child listen to answer specific questions.

11. Teacher must have speech free from defect and should be sensitive to speech sounds.

CHART 5-1 (cont)

Disabilities	Possible Causes	Suggested Teaching Procedures
Emotional mal-adjustments	Emotional imbalance caused by: Auditory impairment, conductive deafness, self-consciousness, over-sensitiveness, speech defect, nervous tensions and frustrations, inferiority feeling toward listening, resulting from child's inability to master listening. Lack of parental interest in child's school life. Tension in school or home. Confusion in classroom. Poor social adjustment to school or to associates. Too much competition. Change of schools and teachers during the year.	1. Discover hearing defect in early stages. 2. Discover as far as possible child's personal anxieties. 3. Confer with parents. 4. Teacher must be a good listener. 5. Teacher should listen attentively and courteously. 6. Avoid sarcasm, ridicule, and disparagement. 7. Give child a sense of security, self-reliance, self-respect, and importance. 8. Provide opportunities for child to establish a feeling of successful accomplishment in listening tasks. 9. Encourage competition with self. 10. Be generous with praise and recognition for child's efforts and progress.

Personality traits	Prejudice. Egocentricity. Narrow-mindedness. Improper attitude toward school, teachers, subjects, speaker, or cause, Antagonism. Resentment of unsympathetic or sarcastic teacher. Boredom. Lack of interest in subject. Nervousness.	1. Cultivate fairmindedness. 2. Provide interest-provoking background.
Retarded mental development	Lack of meaning vocabulary. Inability to get meaning from verbal stimuli.	1. Develop child's speaking, writing, and hearing vocabularies insofar as is possible.
Pedagogical Lack of interest	Meager experience or none at all in listening experience. Unhappy experiences. Material for listening below child's interest level. Material too mature for child's interest level. Failure to recognize purpose for listening.	1. Use material related to child's personal experiences and concerns. 2. Furnish child with materials within his interest level. 3. Have children play listening games, the object of which is to remember proper sequence, to pronounce distinctly, and to listen accurately. 4. Provide audience situations such as plays, charades, programs.
Lack of purpose	Failure to distinguish between listening for pleasure and listening for information.	1. Listen for news. 2. Listen for directions which one expects to follow.

109

CHART 5-1 (cont)

Disabilities	Possible Causes	Suggested Teaching Procedures
		3. Have pupils listen for the answer to a definite question.
		4. Have pupils listen to a question, with the intention to answer.
		5. Listen to an argument in order to answer it.
		6. Listen to form an opinion on a controversial issue.
Half listening	Poor listening habits. Listening without purpose. Expectation of entertainment.	1. Establish good listening habits in classes, clubs, pupil activities.
		2. Be interested in materials that interest the child.
		3. Have pupils understand purpose of listening activity.
		4. Have children use more than a word or sentence in response to a question.
		5. Evaluate quality of listening by observing changes in pupil behavior, habits, attitudes, and ideals.

Failure to listen discriminatively	Does not grasp organization of materials. Fails to grasp significant points. Unable to relate content with purpose. Fails to discriminate between fact and principle, ideal and example, evidence and argument, essential and less important	1. Discuss personal experiences. 2. Listen to story read by teacher. 3. Have pupil read a story. 4. Have a panel discussion. 5. Provide opportunity for purposeful listening, definite notetaking, discriminating judgment in selecting a theme topic, and in using illustrations.
Failure to listen critically	Has inadequate listening vocabulary. Listens to refute arguments with which he disagrees. Listens to support ideas he holds. Does not recognize significance of statements. Does not evaluate worth of statements. Does not discover relationship between ideas.	1. Reserve judgment. 2. Discount bias of speaker. 3. Ask for source of information. 4. Require evidence for statements made. 5. Watch for indefinite emotionalized terms. 6. Distinguish fact from principle, argument from evidence. 7. Detect false inferences and unsupported generalizations. 8. Distinguish relevant from irrelevant material. 9. Detect hidden purposes.

CHART 5-2. Checking up on my listening

	Yes	No
1. Did I remember to get ready for listening?	___	___
a. Was I seated comfortably where I could see and hear?	___	___
b. Were my eyes focused on the speaker?	___	___
2. Was my mind ready to concentrate on what the speaker had to say?	___	___
a. Was I able to push other thoughts out of my mind for the time being?	___	___
b. Was I ready to think about the topic and call to mind the things I already knew about it?	___	___
c. Was I ready to learn more about the topic?	___	___
3. Was I ready for "take-off"?	___	___
a. Did I discover in the first few minutes where the speaker was taking me?	___	___
b. Did I discover his central idea so that I could follow it through the speech?	___	___
4. Was I able to pick out the ideas which supported the main idea?	___	___
a. Did I take advantage of the speaker's clues (such as first, next, etc.) to help organize the ideas in my mind?	___	___
b. Did I use my extra "think" time to summarize and take notes—either mentally or on paper?	___	___
5. After the speaker finished and the facts were all in, did I evaluate what had been said?	___	___
a. Did this new knowledge seem to fit with the knowledge I already had?	___	___
b. Did I weigh each idea to see if I agreed with the speaker?	___	___

If you marked questions NO, decide why you could not honestly answer them YES.

NOTE. From "The Evaluation of Oral Language Activity: Teaching and Learning," by O. W. Kopp. *Elementary English,* 1967, *44,* 114-23. Reprinted with the permission of the National Council of Teachers of English and O. W. Kopp.

Wilt (1957) developed the following criteria for use by upper elementary children in evaluating their own listening powers:

Do I
  Hold the thread of a discussion in mind?
  Listen to content even though it does not affect me directly?

Watch for transitional phrases?
Try to discount bias in a speaker?
Disagree with a speaker courteously?
Reserve judgment in listening to different viewpoints in discussion?
Indicate by my remarks that I have turned over in my mind the ideas of
others?

The alert teacher will find countless opportunities to evaluate listening as children plan units of work, give reports, give directions and make announcements, tell or read stories, and take part in choral reading or speaking.

Of course, teachers and their procedures are an important consideration in the listening art. The following questions might alert the teacher to his responsibility:

- Do I provide a classroom environment (emotional and physical) that encourages good listening?
- Am I a good listener and do I really listen to the pupils?
- Do I use appropriate tone, pitch, volume, and speed in my speaking?
- Do I vary the classroom program to provide lisening experiences (films, discussions, debates, reports) which are of interest to the children?
- Am I aware of opportunities for teaching listening throughout the day?
- Do I help pupils see the purpose for listening in each activity?
- Do I help children see the importance and value of being good listeners?
- Do I build a program in which listening skills are consistently taught and practiced?

Early in the school year the teacher might evaluate the listening skills of the children by keeping such questions as the following in mind:

- How well do the children follow directions?
- How often must I repeat instructions?
- Do the children's responses show that they comprehend what they hear?
- Are the children accurate in recalling information after a listening experience?
- Is there appropriate questioning of content, new words, and concepts?
- Do the children "get ready" for listening?

LISTENING

Analyzing and Recording

To measure listening strengths and weaknesses, planned sessions may be needed with focus upon the specific skills listed below. The listening ability of the pupil can be analyzed in activities like those in Chart 5–3.

CHART 5-3. Activities for analyzing skills

Skill	Pupil Activity
Attitudinal	
1. Understanding difference between hearing and listening	Playing a game, such as "Simon Says"
2. Understanding the importance of listening	Keeping a chart of all things done during the day which involve listening
3. Understanding the responsibilities of a listener	Discussing behaviors, as listeners to a guest speaker
4. Recognizing some factors that affect listening	Experimenting with listening when physical comfort and ability to hear are altered
5. Recognizing poor listening habits	Identifying reasons for inability to answer specific questions
6. Recognizing characteristics of an effective listener	Compiling a list of standards for good listening
Informational	
7. Identifying main idea	Writing one-sentence summary or title for a selection
8. Identifying details	Outlining, with topics and subtopics
9. Recognizing stated cause and effect relationships	Stating causes for a result or vice versa
10. Detecting sequence	Predicting "what next"
11. Drawing conclusions	Writing concluding statements
12. Making generalizations	Writing a generalized statement
13. Recognizing speaker's purpose	Determining if purpose is to inform, entertain, persuade
Appreciative	
14. Enjoying prose	Indentifying author's intended mood or effect
15. Noting pleasing rhyme or rhythm	Suggesting intended mood or effect
16. Sensing images	Analyzing words that produce images
17. Sensing moods	Noting words that reveal mood

CHART 5-3 (cont)

Skill	Pupil Activity
Analytical	
18. Recognizing speaker's bias	Detecting the effect a speaker's bias has on his or her statements
19. Determining speaker's qualifications	Relating a speaker's qualifications for speaking on a particular topic
20. Determining accuracy of information	Selecting proven statements
21. Differentiating fact from opinion	Labeling statements as fact or opinion
22. Recognizing propaganda techniques	Naming specific technique
23. Understanding implied cause and effect relationships	Stating causes for a result or vice versa when not directly stated
24. Visualizing events	Drawing pictures from oral descriptions of events
25. Using material heard to solve problems	Discussing questions such as "How was the problem handled?" "Was the solution a good one?"
26. Predicting outcomes	Forecasting what will happen next based on knowledge of events in the past
27. Modifying what is heard	Elaborating in a new, different manner

Chart 5–4 is a sample of a form for screening purposes and for rechecking listening skills in Chart 5–3. From such information, the teacher can form homogeneous groups on the basis of level of performance on the various types of listening. Listening activities should be planned sequentially, designed for the appropriate level, and based on past learnings.

A LEARNING CENTER FOR LISTENING

The main purpose of a learning center is to provide for individual differences in ability, pace of learning, mode of learning, and interest. The steps in planning a center are:

1. Identify the content area
2. Pretest to diagnose strengths and weaknesses of pupils
3. Determine the skills or learning needed

CHART 5-4. Analysis of listening skills

Skill	Jim	Betty	Joe	Alice
(Attitudinal)				
1. Understanding difference between hearing and listening				
2. Understanding the importance of listening				
3. Understanding the responsibilities of a listener				
4. Recognizing some factors that affect listening				
25. Using material heard to solve problems				
26. Predicting outcomes				
27. Modifying what is heard				

Key: I— No skill; needs introduction and teaching

R— Weak; needs review/reinforcement

S— Satisfactory; regular program adequate satisfactorily at this time

M—Has mastered skill; no more practice needed

4. Establish the sequence of tasks from easiest to most difficult
5. Find different kinds of instructional materials to use and devise varied ways to present them in tasks of graduated difficulty
6. Posttest to evaluate each major segment of the center

Planning the use of the center with the children—perhaps conducting a trial run for the first few tasks—is a prerequisite. The teacher must evaluate and revise the center tasks as they are used by the children.

Four kinds of listening might be a part of the center—attitudinal informational, appreciative, and critical. Choose materials on the basis of an evaluation of the children's listening using standardized tests, informal check lists, or tape recordings.

Listening center supplies might include commercially and teacher-developed tapes, concrete materials, radios, records, television, and books. Some activities might be for individuals, others for pairs, or a group of peers.

Chart 5–5 is a sampling of tasks which might be part of a listening center. Tasks should be graduated in levels of difficulty.

ADDITIONAL CORRECTIVE ACTIVITIES

1. If a child needs further experiences with environmental sounds, provide opportunity for listening attentively to everyday sounds, city and country sounds, pleasant and unpleasant sounds, comforting and frightening sounds, funny and sad sounds, day and night sounds, inside and outside sounds, winter and summer sounds, and the like. These can be supplemented through different recordings. The sounds of animals, machines, and people can also be differentiated.

2. If a child needs further experiences with discrimination skills (recognizing and identifying likenesses and differences in sounds), use primary reading program materials which commonly focus upon recognizing differences in consonant sounds, vowel sounds, rhyming words, and other sound and symbol relationships.

3. The activity source books cited on pages 90–93, the trade (library) books, and the multi level materials, cited on pages 94–100, should be reviewed for books and materials dealing with listening activities.

4. The students may be asked to list some common habits that produce negative listening results and to suggest ways of preventing or remediating such habits. Examples of negative habits are:

- Thinking the topic is uninteresting. (Background is often needed to understand and appreciate what a speaker is saying.)
- Thinking about the speaker rather than the content of the speech. (Both listeners and speakers have responsibilities to help one another.)
- Failing to listen objectively. (Strong emotional reactions to one idea may prevent the listener from processing additional content of a speech. Evaluation should come after there is sufficient evidence for judgment.)
- Listening only for facts. (Good listeners concentrate on getting main ideas.)

CHART 5-5. Task ideas for listening centers

Skills	Tasks	Materials Needed
Attitudinal Listening		
Hearing and listening	Repeat a story	Story record. One child listens to record and tells the story to a second in private. The second child tells a third. Is the story told by third child the same as the one on the record?
Importance of listening	Follow oral directions	"Pin the Tail on the Donkey" game. Teacher gives blindfolded child directions—"move to right, left."
Listener's role	Hold a telephone conversation	Telephones or teletrainers. Check list for attentive and courteous response.
Factors	Explain what affects listening	Tapes of a passage containing ideas and vocabulary above comprehension of listener.
Poor listening	Listen purposefully and selectively	Tape, giving directions once, such as "8-5-2-6-9: Which number is closest to the sum of two plus two?"
Effective listener	Recognize listening attitudes	Pictures of people or animals, listening. Answer questions about what the person or animal is doing, attitude, or characteristics. Draw figures to illustrate poor listening attitudes.

118

Informative Listening		
Main idea	Identify main idea of a passage	Commercial record or tape designed to present main idea.
Details	Find answers to specific questions	Tapes of graded difficulty. Detailed questions to answer.
Stated cause and effect	Relate cause and effect	A taped series of causes such as "He fell in the lake" for listener to relate an effect, as "He got wet."
Sequence	Establish sequence	Taped story. Set of sequential pictures.
Conclusions	Write reasonable ending sentence	Commercial record designed for drawing conclusions; or taped reading of appropriate material.
Generalizations	Make a generalization	Taped or recorded selections from which generalizations can be made.
Speaker's purpose	Recognize purpose of speaker	Taped or recorded talks by speakers to persuade, to inform, or to entertain.
Appreciative Listening		
Reacting to prose	Identify variety of words	Commercial record. Work sheets to write substitute words for trite or "worn out" expressions used on record.
Noting pleasing rhyme or rhythm	Mark stress in a sonnet	Poetry record or tape. Copy of poem to mark stressed and unstressed syllables.

119

Chart 5-5 (cont)

Skills	Tasks	Materials Needed
Sensing images	Describe or illustrate image conveyed in poem or story read aloud	Lyric poem read by a peer.
Sensing moods	Contrast poems written in differing moods	Poetry tape. Crayons, finger paint, paper.
Analytical Listening		
Speaker's bias	Compare two reports of same event	Teacher-made tapes from accounts by two newspapers.
Speaker's qualifications	Compare speakers' qualifications for speaking on a particular topic	A series of speakers.
Accuracy of information	Analyze advertisement	Newspaper or magazine advertisements.
Fact and opinion	Detect clues to opinions	Radio documentary. Identify clues to "opinions."
Propaganda techniques	Recognize specific techniques	Posters naming and illustrating techniques. Taped messages to be labeled.

Implied cause and effect	Relate effect and cause	Taped series of results such as "He ate a dozen hamburgers" for listener to relate an effect, as "He was hungry."
Visualizing events	Sketch scenes or situations from oral presentation	Tapes of a series of paragraphs that vividly describe scenes or situations.
Using material	Analyze solutions	Taped story in which a problem is solved.
Predicting outcomes	Tell continuation of a story	Peer reads a certain part of a book to another.
Modifying ideas	Elaborate on a story	Book to be read aloud. Student writes another episode.

- Faking attention. (Good listening is active—not just assuming a listening pose.)
- Permitting distractions. (Overwhelming distractions need to be tuned out.)
- Failing to use the differential between speech and thought speed. (Plan to use the differential time in recall, relating ideas—not allowing yourself to stray off to unrelated thoughts.)

REVIEW QUESTIONS AND ACTIVITIES

1. Trace the scope and sequence of listening through the charts provided in the Appendix.
2. Develop a systematic lesson plan to teach a specific listening skill, following the model provided in Chapter 2.
3. What are some causes of listening disability of "lack of interest"? Suggest three or four remedial teaching suggestions.
4. Administer an appropriate standardized listening test to a child.
5. Differentiate between the four types of listening.
6. Fully develop one of the tasks that might be presented in a listening learning center.
7. Prepare an activity or game for helping a child who needs further experiences with environmental sounds.
8. Prepare an activity or game for helping a child who needs further experiences with discrimination skills or sounds.
9. Develop a card file of ideas, games, and language arts books focusing on strategies and materials for helping a child with listening disability.
10. Review articles dealing with the diagnosis and correction of difficulties in listening.
11. Review source books, trade books, and multilevel materials that deal specifically with the listening component of the language arts.
12. Develop a teaching plan related to one of the "Additional Corrective Activities."

REFERENCES

Lundsteen, Sara. *Listening: Its impact on reading and other language arts,* rev. ed. Urbana, Ill.: National Council of Teachers of English, 1979.

Wilt, M.E. "Let's teach listening." In *Creative ways of teaching the language arts.* Champaign, Ill.: National Council of Teachers of English, 1957, p. 88.

6
Oral Communication

Although the importance of oral communication is generally recognized, it is not always recognized that children should have opportunities to talk in the classroom. Sometimes they are even discouraged from talking.

Some ways to develop oral language abilities are:

- Provide opportunities for talking so that children can use their language skills.
- Discuss standards for speech and suggest improvements.
- Plan with the child before a performance.
- Stress the importance of a good audience-speaker relationship.
- Evaluate, diagnose, and identify individual deficiencies.

In addition, the teacher should set a good example and the atmosphere must be informal and relaxed.

To develop oral language competence, much time must be allowed for groups of children, drawn together by common interests, to talk together about their activities. When the whole group works together, only one person can talk at a time, and that person is too often the teacher. In small groups, many children can participate in the discussion, and the teacher can take time to circulate and listen. This provides an opportunity for noting individual competencies and needs. On the basis of this information, children can be regrouped for specific purposes.

Informal techniques for diagnosing oral expression should continue throughout the year. These might include anecdotal records, interviews, casual and structured observations of speech habits, and criteria and standards prepared cooperatively by the teacher and pupils. Only through a comprehensive program of diagnosis can the teacher secure a true and complete analysis of pupil performance upon which to base corrective treatment.

INFORMAL ASSESSMENT OF
ORAL LANGUAGE DEVELOPMENT

An informal language inventory is a way of measuring growth in children's everyday speech. An evaluation procedure for young children, as reported by Melear (1974), involves the steps below. (Remember, the child's response can be limited by the drawing he makes.)

Instruct the child to draw a picture of anything he wants to draw. (10 minutes)
Turn on a tape recorder.
Ask, "Would you like to tell me about this picture?" (Wait 45 seconds for a response.)
If the child responds, say, "That was very good."
Transcribe the recording.
Record the number of morphemes.
Record the number of sentences.
Record the number of grammatically correct sentences.
Record the percentage of correct sentences.
Record the number of descriptive terms.
Record the number of modifying phrases.

The number of "mazes" in the learner's oral language is also an important item to note. (Mazes are confused and tangled groups of words characterized by hesitations, false starts, and meaningless repetitions. In other words they are unattached fragments that do not constitute a meaningful communication unit—for example, "and uh . . . , uh . . . yeah, uh . . . ," etc.) Record these data for mazes:

The number of mazes.
The number of words in the mazes.
Average number of words per maze.
The percent that maze words are of total words.

Stauffer and Pikulski (1974) have analyzed oral language in the dictated stories of first graders who were being taught by the language-experience approach. The technique can be helpful at any level where the language-experience approach is used.

The language-experience approach uses student-produced materials. The students write or dictate stories based upon their personal experiences. The stories may be written by individuals or small groups and may be based upon in-class or out-of-class experiences. These stories may be used by the teacher to teach such language arts skills as planning what to say, organizing a logical sequence, choosing the words to convey the exact meaning intended, and learning about the conventions of writing.

This approach is especially effective as corrective instruction for several reasons:

Because the stories are produced by the students themselves, the students are motivated to study them. It is ego-satisfying to study something they have produced themselves.

Because the students' own language is used, the material is meaningful to them. Frequently, stories from language arts texts are not meaningful to all students.

Even though the language patterns in students' stories are frequently more mature than those found in text materials, the students seem to find their own language patterns easier to work with.

Older students are not exposed to material that they may view as "baby stuff." The stories are on the maturity levels of the students who compose them.

The approach offers something in all learning modes (visual, auditory, kinesthetic, or tactile) because all modes are incorporated. The learner uses the auditory mode when stories are dictated or read aloud, the visual mode when stories are read and analyzed, and the kinesthetic and tactile modes when stories are written.

With the language-experience approach, language study grows out of natural, ongoing activities. Pupils can see the relationships between reading and their oral language, writing and the spelling of words.

This approach promotes a good self-concept. It shows the student that what he or she has to say is important enough to write down.

There are some disadvantages to using this approach. It may not offer a systematic development of language arts skills. The stories may be lacking in literary quality, and repeated work with the same story may become boring to students. Producing the stories in type-written or other forms can be time consuming for the teacher.

If each child is given a notebook in which his dictations are placed, the teacher can monitor his language progress on a regular basis for these evidences of growth:

average number of words
average number of sentences
average number of short sentences
average number of long sentences
average number of pronouns
average number of prepositions

An excellent reference for the language experience approach is *Teaching Reading as a Language Experience,* 2nd edition, by Marianne Hall (Columbus, Ohio: Charles E. Merrill, 1976.)

DIAGNOSIS OF PRONUNCIATION AND ARTICULATION

The most frequent errors of pronunciation easily detected in oral speech, according to Abney, (1944), are

incorrect vowel quality, as in *get, catch, just.*
incorrect consonant quality, as in *what, immediately, walking.*
misplaced accent, as in *research, discharge.*
omission of requisite sounds, as in *recognize, really, February.*
sounding silent letters, as in *often, toward, corps.*
the addition of superfluous sounds, as in *athlete, once, elm.*
the utterance of sounds in improper order, as *children, hundred.*

Remember, dialects must be taken into account in deciding what is a pronunciation error.

According to McKee (1939) some of the most common difficulties in articulation are the *s* lisp; *t* for *k; d* for *g, th, r, l; w* for *wh;* and *n* for *ing.*

Other common features of some children's speech include dropped endings of words (*goin'*); lack of distinction of the vowels before "r" (*far; fir*); distortions of sounds (*cidy* for *city*); and mispronunciations of words (*duh* for *the*).

The value of group practice in speech has long been established. The teacher of young children can make this practice incidental to the use of rhymes, stories, and songs. More formal lessons organized around the speech sounds that are most likely to be defective may be planned where observation indicates a need. Some of the most common error patterns are readily identified by the teacher who trained himself to listen: *w* for *r* and *l,* as in *red* and *lamp;* voiceless *th* for *s,* in *sun;* voiced *th* for *z,* as in *zebra;* *f* for the voiceless *th,* as in *thumb;* *d* for the voiced *th* and *g,* as in *this* and *get;* *b* for *v,* as in *valentine;* *s* or *ch* for *sh,* as in *shoe;* and *t* for *k* as in *candy.* Every experience in which language is used may become an opportunity for informal speech development.

GENERAL OR PERVASIVE ORAL DEFICIENCIES

At the beginning of the school year, the teacher may find the method described here helpful in categorizing common class weaknesses and detecting individual deficiences. Delawter and Eash (1966) asked children to complete stories and tape-recorded the endings. The investigators detected seven types of errors:

a. failure to focus
b. poor organization of ideas
c. failure to clarify the question (that is, hasty replies that have little relationship to the question)
d. lack of supporting ideas
e. inadequate description
f. lack of subordination
g. stereotyped vocabulary

While there is nothing absolute about these classifications, a grouping of deficiencies does give a starting point. Based upon his findings, the teacher can plan for small group work which would help to correct the deficiencies. Teachers who have used Delawter and Eash's technique report that it gives purpose to their instruction, allowing them to aim at specific deficiencies. Some activities for the seven types of errors are

Errors a-b. To strengthen focus and logical organization, children may
arrange pictures in correct sequence to tell a story
describe events in a story in sequential order
list things seen on a field trip, organizing them in sequence by categories
outline the main points of a simple talk
tell stories, recalling events in the order in which they happened
dramatize stories in logical order

explain a process in science or give directions for a game
choose a topic and limit its scope to a certain number of points.

Errors c-d. To clarify and support ideas, children may
outline the main points of a simple talk, with supporting ideas for each main point
invent endings for incomplete stories or poems and show the relevancy of supporting details
expand a topic sentence into a short talk
develop functional speaking situations such as supporting detail for announcements, directions, and explanations.

Errors e-g. To strengthen description, subordination, and vocabulary, children may
listen to and make lists of descriptive words (such as "quiet" words) or words that apply to different moods ("angry" words)
look for alternatives to overused words, such as *nice*
suggest words that aptly describe objects or events in a picture
study synonyms, antonyms, word histories
look for figures of speech
discuss multiple or unusual meanings of common words, such as *run* and *fall*
listen for new or interesting words
practice expanding simple sentences through the use of modifiers
collect examples of the various sentence types
combine short sentences into compound or complex sentences or change a basic sentence into another form (transformations)

SPECIAL EXPERIENCES IN ORAL EXPRESSION

The six most significant experiences in oral expression include:

- conversation
- discussion
- description, comparison, evaluation
- reporting
- storytelling
- creative drama and choral reading or speaking

Criteria for good oral performance should be developed by the teacher and children. These are often referred to as "standards" or "performance criteria" or "behavioral objectives." They can facilitate both instruction and evaluation: reference to the criteria can be made when the teacher and pupils analyze techniques involved in the experiences.

There are at least two basic types of feasible criteria that a teacher should consider maintaining in helping pupils exhibit the desired skills. The first is a check list of speaking skills which permeate most, if not all, speaking situations (Chart 6-1).

CHART 6-1. Analysis of general speaking qualities

Qualities	Child A	Child B	Child C	Child D
Ideas are worthy				
Expresses ideas clearly and with variety				
Selects and organizes ideas effectively				
Usage appropriate for situation				
Appropriate voice and articulation				
Appropriate posture and body actions				

Key: S—satisfactory
E—enrichment and extension are appropriate
I—needs instruction
R—needs review and practice

Such analysis two or three times per year should indicate the effect of the program for each child. While Chart 6-1 focuses upon important overall goals, Chart 6-2 isolates desired qualities of a particular form of oral expression.

Similar check lists should be available for other types of oral experiences: for example, the following items might be part of the discussion check list:

Keeps to topic
Listens closely
Participates
Supports opinions with reasons
Asks for explanations politely
Encourages reserved members

CHART 6-2. Conversation analysis

	October	January	April
Talks softly			
Helps others take part			
Interjects questions politely			
Supports opinions with reasons			
Listens to others			
Reacts tactfully to opinions with which he disagrees			
Politely asks speaker to repeat or explain			

Key: X-deficiency; ✓-improvement noted; 0-no deficiency

Name of pupil:_____

Literature is a valuable tool for helping children develop their abilities to describe, to compare, and to value. Describing involves giving the basic facts about an object, place, animal, person, or event. In comparing likenesses and differences of objects, places, animals, persons, or events are provided with supporting evidence as to how or why. Evaluation involves making a choice among objects, places, animals, persons, or events and giving reasons orally for choosing one above another.

The following items would be appropriate for an oral reporting check list:

Chooses interesting topic
Gathers information from various sources
Takes notes from readings
Arranges ideas in logical sequence
Begins with interesting sentences
Uses varied ways of presenting materials
Uses acceptable language patterns and voice
Summarizes with an interesting conclusion

The following questions are typical of those which a class might construct to evaluate individual and class progress in the art of storytelling.

Does the storyteller

speak distinctly so that all could understand as well as hear?
have good eye contact with the audience?

change voice to fit the characters, the setting, and the action in the story?

show enough expression, excitement, and enthusiasm in the right places to hold the attention of the audience?

choose a story with the audience in mind as well as his personal enjoyment?

have a good beginning for the story?

tell the story in an order that was easy for the audience to follow?

paint visual pictures for the audience with vivid words, actions, and symbols?

take only the required time to tell the story appropriately?

use appropriate gestures and body movements?

use appropriate facial expressions?

have a good ending for the story?

A rating scale to evaluate individual or group performance in choral reading and speaking might include the following items:

Voice Quality
    volume appropriate for selection
    volume varied for specific effect
    tone appropriate for selection
    tone varied for specific effect
Tempo
    appropriate for selection
    varied to add to interpretation
    timing sharp and accurate
Clarity
    clear understandable production
    vowels sharp and clear
    unison in phrasing
    enunciation clear but not overstressed
    pronunciation natural for the geographic region
Rhythm
    distinct rhythm, not singsong
    rhythm melodic, not overstressed
Interpretation
    intelligent interpretation
    mood of poem expressed in voice and tempo
    phrasing expresses meaning
    inflection reinforces meaning
Group Cooperation
    follows hand directions

works cooperatively with group members
displays a positive attitude
Casting and Selecting
    identifies high, low, medium voices
    identifies words with special emotional quality
    recognizes poems appropriate for different patterns of presenta-
        tion (refrain, dialogue, single voice, cumulative)
    selects appropriate poems (of good quality and of interest for
        age level or audience)

Other oral expression experiences include:

Making announcements
Giving messages, directions, explanations
Giving reviews of books, movies, and television programs
Using the telephone
Making introductions and observing social courtesies
Conducting meetings
Conducting interviews

A check list for each of the above experiences should be con-
structed as a way of evaluating individual and class progress. Some
points to remember in developing such check lists are—

- In making announcement of meetings, children should tell what
  the event is, who is invited, the date, the time, the place, and the
  price of admission.
- In carrying a message from one person to another, the child
  should know who is sending the message and who is to receive
  it, and he must be able to state the message accurately. In giving
  directions, he must learn to include all the steps in the proper
  order. Explanations will require skills similar to those for messages and directions and often call for reasons for doing something.
- Book reports will vary in complexity from the early primary years
  to the intermediate school years. At the intermediate years, the
  child should give such information as the title of the book, author,
  publisher, kind of story, the setting, and the main characters and
  discuss and evaluate the book.
- Movie reviews include attention to such items as the title, the
  name of the theatre where it can be seen, the names of the main
  actors, whether the picture is in color or black and white, the
  plot, whether it is make-believe or based on facts, funny or seri-

ous, and why he enjoyed it, without revealing any surprise for those who plan to see it later.

- Telephoning involves finding a number in the directory, dialing, using the Yellow Pages, long distance dialing, and the use of area code numbers. Good manners in telephoning require identifying oneself, speaking clearly, stating the purpose of the call, keeping the message brief and to the point, responding when the call is for another person, taking messages accurately, and apologizing for a wrong number.
- In making introductions, the child should speak slowly and clearly, know which name to give first, make appropriate responses to introductions, and use the name of the person when speaking to him or her.
- For conducting meetings, a parliamentary guide should be adapted for use by the class. Guidelines for interviewing include such points as making an appointment at the time most convenient for the person to be interviewed, being polite, planning questions carefully and stating them clearly, taking notes, avoiding taking too much of the person's time, and thanking the person for granting the interview.

The assessment of performance, as suggested in this and other chapters, is necessary for effective instruction. But again, the best diagnosis is useless unless it is used as a blueprint for instruction.

A systematic or mastery lesson, dealing with the topic of reviewing television programs, is provided below to indicate the close relationship between diagnosis and instruction.

Performance Objective
Given an opportunity to orally review a television program, the learner will include the eight basic items of information.
Diagnostic Pretest.
Read aloud a prepared review of a television program to a child. When completed, ask him for the number of basic items supplied.

title	length
name of main performer	kind of program
station or channel	something interesting
time	why it was liked

Criterion for mastery is 80%. The purpose for this task is to teach the learner the eight items in a television or radio program review.
Teaching Suggestion.
Before a television review is given by a pupil, put the eight items on the chalkboard and ask him to use them as guide.

Mastery or Posttest Suggestions.
 1. Prior to giving his television program review, ask the pupil to list the eight items in his report.
 2. The suggestions provided in the pretest may be adapted and used in the posttest.

Reteaching Suggestions.
 1. Before the student listens to a review of a television program, give him a specific reason to listen by asking him to make a tally mark on his paper for each of the basic items he hears.
 2. Ask the learner to list key words (for the basic items) as he prepares a review of a television or radio program.

It is important to remember that no pupil reveals all there is to know about his oral expression ability in any single sample of his behavior. When diagnosis is continuous, patterns of error become more apparent. Something can be learned each time the child speaks. Diagnosis should not be considered a prelude, but rather a part of the whole instructional process.

DIALECT AND USAGE PATTERNS

The language used by pupils reflects their geographic origin. The teacher should become familiar with the local dialect patterns so that he will not waste time trying to modify them. Of course, he should teach about dialects and promote interest and acceptance of the speech patterns of other people.

The language used by an individual also yields information about his social and educational level. The choice of words will vary in accordance with the speaker's purpose and situation. For these reasons, it is well for the teacher to avoid the labels "right" and "wrong," for language habits, and replace them with the terms "appropriate" and "inappropriate."

The time to develop alternate speech patterns is not the early years of elementary school. Oral English comes in a variety of packages and the teacher should build upon the package the child brings with him rather than alienating him from it. If the teacher places immediate restrictions on the child's expression, he may only succeed in making the child feel insecure in self-expression. Certainly, negative and derogatory statements are out of place, for they only serve to alienate. The child's language is one of his most intimate and personal possessions, and the teacher is obligated to accept and respect its individuality.

In order to help the older child who recognizes the need to acquire standard speech patterns for speaking and writing, the teacher needs to keep records of the deviations in the phonological and grammatical aspects of each child's speech. (Vocabulary deviations are of lesser import—a speaker's choice of "blinds" for "window shades" is more widely accepted by listeners.) It must be recognized that traditional "corrective" instructional procedures have demonstrated only remarkable and consistent failure, their effect being possibly more harmful than helpful. Learning parts of speech, analyzing sentences, doing written drills, and reading descriptions of language as it should be are unrewarding practices in changing speech patterns. Language is learned by hearing and imitating the sounds of models. This is how language is originally learned, and the same is true for adding to one's oral English repertoire.

The recommended audio-lingual approach includes at least five teaching steps:

- The child must learn to recognize differences between his dialect and the dialect being taught.
- The child must *hear* the standard English sound or pattern being taught (*that* for *dat*).
- The child must be able to discriminate between the standard English sound or patterns and the corresponding sound or patterns in nonstandard dialect (/th/ in *this* from /d/ in *dog*).
- The child must be given pattern drills which help him to reproduce the standard English.
- The child must be afforded the opportunity—often through role-playing situations—to use the standard sound or pattern.

Usage Choices

If a formal usage test is administered in the fall of the school year, the teacher can refer to the manual for possible reasons for low test scores and suggested corrective treatment. One such source is the *Manual for Interpreting the Iowa Language Abilities Test,* which provides general information listed in Chart 6–3.

The observation of children's speech during free activity periods, club meetings, and similar occasions for uninhibited expression is a productive way of securing data on language patterns. Some of the variations that are peculiar to nonstandard oral speech of children are:

Verbs

wrong verbs, as *learn* for *teach* or *leave* for *let*

inappropriate tense form, as *seen* for *saw* (*gave, took, bought, brought, stuck*)

perfect participle for past tense and reverse, as *he* done *or* have came

inappropriate tense—present for past, as *come* for *came* or *jump* for *jumped*

failure of verb to agree with subject in number, as *he don't* or *John run* (*is, are, was, were*)

omission of auxiliary verbs, as *he playing there*

first personal pronoun standing first in series, as *I and my sister*

objective pronoun for subject, as *Bill and me* or *Her went* . . .

pronoun for demonstrative adjective, as *them* for *these*

object of preposition not in objective case, as *with Susan and I*

wrong form of pronoun, *as hisself, his'n*

Adjectives and Adverbs

confusion of adjective and adverb, as *good* for *well*

wrong article, as *a* for *an*

double comparison, as *more stronger*

wrong comparison, as *gooder*

Negatives, as *haven't no* for *haven't any*

Syntactical redundancy, as *my mother, she* or *this here* and *that there*

Illiteracies, as *ain't, his'n, her'n, our'n*

Classroom teachers should prepare record-keeping charts such as Chart 6–4 to survey the oral speech of children: Chart 6–4 is a model only; specific items should be modified to fit the speech patterns of the locale.

A special analysis may be made of the speech characteristics of children whose speech indicates many deviations from standard English. This form of analysis is more time-consuming than paper-and-pencil tests of knowledge of correct forms of speech. However, it allows the teacher to test the oral speech characteristics of children in normal and natural social situations.

The essential items should receive attention first. After these have been mastered, attention should be devoted to usage items of lesser consequence. The group instructional program will include inappropriate usages common to most class members—those which appear

CHART 6-3. Language usage: Diagnostic and remedial suggestions

Possible Causes of Low Test Scores	Additional Evidence of Deficiency	Suggested Remedial Treatment
1. Failure to comprehend testing technique.	Midunderstanding of method of recording responses to items.	Prepare and use drill exercises similar to those used in test. Work with pupil until he understands technique.
2. Poor control over special language usages.	Observation and check on daily habits of oral and written expression.	Check pupil's test paper to identify types of usages missed. Check with text and course of study for grade emphasis. Emphasize individual drill on specific errors. Contrast correct forms with those to be avoided. Supplement with oral drill.
3. Poor language background.	Careless, inaccurate usage in oral and written expression.	Corrective instruction is the only remedy here. Select a limited number of usages and proceed as in No. 2 above.
4. Foreign language in the home.	Observed foreign accents. Evidence of two languages in the home.	Use direct corrective instruction here. Follow suggestions in No. 2 above.
5. Poor general reading comprehension.	Erratic response to test items; poor reading ability in other subjects.	Drill on sentence and total meaning comprehension as required for general improvement in reading.
6. Low mental ability.	Difficulty in following directions; erratic response to difficulty with common usages; low MA and IQ shown by reliable mental test.	Follow general procedure as outlined in Nos. 2 and 3 above. Have pupil prepare and memorize a key sentence for troublesome usages.

7. Careless language habits.	Erratic responses to test items; carelessness in informal expression.	Develop self-critical attitude toward usage errors. Bring pressure to bear favoring correct usages. Stress proofreading all written work.
8. Confusion caused by emphasis on formal rather than functional usages.	Inaccurate responses to items emphasized mainly through rules.	Emphasize individual drills; stress definite habits of correct response to important usages.

NOTE. Reproduced from the *Iowa Language Abilities Test.* Copyright 1948, renewed 1976 by Harcourt Brace Jovanovich, Inc. Reproduced by special permission of the publisher.

CHART 6-4. Analysis of nonstandard usage

Date: October 19___

Pupils	Verbs	Pronouns	Adjectives Adverbs	Negatives	Redundancy	Illiteracies
Alice	have came	Betty and me	gooder	don't have no	John he	hain't
Jeff						
Doug						
Lisa						

most frequently in pupils' oral and written expressions. The other usage items will be treated in small groups or individualized instruction.

Practice should not be devoted to skills unless a weakness has been identified. Generally speaking, exercises should be given to each pupil according to his need and not to the class as a whole. A relatively small number of items will be attacked each year—but these should be treated thoroughly in order to lessen the amount of re-teaching needed in later years.

Providing Time for Individual Needs

The teacher's time must be organized to allow for attention to individual differences. The first step is pretesting on usage. The pretest enables the teacher to detect those pupils who are having difficulty with standard usage. Pupils who already appropriately use the items to be presented may be excused from the lessons and allowed to do independent work. When some pupils need further practice on previously taught items, those pupils who do not need the additional practice should be excused for independent activity.

While there can be no doubt that practice on conventions for maintenance purposes is necessary for many pupils, much of this should take place in the content subjects. For example, discussion skills can be practiced in social studies, science, reading, mathematics, and practically all school activities; oral reports are prepared in connection with other school subjects and the standards developed in the English lesson should be recalled and applied in those situations. Practical application is more valuable than any contrived practice from a textbook.

ADDITIONAL CORRECTIVE ACTIVITIES

1. During sharing periods, the teacher should use questioning techniques that will stimulate oral expression. Seven major types of questions that are useful to include are:

Main idea—questions that ask the child to identify the central theme of his thought
Detail—questions that ask for bits of information
Vocabulary—questions that ask for the meaning of words used
Sequence—questions that require knowledge of events in their order of occurrence
Inference—questions that ask for information that is implied, but not directly stated

Evaluation—questions that ask for judgments
Creative—questions that ask the child to create new ideas based on ideas presented

2. Four features of morphology, or patterns in word formation, usually appear after the child has started school: formation of (a) plurals for /s/, /z/, /əz/ as *bets, beds, matches;* (b) possessives (Bill's bat); (c) third-person singular of the verb (*wishes*); and inflections for the past tense of regular verbs—/t/, /d/, /əd/ as in *asked* (askt), *begged* (begd), and *dusted* (dust-ed).

Considerable growth in syntactic structure also occurs during the elementary school years, such as referents of pronouns in sentences, passive voice, and use of connectives (*as, because, then, therefore, but, although, and*).

In terms of semantics, children increase their vocabulary at a rapid rate during the elementary school years. It has been estimated that the typical child increases his vocabulary at a rate of about 1,000 words a year in the primary grades, and 2,000 words a year in the intermediate grades. In terms of word meanings, children need instruction in homonyms, homographs, synonyms, antonyms, and relational words.

These two books will be helpful in clarifying these ideas:

Dale, Philip, *Language Development, Structure and Function,* 2nd edition. New York: Holt, Rinehart, 1976.

Malmstrom, Jean, *Understanding Language: A Primer for the Language Arts Teacher.* New York: St. Martin's Press, 1977.

3. Deficiencies in understanding word meaning need much attention through a variety of procedures:

- providing direct and vicarious experiences
- encouraging reading
- providing instruction in finding context clues
- providing instruction in content area vocabulary
- encouraging variety in oral and written expression
- serving as a model
- engaging in morphology study
- teaching connectives as well as substantive words
- using other procedures that promote sensitivity to and excitement about words (develop a system for individualized word study, using library books that deal with words and provide many ideas for activities and word games)
- utilizing the dictionary.

4. The teacher should become familiar with widely used language development materials, such as

Peabody Language Development Kits by L. Dunn and J.O. Smith (Circle Pines, Minn.: American Guidance Services). Four kits emphasize sensation, expression, and conceptualization. Sensory experiences are provided that stimulate sight, hearing, and touch. Vocal and motor (writing) expression are encouraged. Exercises concentrate on intellectual development. The kits stress an overall oral program. No reading or writing is required.

New Distar Language Program by Siegfried Engelmann and J. Osborn (Chicago: Science Research Associates). Distar is a system of language arts instructional materials designed to teach skills to children with below-average communication abilities. It is highly structured: everything that the teacher should say and do is described in detail in the teacher's manual. The program is administered to small groups of children. The teacher presents a 30-minute lesson to each group each day, following the manual directions exactly. The manual specifies exact words, tone of voice, and gestures to be used and ways of reinforcing correct responses and correcting incorrect responses. Because of the highly structured presentations necessary to this approach, training films are available. Some teachers find the program to be too rigid and regimented for their teaching styles. Many teachers, however, cite encouraging results when using the program, especially with bilingual or disadvantaged children.

English Now by Irvin Fiegenbaum (New York: New Century). Fiegenbaum's materials include workbooks, manuals, and cassette tapes. An oral approach is used in teaching standard English as a second dialect the same way English is taught as a second language. Sound discrimination drills are employed, as are identification drills and translation drills. The final drills deal with the pronunciation of the standard English.

Other widely used materials include *Goal: Language Development Games Oriented Activities for Learning* by Karnes, (Springfield, Mass.: Milton Bradley), *MWM Program for Developing Language Abilities* by Minskoff and others (Ridgefield, N.J.; Educational Performance Associates) and *SYNPRO (Syntax Programmer)* by Peterson (St. Louis: Division of EMT Labs).

REVIEW QUESTIONS AND ACTIVITIES

1. Make an informal assessment of the oral language development of a child.

2. Develop an analysis chart for one of the following types of oral expression: making announcements; giving messages; directions; explanations; giving reviews of books, movies, and television programs; using the telephone; making introductions and observing social courtesies; conducting meetings; or conducting interviews.

3. Develop a systematic or mastery lesson for one of the types of oral expression cited in Question 2 above.

4. Develop a lesson plan to teach a feature of standard English, using the recommended audio-lingual approach explained in this chapter.

5. What are some possible causes of low test scores on usage tests? Provide one suggested remedial treatment for each cause you cite.

6. Become familiar with one of the types of materials cited on page 142 and explain it to a group of peers.

7. Trace the scope and sequence of oral expression experiences through the charts provided in the Appendix.

8. Develop a card file of ideas, games, language arts books focusing on strategies and materials for helping a child with oral language difficulties.

9. Review articles dealing with the diagnosis and correction of language arts difficulties in the area of oral expression.

10. Review source books, trade books, and multilevel materials that deal specifically with the oral expression component of the language arts.

11. Prepare an activity or game for helping a child who needs further experiences in some aspect of oral expression.

12. Develop a teaching plan related to one of the "Additional Corrective Activities".

13. There are a number of professional references which deal with the topic of this chapter and contain many ideas which can be applied. Read such a reference and develop a set of practical classroom ideas. Here are five such references:

Anastasiow, Nicholas. *Oral Language: Expression of Thought,* rev. ed. Newark, Del.: International Reading Association, 1979.

Halliday, Michael, *Functions of Language.* New York: Elsevier-North Holland Publishing Co., 1977.

Klein, Marvin, *Talk in the Language Arts Classroom.* Urbana, Ill.: National Council of Teachers of English, 1977.

Loban, Walter D. *Language Development: Kindergarten Through Grade 12.*
    Urbana, Ill.: National Council of Teachers of English, 1976.
Tough, Joan, *Talking, Thinking, Growing: Language With the Young Child.*
    New York: Schocken Books, 1974.

14. Read: "A Practical Approach to Analyzing Children's Talk in the
    Classroom," by *Language Arts,* May 1977, *54,* 506–510. Try out
    the ideas with two or three children and report your findings to
    the class.

15. Here is how Michael Halliday (*Learning How to Mean: Explora-
    tions in Development of Language,* London: Edward Arnold,
    1975) categorizes children's functions of language:

    Instrumental language (to get things, such as "I want . . ." or
    "May I . . . ?")
    Regulatory language (to control others, such as "Don't do that." or
    "Let's do this.")
    Interactional language (to maintain personal relationships, such as
    use of names, greetings)
    Personal language (to express personality or individuality, such as
    "I'm going to be a movie actress" or "I like swimming better than
    anything else.")
    Imaginative language (to create one's own words, as "Once upon a
    time . . .")
    Informative language (to convey information, such as giving re-
    ports, telling of observations)
    Heuristic language (to find out things, such as "Why . . .", "What
    for?", "I wonder if . . .?"

    Use this listing for observing the functions of language of a child
    or a small group of children. Describe how you, as a teacher,
    could stimulate a variety of language functions and provide
    maximum support for language development.

16. Compare the oral language of these two first graders describing
    different pictures:

    a. "This is a sunny picture. There are pretty flowers. The rainbow is
       falling down. The picture is pretty. It is spring. The flowers are
       blooming. The flowers is come. The little thing inside will come.
       One of them little things inside will come down and touch another
       one. Then there will be a seed."

    b. "There are some twins jumping in the water. These boys went to
       play in the water and one of them said, "This is cold." The other one

said, "This is cold." The other one said, "Wait a minute. I'll be in there to see." Then they found out it was cold. Then they both got out and dived again and they were freezing cold and got out. Then they went back in and then they had a party after that. Then they had watermelon, peaches, oranges, lemons, grapes, and tea, and they said, "How about going fishing?" Then they're going fishing here. They're going row in a boat. Then they're going fall out of the boat. That's all."

REFERENCES

Abney, L. *Teaching language in the elementary school,* 43rd Yearbook of the National Society for the Study of Education, Part II. Chicago: University of Chicago Press, 1944, p. 186.

Delawter, J.A., & Eash, M.J. Focus on oral communication, *Elementary English 43* (Dec. 1966): 880–83.

McKee, P. *Language in the elementary school.* Boston: Houghton-Mifflin Co., 1939, p. 318.

Mclear, J.D. An informal language inventory, *Elementary English 41* (Apr. 1974): 508–11.

Stauffer, R.G., & Pikulski, J.J. A comparison and measure of oral language growth, *Elementary English 51* (Nov./Dec. 1974): 1151–55.

7
Written Communication

Composing begins with the teacher writing down the child's thoughts and reading them back to him. As this occurs time and again, children come to understand that what they can think about they can talk about, and what they say can be written down and read back.

Shortly after children can read back what the teacher has written at their dictation, they may want to write. They might learn to do this by copying the story the teacher has written for them. Gradually, the children should be able to write their own stories independently. Some children will move ahead quickly in this process; others will move more slowly.

As the amount of writing increases, it can be bound into books. The teacher may use the writings to illustrate likenesses and differences in words, the fact that sentences start with a capital and end with a period, and, as the children are ready, other language skills involved in written composition. In the primary years more attention should be focused upon children's interest in writing and independence in writing than upon technical skills.

ANALYSIS OF PUPIL WORK

Even though a pupil may be able to give a definition of an adjective, this is no assurance that he can or does make effective use of descriptive words. Only those skills which actually appear in a pupil's daily performance can be considered learned.

Once again, record keeping is essential. A review of these records will reveal which children are having similar problems with punctuation, run-on sentences, or descriptive words.

Whatever the common problems may be, seminars in writing are a good way to treat them. Children who are working at the same skills at the same time can be grouped together to help each other, and to get needed assistance from the teacher. As children gain the new skill, they may leave the group to return to other activities. On successive days, all or part of the group may meet again as needed.

Similar procedures can be used at the intermediate level. For instance, the teacher might study a set of written compositions, one from each pupil, and compile a series of notes upon which language teaching could be based. A record-keeping sheet for such purposes would include:

- names of pupils and their weaknesses
- names of children who need help with capitalization, punctuation, sentence sense, or paragraph sense
- usage problems (general for the class; specific difficulties for individuals)
- spelling difficulties (specific words for specific children)
- handwriting deficiencies (specific points for the name of each child appearing on the list)

Chart 7-1 is a sample individual and class profile. It will help the teacher keep track of all class members, assign appropriate study materials, and retain a record for later evaluations. In effect, the teacher teaches only what needs to be taught and only to those needing it; there is no repetition for the able. Those who know how to write correctly are not held back by those who need help. Items for study can be isolated and analyzed so that the teacher can plan appropriate lessons for individuals and for small groups.

With the exception of the final section, devoted to creative writing, the remaining sections of this chapter are organized around the elements cited in Chart 7-1.

ANALYSIS OF COMPOSING AND SOME INSTRUCTIONAL PROCEDURES

Rating scales can be used to help children judge their own compositions and those of others. Analysis of syntax in children's oral and written composition can be made by the teacher.

CHART 7-1. Analysis of composition elements

Pupils' Names	Composing					Mechanics					Usage	Spelling	Handwriting
	Topic Selection Scope	Ideas	Organization	Details	Word Choice	Revision Proofreading	Capitalization	Punctuation	Sentence	Paragraph			

Rating Scales

Four components are generally agreed upon as important ingredients in composition:

Vocabulary
  exact words
  synonyms
  sensory words
  descriptive words
  unusual expressions
Elaboration
  related ideas
  vivid details
Organization
  effective sequencing
  building to a climax
Structure
  use of a variety of sentence types
  no run-on sentences or sentence fragments

Gradually, children should become aware of these four components and their meaning. A scale, worded so the pupils can understand it, could be developed, with a 4-point value (3, 2, 1, and 0) to indicate the degree to which each component has been achieved. Through instruction and practice, children can learn to use the scale to rate compositions. In doing so, they would likely improve the quality of their writing over a period of time. One such commercially available program is *Reading, Writing, and Rating Stories* by Carol Sager Curriculum Associates, 8 Henshaw Street, Woburn, Mass. 01801.

A standardized *Test of Written Language* (TOWL) by Donald D. Hammill and Stephen C. Larsen (Austin, Texas: Pro-Ed) consists of seven subtests:

Word Usage—standard verb tenses, plurals, pronouns, and other grammatical forms
Style—conventions of punctuation and capitalization
Spelling—regular and irregular words
Thematic maturity—meaningful story on a given theme
Vocabulary—complexity of words used
Thought units—number of complete sentences
Handwriting—legibility of the written story

Analysis

Based on studies by Hunt (1965), a good index for determining a student's maturity in composition is the T-unit length. Hunt defines a T-unit "as one main clause expanded at any or many different points by structures that are modified or complements or substitutes for words in the main clause". Accordingly, younger children do the greatest proportion of their writing in short T-units, with T-units becoming progressively longer with increased writing maturity.

The example, which is analyzed below, follows the procedures recommended by Jung (1971).

1. Divide all the sentences of a pupil's composition into T-units.
2. Divide the total number of words in the composition by the total number of T-units. This will reveal the average length of the pupil's T-units, a very important measure for evaluating composition maturity.
3. Analyze each sentence in the composition in terms of the number of T-units, number of words per T-unit, ways in which subordination and coordination are indicated, means for the development of characterization, nominals, adverbials, and any other measures which affect T-unit length.
4. Prepare a summary outline based on the analysis of sentences including T-unit measures, features of the pupil's syntax, methods utilized for developing characterizations, plot structure, analysis, and story interpretation.
5. Write an evaluation based on the data obtained in steps one to four.

A single sentence was presented to the class from which the example below was obtained. The sentence: "Slumping in the lifeboat, the survivors watched the ship slip from sight." The students were directed to develop a story based on this sentence. A brief discussion period was held in which several suggestions were made about possible location, situations, and characters. One child's composition appears in italics. The analysis appears after each sentence. The numbers in parenthesis are: first number shows number of sentences, the second number is T-units, and the third, number of words in T-units.

1. *It was wintertime.* (1;1;3)
   a. Statement of time
   b. Shortest T-unit

2. *The snow lay thick and deep on the ground of the Robinson's front yard.* (1;1;14)
   a. Compounding of adjective ("thick and deep")
   b. Prepositional phrase, adverbial of place ("on the ground")
   c. Prepositional phrase ("of the Robinson's front yard")
   d. Introduction of central characters
3. *This winter they planned to go on a cruise to the Carribean.* (1;1;12)
   a. Initial statement of time ("this winter")
   b. Infinitive ("to go")
   c. Prepositional phrase, adverbial of place ("on a cruise")
   d. Prepositional phrase, adverbial of place ("to the Carribean")
4. *They won the cruise when their mother was on "Let's Make a Deal" about two months earlier.* (1;1;17)
   a. Adverbial of time "when" clause in final position
   b. Prepositional phrase, adverbial of place ("on Let's Make a Deal")
   c. Prepositional phrase, adverbial of time ("about two months")
   d. Adverbial of time ("earlier")
5. *The trip was only two weeks away and they were very excited.* (1;2;7 + 5)
   a. Adverb of degree ("only")
   b. Compound sentence, "and", compounding of T-units
   c. Adverb of degree ("very")
6. *They knew, however, they would probably encounter danger in the wintertime.* (1;1;11)
   a. "That" clause in final position ("that" understood)
   b. Adverb of degree ("probably")
   c. Prepositional phrase, adverbial of time ("in the wintertime")
7. *The snow began to melt as the sun's rays shone on it as though it were gold.* (1;1;17)
   a. Infinitive ("to melt")
   b. Adverbial of time "as" clause in medial position
   c. Prepositional phrase, adverbial of place ("on it")
   d. Adverbial "as" clause in final position
8. *There was not much time left to pack and winterize their house.* (1;1;12)
   a. Adverb of degree ("much")
   b. Compounding of infinitive ("to pack and winterize")
9. *They would be gone three weeks in December.* (1;1;8)
   a. Prepositional phrase, adverbial of time ("in December")

10. *The day had come at last.* (1;1;6)
    a. Prepositional phrase, adverbial of time ("at last")
11. *Everyone was hurrying so they wouldn't miss the boat.* (1;1;9)
    a. Indefinite pronoun ("everyone")
    b. Be + ing verb
    c. Adverbial "so" clause in final position
12. *They arrived at the docks at exactly 9:00 A.M.* (1;1;9)
    a. Prepositional phrase, adverbial of place ("at the docks")
    b. Prepositional phrase, adverbial of time ("at exactly 9:00 A.M.")
    c. Adverb of degree ("exactly")
13. *The voyage started at 9:30.* (1;1;5)
    a. Prepositional phrase, adverbial of time ("at 9:30")
14. *They were off!* (1;1;3)
    a. Adverbial of place ("off")
    b. Shortest T-unit
15. *About three days after they had started, they ran into icebergs.* (1;1;11)
    a. Prepositional phrase, adverbial of time ("about three days")
    b. Adverbial of time "after" clause in medial position
    c. Prepositional phrase, adverbial of place ("into icebergs")
    d. Introduction of central problem
16. *The ship hit a huge iceberg which tore a big hole in the hull of the ship.* (1;1;17)
    a. Description by adjective in det. + _____ + object noun slot ("a huge iceberg")
    b. "Which" clause in final position
    c. Description by det. + _____ + object noun slot ("a big hole")
    d. Prepositional phrase, adverbial of place ("in the hull")
    e. Prepositional phrase, adverbial of place ("of the ship")
17. *The Robinsons were swept overboard onto an iceberg.* (1;1;8)
    a. Adverbial of place ("overboard")
    b. Prepositional phrase, adverbial of place ("onto an iceberg")
18. *The lifeboats were floating and attempting to rescue survivors as the ship slowly sank to the ocean bottom.* (1;1;18)
    a. Compounding of verb ("were floating and attempting")
    b. Infinitive phrase ("to rescue survivors")
    c. Adverbial of time "as" clause in final position
    d. Adverbial of degree ("slowly")
    e. Prepositional phrase, adverbial of place ("to the ocean bottom")
    f. Longest T-unit

19. *Although they weren't far from the shore, the lifeboat didn't see them.* (1;1;12)
   a. Adverbial "although" clause in initial position
   b. Prepositional phrase, adverbial of place ("from the shore")
20. *The survivors watched as the ship slipped from sight.* (1;1;9)
   a. Adverbial of time "as" clause in final position
   b. Prepositional phrase ("from sight")
21. *Later that day an airplane passed over the area where they were located.* (1;1;13)
   a. Initial time reference ("later that day")
   b. Prepositional phrase, adverbial of place ("over the area")
   c. Adverbial of place "where" clause in final position
22. *Luckily their father was wearing a red shirt.* (1;1;8)
   a. Be + ing verb form
   b. Description by adjective in det. + _____ + object noun slot ("a red shirt")
23. *He took it off and waved it in the air to get the plane's attention.* (1;1;15)
   a. Compounding of verb ("took . . . and waved")
   b. Prepositional phrase, adverbial of place ("in the air")
   c. Infinitive phrase ("to get the plane's attention")
24. *The plane saw it and returned their signal.* (1;1;8)
   a. Compounding of verb ("saw . . . and returned")
   b. Solution of central conflict
25. *Later a helicopter came and picked them up after they were half-frozen.* (1;1;12)
   a. Initial time reference ("later")
   b. Compounding of verb ("came and picked")
   c. Adverbial of time "after" clause in final position
26. *The trip hadn't turned out quite so well after all.* (1;1;10)
   a. Adverb of degree ("so")
   b. Prepositional phrase ("after all")

Summary of Composition Characteristics:
1. Lengths
   26 sentences total
   27 T-units total
   219 words
   10.3 words/T-unit average
   18 words/T-unit maximum
   3 words/T-unit minimum
2. Syntax
   Subordinate clauses occur in 11 out of 26 sentences, two occurring in S. 7:

(1) "When" clause in final position; "that" clause in final position; "as" clause in medial position; "as" clause in final position; "so" clause in final position; "after" clause in medial position; "'which" clause in final position; "although" clause in initial position; "as" clause in final position; "where" clause in final position; "after" clause in final position; "as" clause in final position.

(2) Length of about half of long sentences comes from subordinate clauses.
Compounded verbs (4 of 26 sentences)
Compounded adjectives (1 of 26)
Compounded infinitives (1 of 26)
Compounded sentences (1 of 26)
Adjectives in det. + _____ + noun slot (2 of 26)
Use of infinitives (4 of 26)
Extensive use of prepositional phrases (17 of 26)

3. Characterization
Main characters introduced with very limited characterization (emotional references)
Human characters only
Innate desire for survival

4. Plot Development
Introduction of characters and locations (S.1–10)
Account of events leading to central conflict (S.11–14)
Central conflict arises (S.15–19)
Account of events (S.20)
Resolution of conflict (S.21–25)
Statement of outcome (S.26)

What are the effects of this type of analysis on instruction? Such analysis forces the teacher to focus on the child and his writing. It can provide a means for the teacher to become more sensitive to the need for close observation of the linguistic features of children's writing. Through the study of specific features of language, attention can be pinpointed on specifics rather than general impressions. Such analysis can provide data about the development of an individual child. It also permits the teacher to comment on things well done.

Revision and Proofreading

A paragraph written on the board or placed on the overhead projector serves as a model for illustrating the process of revision. The teacher might ask the students to think of ways the paragraph could be improved and suggest the questions such as those in Chart 7–2.

CHART 7-2. Revision guide

Does it keep to the subject? Is there a good topic sentence?
Is each detail interesting to those who read it? Do all details relate to the topic?
Has enough been written about the subject?
Are sentences in correct order? Is the paragraph well organized?
Does each sentence say what it intends to say?
Are there any empty sentences? Added sentences?
Is there a good beginning, a good ending, a catchy title?
Does the concluding sentence bring the ideas to a satisfactory conclusion?

As with revision, proofreading must be practiced at repeated intervals in order to be sure that pupils are asking themselves pertinent questions. Practical and specific suggestions about what to look for, such as those in Chart 7–3 below, are needed.

CHART 7-3. Proofreading guide

Listen and look at each group of words to be sure it is a good sentence. Make sure that you kept your sentences apart.
Listen and look for mistakes in punctuation. Be sure that you have put in punctuation marks only where they are needed. Did you end sentences with the mark required?
Listen and look for mistakes in using words correctly. Be sure that you have said what you mean and that each word is used correctly with other words. Is there any incorrect verb or pronoun usage?
Look for mistakes in using capital letters. Did you capitalize the first word and all important words in the title? Did you begin each sentence with a capital letter?
Look for misspelled words. Use the dictionary to check the spelling of any word about which you are not sure.
Check legibility of writing and directions around spacing, title, and the like.

NOTE. Charts 7-2 and 7-3 from *Language Arts in Childhood Education,* 3rd edition, by Paul C. Burns and Betty L. Broman. Copyright 1975 by Rand McNally and Co., pp. 286-87. Used with permission.

The pupil may find it helpful to reread his material several times with a different purpose in mind each time. For example:

Proofreading 1: Reading for sentence sense
Proofreading 2: Reading for punctuation
Proofreading 3: Reading to make general terms specific and vague words clear
Proofreading 4: Reading for capitalization
Proofreading 5: Reading for misspelled words
Proofreading 6: Checking such items as margin, title, and the like

Some teachers have found interviews and a sequence of steps in correcting papers helpful in leading the child toward independence in proofreading.

Correction of error
Placing a symbol at the point of error.
Noting the number of errors at the line of error (2x)
Indicating the total and type of error (2 *p*, 2 c, 2 *u*–meaning 2 punctuation, 2 capitalization, and 2 usage errors)
Noting the total number of errors, without indicating the type (2)

The group correction lesson is another effective device. The teacher selects a few sentences from pupils' papers which include the items he wishes to bring to the pupils' attention and projects them on the screen or provides copies for all pupils. The teacher then uses these sentences as a basis of instruction for a group of pupils, or the whole class. Here use may be made of the handbook often provided in the pupil textbooks.

Keeping records of pupil work over a period of time, including samples of different kinds filed by dates, can be one of the strongest and most effective means of encouraging revision and proofreading. Displaying students' work is an additional motivator for revising and proofreading.

WRITING CONVENTIONS

The technical conventions of capitalization, punctuation, sentence sense, and paragraph sense cut across all writing tasks.

Capitalization

A guide to the sequence of capitalization skills is needed by teachers. The list of minimal capitalization skills in Chart 7–4 is suggestive only, but it does take into account the needs of children in writing and the relative difficulty of the various items.

There are a number of ways to develop capitalization skills. Certainly the teacher will study the pupil's written work, noting and possibly tabulating the types of errors for further teaching and study in the manner suggested by Chart 7–5. Group and individual dictation drills emphasizing capitalizations that seem difficult for the pupil may be used. Group proofreading of a paper for capitalization is possible through the use of an opaque or overhead projector or the chalkboard. Five-minute individual practice periods near the end of the school day may be devoted to capitalization errors observed during the day.

CHART 7-4. Capitalization skills

Primary Years
The first word of a sentence
The child's first and last names
The name of teacher, school, town, street
The word "I"
The date
First and important words of titles of books the children read
Proper names used in children's writings
Titles of compositions
Names of titles: "Mr.," "Mrs.," "Miss," "Ms."
Proper names: month, day, common holidays
First word in a line of verse
First and important words in titles of books, stories, poems
First word of salutation in an informal note ("Dear")
First word of closing of informal note ("Yours")

Intermediate Years
All that is listed for preceding years
Names of cities and states
Names of organizations to which children belong, such as Boy Scouts, Grade
    Four
Mother or Father, when used in place of the name
Local geographical names
Names of streets
Names of all places and persons, countries, oceans
Capitalization used in outlining
Titles when used with names, such as President Lincoln
Commercial trade names
Names of the Deity and the Bible
First word of quoted sentences
Proper adjectives, showing race, nationality
Abbreviations of proper nouns and titles

NOTE: From *Developing Language Skills in Elementary Schools,* 5th edition, by Harry Greene and Walter T. Petty. Boston: Allyn and Bacon, Inc., 1976, pp. 304–5. Used with permission.

In addition, the general diagnostic and remedial suggestions in Chart 7–6 should be used by the teacher.

Punctuation

Punctuation errors have been cited as the most common type of mechanical mistake pupils make in written composition. Chart 7–7 suggests punctuation items that should receive attention in the elementary school years.

CHART 7-5. Analysis of capitalization items

Pupils' names	Beginning of sentence	Proper nouns	Days, months, places, holidays	Titles	Beginning line in verse	Salutation/closing of letters	Organization	Trade names	Beginning of quoted sentences	Proper adjectives

McKee (1934) found the following punctuation errors were the greatest stumbling blocks for elementary school pupils:

No period at end of a sentence
No period after abbreviations
Failure to use a colon
No question mark at the end of a question
Failure to set off nonrestrictive clauses by commas
Failure to set off a series by commas
Lack of commas in setting off an appositive

One procedure for analysis of punctuation is dictation of both studied and unstudied material. The teacher dictates short sentences or paragraphs which contain the punctuation marks to be tested. The

CHART 7-6. Capitalization: diagnostic and remedial suggestions

Possible Causes of Low Test Scores	Additional Evidence of Deficiency	Suggested Remedial Treatment
1. Lack of knowledge of capitalization situations.	Analysis of pupil's test paper and other written work to determine types of errors made.	Identify specific capitalization skills missed by pupil and teach these. Stress proofreading drills on skills in which pupil is weak.
2. Limited knowledge of exceptions and irregularities in capitalization.	Analysis of test paper and daily written work; tendency to overcapitalize. High correction for overcapitalization in test.	Give direct practice on capitalization skills taught in this grade. Point out exceptions and irregularities in the use of capitals. Inspect test paper and written work for excessive use of capitals. Use dictation and proofreading designed to emphasize correct use of capitals.
3. Tendency to overcapitalize.	High correction for overcapitalization in test.	Inspect test paper and written work for excessive use of capitals. Use dictation and proofreading design to emphasize correct use of capitals.
4. Lack of self-critical attitude toward capitalization. Poor proofreading ability.	Erratic and careless written work in other subjects; limited ability to note errors in own or other written copy.	Emphasize need for self-critical attitude toward own written work. Use proofreading exercises designed to emphasize use of capitals.
5. Poorly developed sentence sense.	Low scores on sentence sense tests.	Use suggestions in remedial chart for sentence sense. (See Chart 7–11.)
6. Carelessness in writing.	Analysis of handwriting characteristics in daily work.	Practice capital letters and small letters which analysis shows cause trouble.

NOTE: Reproduced from the *Iowa Language Abilities Test.* Copyright 1948, renewed 1976 by Harcourt Brace Jovanovich, Inc. Reproduced by special permission of the publisher.

CHART 7-7.   Punctuation skills in elementary grades

Primary Years
1. Period at the end of a sentence
2. Period after numbers in any kind of list
3. Question mark at the close of a question
4. Comma after salutation of a friendly note or letter
5. Comma after closing of a friendly note or letter
6. Comma between the day of the month and the year
7. Comma between name of city and state
8. Period after abbreviations
9. Period after an initial
10. Use of an apostrophe in common contractions such as isn't, aren't
11. Commas in a list

Intermediate Years
    (All items listed for previous years)
12. Apostrophe to show possession
13. Hyphen separating parts of a word divided at end of line
14. Period following a command
15. Exclamation point at the end of a word or group of words that makes an exclamation
16. Commas setting off an appositive
17. Colon after the salutation of a business letter
18. Quotation marks before and after a direct quotation
19. Comma between explanatory words and a quotation
20. Period after outline Roman numeral
21. Colon in writing time
22. Comma to indicate changed word order
23. Quotation marks around the title of a booklet, pamphlet, the chapter of a book, and the title of a poem or story
24. Underlining the title of a book
25. Comma to set off nouns in direct address
26. Hyphen in compound numbers
27. Colon to set off a list
28. Comma in sentences to aid in making meaning clear

NOTE. From Greene and Petty, *op. cit.,* pp. 303–4. Used with permission.

children's written work will reveal any weaknesses. The dictation of new or unstudied material approximates spontaneous writing. Studied dictation differs in that pupils have the opportunity to study the selections—paying particular attention to various aspects of the written form—prior to dictation.

Systematic record keeping of the types of punctuation errors made by individual children is strongly recommended in order to plan les-

CHART 7-8. Analysis of punctuation items

Pupils' Names	Period	Comma	Semicolon	Colon	Quotation Mark	Apostrophe	Question Mark	Hyphen	Underlining

KEY: Use numerals (1-28) to correlate with Chart 7-7 which lists punctuation items to be taught in the elementary school years.

sons, assign appropriate study materials, and evaluate growth. Notice that Chart 7–8 is designed in conjunction with the list of punctuation items recommended for attention at the elementary school level (Chart 7–7).

The general diagnostic and remedial teaching suggestions in Chart 7–9 should be useful to the teacher.

Another technique in teaching punctuation is the detailed test of certain punctuation usages, based on the results of a general survey test. A sample set of questions from such a test appears below. Two specific usages are being tested: the use of the question mark (1) after a direct question and (2) after a direct question within the sentence.

These are exercises dealing with the question mark. Each sentence illustrates one usage of the question mark. Insert the needed question mark for each.
1. Is this your dog
2. "Are you ready," the man asked.

CHART 7-9. Punctuation: diagnosis and remediation

Possible Causes of Low Test Scores	Additional Evidence of Deficiency	Suggested Remedial Action
1. Lack of knowledge of specific punctuation skills.	Examination of test papers to determine types of skills missed; observation of daily written work.	Check punctuation items missed in test with textbook and course of study. Use proofreading drills on skills missed pupil. Stress correct punctuation, avoiding over-punctuation, and self-editing of own copy.
2. Tendency to overpunctuate.	Analysis of test and daily work for evidence of overpunctuation, especially commas.	Use dictation and proofreading for the elimination of improper or excessive punctuation.
3. Lack of self-critical attitude toward own written work.	Careless punctuation in daily work; failure to note errors in own or in other written copy.	Emphasize self-criticism of own daily written work. Use proofreading exercises to emphasize correct use of punctuation marks.
4. Poor general comprehension in reading.	Low scores on comprehension tests; poor reading in other subjects.	Give attention to punctuation during oral reading. Use content from varied subject-matter fields.
5. Poor vision or hearing.	Observation of pupil at work; nurse's or doctor's examination.	Refer pupil to doctor for medical attention. Move pupil to front of room. Encourage pupil to make special effort to write carefully and to make punctuation marks distinctly.

6. Poorly developed sentence sense.	Observation of pupil's daily usage.	Explain types of sentences and the relation of sentence structure to punctuation. Stress practice in writing sentences and punctuating them correctly. Use dictation and proofreading exercises calling for punctuation.
7. Carelessness in matters of form in written expression.	Observation and analysis of characteristics of handwriting and punctuation.	Stress essentials of good form in written work. Insist that pupils edit and proofread all written work.

NOTE: Reproduced from the *Iowa Language Abilities Test*. Copyright 1948, renewed 1976 by Harcourt Brace Jovanovich, Inc. Reproduced by special permission of the publisher.

A series of such specialized tests can be made available to the pupils. Pupils can take some or all of the tests. Items missed on any test should be discussed with the pupil so that he can become aware of what he is doing wrong.

For each test there should be a package of follow-up materials and exercises. Such packages may come from workbooks, other textbooks, or teacher-made materials.

Punctuation tests can be interspersed with regularly scheduled instruction. The important thing is to create a situation whereby pupils realize their deficiencies and have an opportunity to restudy some topics. Some special study projects can be carried out during regular classroom periods by pupils who volunteer and are in need of the study.

An idea of the type of exercise used on the worksheets may be gathered from the sample items presented in Chart 7–10.

CHART 7-10. Corrective work sheet in punctuation: The question mark

Directions: These exercises will give you practice in two uses of the question mark. Read each sentence carefully and think about your answer before you mark or write.

1. Study each sentence below. Notice each circled question mark. Try to figure out why it is used in each case.
   (a) Do you think we can go⟨?⟩
   (b) "Do you expect her today"⟨?⟩ questioned father.
2. Is the question mark used in 1 (a) at the end of a direct question? Place question marks in each of these sentences.
   (a) Do cats like fish
   (b) Where does Mary live
   (c) Is John a good baseball player
3. Read aloud the statements in 2. Was there a quick rise in your voice and then a drop back to the basic level? Is the drop where you put the question mark?
4. Is the question mark used in 1 (b) after a direct question but within the sentence? Place question marks in each of these sentences.
   (a) "Can we go" asked Joe.
   (b) "Will you help us" the men asked.
   (c) "Is this your ball" questioned Bill.
5. Write two sentences to show the two uses of the question mark studied in this worksheet.
6. Find examples of the two uses of the question mark in your reading book.
7. If you would like more work with the question mark, see your language textbook, p. _____.

Pupils should be encouraged to use as many work sheets as they want to use, or repeat any work sheet. The teacher should help the children get started with the exercises and show interest in what they are doing. The teacher might also use content from the work sheets in oral exercises for the entire class.

Some workbooks contain materials that will be helpful for some of the noted deficiencies. Specifically designed for corrective work, the series of workbooks entitled *Individual Corrective English* (Books 2, 3, 4, 5, and 6) (Cincinnati, Ohio: McCormick-Mathers Publishing Company.) contains a wealth of material for practice in punctuation and capitalization. Beginning with Book 4, a survey test precedes each unit, and in all books, a pupil's self-test follows the practice assignments. Accompanying the workbooks are a set of achievement tests which are valuable in diagnosing weaknesses of pupils.

Sentence Sense

Even in the primary years, teachers can help children understand and write well-formed sentences. When children dictate stories, the teacher can focus attention on sentences by comments such as "That's a good beginning sentence. What should our next sentence be?" "Yes, that's another sentence. We will begin it with a capital letter and put a period at the end." Oral reading also helps pupils to develop sentence sense.

One-sentence compositions, about a picture or object, a pet, a trip, will also be helpful. From the one-sentence composition, pupils can move to the two- and three-sentence composition as sentence skill develops.

The *run-on* sentence and the choppy sentence are frequently found in the writing of older children as they attempt to write complex sentences and experiment with new forms of expression. Such difficulties may be considered related to general linguistic and intellectual development of children. While all such difficulties with sentence formation cannot be eliminated overnight, there are some instructional procedures that hold promise of alleviating the common sentence difficulties, such as:

a. Exercises in understanding the sentence, sentence intonation patterns, and sentence-building.
b. Practice in various ways of adjusting run-on sentences through separation, sentence connectors, conjunctions, or subordination.

c. Exercises in ways to combine short sentences and the use of connectives other than *and* to add variety to sentences.

Further general diagnostic and remedial teaching suggestions are provided in Chart 7–11

Paragraph Sense

A prerequisite for individuals or small group lessons is knowledge of the goals for the particular skill and instructional approaches for attaining them. In expository writing, children need to learn these features of a well-organized paragraph.

A paragraph should deal with a single topic.
A paragraph typically has a topic sentence.
A paragraph develops a topic.
Sentences in a paragraph are related to each other.
A long paragraph should be concluded with a general sentence related to the topic or beginning sentence. The last sentence of one paragraph may lead into the next paragraph.

With a guide like this in mind, the intermediate-level teacher can form a teaching program according to the needs and abilities of his pupils. (The above outline should not suggest that paragraph features need to be studied as an isolated unit—the ideas may better be acquired through report writing, for example.) Moreover, the points made about the paragraph are not standards all pupils are expected to attain, but rather guidelines to help the teacher select and plan appropriate goals and learning activities.

Some teachers choose to prepare material which can be used by individuals to supplement the small group instruction. The Individualized Study Plan (ISP), one possible technique, is explained below with reference to the paragraph.

The ISP attempts to deal with a single idea, skill, or attitude. The plan may be used with one pupil or a whole class of pupils individually. It is a design for independent work with a choice of activities to fit the pupils' learning styles. It includes pretesting, self-testing and post-testing.

An analysis of the following sample of ISP shows the need for (a) selecting a learning concept, skill, or attitude, and breaking it into components which in turn are composed of specific ideas; (b) stating learning objectives in behavioral terms (that is, behaviors that are observable or measurable, such as "identify," "distinguish," "con-

CHART 7-11. Sentence sense: Assessment and correction suggestions

Possible Causes of Low Test Scores	Additional Evidence of Deficiency	Suggested Remedial Treatment
1. Limited meaning vocabulary.	Low scores on vocabulary tests; pupil's use of words in oral and written work.	Teach new vocabulary. Develop different meanings of common words. Stress using words in sentences demonstrating differences in meanings.
2. Poor reading comprehension.	Low scores on information and reading comprehension tests.	Give practice on word meanings, sentence and paragraph meanings, and comprehension of total meaning of content suitable for the grade.
3. Inability to recognize subjects and predicates of sentences, and to sense what is missing in a fragment.	Presence of many fragments in pupil's speech and writing.	Use matching exercises made up of subjects in one column and predicates in parallel column.
4. Failure to think of sentence as complete unit of expression.	Sentence errors in pupil's spoken and written work.	Stress use of sentences in daily oral and written work. Point out that there are times when fragments may be used but that they must be recognized as such. Practice on completion of exercises in which either the subject or predicate is missing. Use exercises calling for identification of fragments and sentences.
5. Use of "run-on" sentences; loose and.	Analysis of pupil's expression for use of loose and's and "run-on's."	Explain and illustrate various types of incorrect sentences. Stress individual practice in writing good sentences. Practice on identifying poor sentence structure and in recasting poor sentences.

NOTE: Reproduced from the *Iowa Language Abilities Test*. Copyright 1948, renewed 1976 by Harcourt Brace Jovanovich, Inc. Reproduced by special permission.

struct," "name," "arrange in order," "describe," "state a rule," "apply a rule," "demonstrate," "interpret"); (c) developing lessons around the learning objectives; and (d) developing subsequent lessons, tests, and optional activities.

CHART 7-12. A partially developed sample ISP lesson

A. *Major skill: Informative Paragraph Composition*
B. *Component skills*
   1. The one topic principle. (Identification of the paragraph by its shape, and identification of a paragraph by the idea that it usually deals with a single topic.)
   2. The topic and subtopics of a paragraph. (Understanding what is meant by "topic" and "subtopic" and "details"; ability to find such items in a paragraph; knowledge that not every paragraph has a topic sentence and that the topic sentence may not be the first sentence; and the difference between "topic" and "main topic," where a paragraph tells about two or more topics. Outlining is an associated component.)
   3. The development of a paragraph. (Use of description or details, examples, anecdotes, reasons, or explanations.)
   4. The relatedness of sentences within a paragraph. Avoid sentences which do not keep to the topic, or sentences not arranged in logical order. Syntactic as well as semantic cues are useful here: e.g., "links" such as clear noun references from one sentence to another, pronoun references, transitional phrases—*therefore, otherwise;* repetition or synonymity of words; contrast words—*but, yet, however;* time words—*meantime, soon;* and place words—*here, nearby.*
   5. Beginning and ending sentences of a paragraph. (The beginning sentence often tells what the paragraph is about; is general; may arouse interest; is capable of being developed. The concluding sentence often amplifies the beginning sentence; serves as a unifying generalization; or may lead into the next paragraph.)
C. *Pretest* (A paragraph may be assigned about a topic being studied by the children.)
D. *Whom the unit is designed for:* The sequence of Component Ideas (B_1-B_5) proceeds from the simple to the more difficult. Component Idea B_1 would be appropriate for the average 8- or 9-year-old child who is consciously striving to make use of such ideas in his writing. The child who has already mastered B_1 does not need the lesson and can begin with the concept in Component Ideas B_2-B_5 which he is attempting unsuccessfully to incorporate into his informative paragraph writing. This statement also suggests the "next step" for pupils who begin with Component Idea B_1. Materials needed include an English textbook and subject content textbooks.
E. *Learning Objectives for Component Idea B_1:*
   1. Lesson One. Given a selection containing several paragraphs, the learner should be able to bracket each paragraph with 100 per cent accuracy.

CHART 7-12 (cont)

2. Lesson Two. Given a set of well-constructed paragraphs, the learner should be able to identify the topic of the paragraphs.
3. Lesson Three. Given a choice of several topics, the learner can write a paragraph, appropriately each of the preceding ideas in his own paragraph composition.

F. *Study Instructions:* Choose any or all.
1. *Lesson One:* Make a diagram of the paragraphs on page _____ of your language textbook.
2. Identify the number of paragraphs on pages _____ to _____ of your social studies textbook.
   Self-evaluation: Answer the following question: How can you tell one paragraph from another?
3. *Lesson Two:* Read the instructions about paragraph composition in your language textbook, p. _____.
4. Write a word or group of words that tells the topic for the paragraph appearing on page _____ of your science textbook.
5. Write a question which is answered by the paragraph on page _____ of your language textbook.
   Self-evaluation: Answer the following question: What is meant by the topic in a paragraph?
6. *Lesson Three:* Write an informative paragraph about some important safety rules to remember in bicycle riding. Compare it with the one in your health textbook on page _____. (Or write an informative paragraph about the way the beavers build a dam. Compare it with the one in your science textbook on page _____.)

G. *Post-test for Component I* (See pre-test for an idea)
H. *Learning Objectives Stated for Components* B_2, B_3, B_4, B_5
I. *Subsequent Lessons on Components* B_2, B_3, B_4, and B_5
J. *Post-tests for Components* B_1-B_5 (A demonstration of the behaviors suggested within each Component.)
K. *Further Activities* (Where appropriate, such as "Construct a two-step outline on a topic from a content field. Write a paragraph from the outline." Other ideas would involve analysis of paragraph structure of other types of composition.)

Major Parts of Teacher's ISP. Four major parts represent the teacher's plan. First, there is a statement of the idea, skill, or attitude to be learned. The major learning is subdivided into several (normally two to six) principal parts. Second, the learning objectives are stated in behavioral terms (e.g., "Given _____ the pupil will _____ with _____ degree of success."). Third, the teacher writes a statement about the pupil for whom the ISP is designed, suggests what might precede and follow the ISP, and describes the sorts of equipment, materials, or media needed. Fourth, a comprehensive test is needed to cover the objectives. The pretest and posttest may be the same or similar. Successful completion of either pre- or post-test frees the learner to proceed with other activities

Major Parts of Learner's ISP. First, along with a short title and statement of the skill to be learned, an introduction points up the relevance of the desired learning to the larger goal. Second, a series of lessons includes the component ideas, objectives, choices of learning activities to appeal to various learning styles, and self-evaluations. A self-administered quiz should be provided at the end of each lesson so that the learner may check himself. Upon completion of the first lesson, the learner proceeds to the next lesson in the study plan. After satisfactory completion of work for each component, the pupil asks the instructor to administer a posttest. Optional activities which appeal to the learner (quest activities) may be undertaken to pursue the subject or apply it to other situations.

The ISP is designed as one means of individualizing instruction for any subject. It is adaptable for elementary school pupils (e.g., if put on tape, with accompanying pictures and objects, for oral or motor responses, it can be suited to primary level children). It is considered only one portion of the child's total instructional program—not utilized to the exclusion of large and small group situations. ISP might lend itself to various aspects of the language arts programs, such as oral and written expression, spelling, and handwriting.

Usage

An analysis chart can be helpful in tabulating various types of usage errors in a systematic manner. Errors can be treated individually or combined into categories: Chart 7–13 provides a brief list of the types of errors that might be included. The teacher may choose to record the specific example of error, or simply the number of times the error is made. The teacher may wish to provide examples such as the following for the analysis chart.

> *Verbs*
>> Tense form: *He seen it,* or *I have came home,* or *Bill come home.*
>> Tense: Inappropriate shift between sentences
>> Agreement: *They was here.*
>> Auxiliary missing: *He standing there.*
>
> *Pronouns*
>> Subject or preposition object: *Him did it,* or . . . *with Sam and I.*
>> Demonstrative adjective: *Them books are mine.*
>> Unclear antecedents: *Mary and Jane were there and she saw him do it.*

CHART 7-13. Analysis of Written Usage Items

Pupil's Names	Verbs				Pronouns				Adjective/ Adverb			Words				
	Tense form	Tense shift	Agreement	Auxiliary missing	Subject or object position	Pronoun adjective	Antecedents	Form	Confusion	Article	Comparison	Addition	Omission	Substitution	Plural	Nonstandard

Form: *our'n, her'n*
Adjectives and Adverbs
  Confusion: *good* for *well*
  Article: *a* for *an*
  Double comparison: *more bigger*
Words
  Additions: *My cat she meowed,* or *This here dog is pretty.*
  Omissions: *She went the movie.*
  Substitutions: *Sally sat on the there.*
  Plurals: *The two boy played.*
  Nonstandard: *ain't*

SPECIAL EXPERIENCES IN WRITTEN EXPRESSION

Awareness of the special characteristics of each of the major writing areas is a first step in diagnostic teaching. The major composing tasks appropriate for elementary school pupils are:

letter writing
reports and reviews
announcements and notices
records
filling-in forms
bibliographies

The parts of a friendly letter and a business letter and the required capitalization and punctuation, along with addressing of envelopes, need to be analyzed.

What are the skills involved in writing a report? The following list is suggestive.

choosing a topic
using one reference source
introducing the report
organizing the main topics and subtopics
using more than one reference source
notetaking
paraphrasing
presenting by various means

The teacher may phrase objectives behaviorally, as illustrated below, for reviewing a movie.

After seeing a movie, the pupil will be able to write a review in which
he or she
tells the title of the picture, the name of the theatre where it can be
seen, the names of the main actors, and whether or not the picture is
in color
tells what the movie is about, whether it is based on an actual event
or make-believe, and whether it is funny or serious
tells nothing about the picture that would spoil any surprise for those
who plan to see it later
tells whether or not he enjoyed the movie, and why he did or did not
enjoy it.

From either form of listing—skills or behavior—analysis charts of
the type illustrated throughout this chapter may be prepared and
maintained for each of the major composing tasks.

Written notices need to answer these questions: who? what? when?
where? why? how? The same is true of news articles and want ads. A
child needs to learn to be accurate and specific, giving dates and
pertinent details in record keeping.

Filling-in of forms requires ability to give information such as age,
date and place of birth, sex, parents' names and occupations, telephone number, height and weight.

The preceding paragraphs have focused upon matters of form. The
level of ideas must be considered, as well as sequential organization
of the ideas, presentation of details, and word choice for expressing
ideas.

CREATIVE WRITING

Three common creative writing activities in the elementary grades
are (a) story writing (b) poetry writing, and (c) nonstory narrative
(individual expressive, personal writing).

What elements of story writing deserve attention at the elementary
school level? The following list is suggestive; each major item can be
divided into subskills.

description
introduction and conclusion
character development
plot
variation

What qualities of poetry writing deserve attention at the elementary
school level? Again the listing is merely suggestive; each major item
can be divided into subskills.

theme
precise words
words for sound
rhythm
imagery (descriptive words)
lines for effect

Specific types of poems—couplets, triplets, quatrains, limericks, lanternes, sept, haiku, and cinquain—which have special characteristics can be isolated for study.

Marcus (1974) has described how the cinquain, used as a diagnostic and instructional technique, achieved the following objectives:

- In specific categories student vocabulary was elicited and extended.
- Sentence patterning was the basis for word selection. Therefore sentence patterning afforded an opportunity for the nonstandard speaker to use appropriate verb forms and phoneme.
- Each line led the student higher up the ladder of abstraction.
- The students created their own poem.

In other words, the cinquain is not just a loose collection of words. The words in each line have similar relationships. Line 2 consists of words used as adjective complements of the linking verb to be; line 3 requires the present participle form; line 4 requires words that label emotions or personal conditions. Each line leads the student to higher levels of abstractions, culminating with line 5 which contains one abstract noun encompassing the total content of the cinquain.

Lessons for individuals and small groups, encompassing a variety of instructional approaches to writing stories and poems, should be a part of the repertoire of every elementary school teacher. After a teacher has successfully stimulated creative writing, diagnostic teaching becomes more prominent in the attempt to make valid judgments about the child's original work. The teacher must know something about the child's maturity, background and experiences. What is an unsatisfactory product for one child may be excellent for another. In brief, standards must be flexible and adapted to the child.

For story writing, the use of scales such as Carlson's (1964) and Yamamato's (1961) can help the teacher evaluate strengths and weaknesses in such items as ideas and ingenuity. Illustrative samples for the ratings are included in both scales. However, most scales have the disadvantage of requiring much scoring time. Perhaps the most practical scale is one that includes attention to vocabulary, originality, organization and elaborative writing, as shown in Chart 7-14.

CHART 7-14. Scale for rating vocabulary, originality, organization, and elaborative writing

---

Vocabulary
Definition: Use of words to express a particular thought or idea.
Rate 3 if the composition contains the following:
A variety of clear, precise words and/or unusually descriptive and vivid words—
  words that appeal to the senses
  choice selective words which develop shades of meaning
  action clearly shown by the specific words
  synonyms and antonyms which enhance word pictures
  colorful, picturesque, effective similes and/or metaphors
Rate 2 if the composition contains the following:
Words that are adequately descriptive but lack overall excellence—
  sporadic use of vivid words or phrases
  some good similes and/or metaphors
Rate 1 if the composition contains the following:
Some appropriate words with little variety of word choice—
  very few descriptive or picture words
  common overworked similes and/or metaphors
  words that produce vague impressions
Rate 0 if the composition contains the following:
Only commonplace words without variety—
  trite, ineffective, dull words which are monotonous

Originality
Definition: An original composition contains unusual thoughts or unique arrangements of ordinary words to give freshness to a common idea.
Rate 3 if the composition contains the following:
Unique, different, or unexpected ideas, or words arranged throughout to produce an unusual effect—
  individual interpretations of ordinary thoughts
  new ways of telling something
  unusual placement of words
  fresh interpretation of an old idea by unusual play on words or word order
Rate 2 if the composition contains the following:
Frequent use of original ideas or frequent use of words arranged so as to produce an unusual effect
Rate 1 if the composition contains the following:
Occasional use of original ideas or occasional use of words arranged so as to produce an unusual effect

Chart 7-14 (cont.)

Rate 0 if the composition contains the following:
   Conventional ideas and commonplace word patterns
Organization
Definition: Organization is the sequential arrangement of ideas.
Rate 3 if the composition contains the following:
   Continuity and logical clear arrangement of relevant thoughts—
      no irrelevant details.
      buildup of ideas exactly suitable to express mood of story
      main idea fully expressed
      all minor ideas supporting major idea
Rate 2 if the composition contains the following:
   Main idea clearly stated, but relevant thoughts lack continuity and logical
   clear arrangement—
      no irrelevant ideas
      no consistency in buildup of ideas that express the mood created
      main idea fully expressed
      some minor ideas poorly arranged
Rate 1 if the composition contains the following:
   A main idea with some irrelevant ideas—
      relevant ideas poorly developed and illogically arranged
      jumbled arrangement of thoughts which detract from mood
      important elements of composition placed where they are least effective
Rate 0 if the composition contains the following:
   Overall impression of disorder because of illogical sequence of ideas—
      disorganized, needless digression
      irrelevant material more prominent than topic
      minor ideas dwarfing major ideas

Elaborative Writing
Definition: Elaborative writing is an abundance of appropriately
            related ideas fluently expressed.
Rate 3 if the composition contains the following:
   A wealth of ideas which have depth, scope, and feeling—
      full treatment of the subject through ample, unrestrained details which
      give clarity and color.
      associated ideas which are fully developed and follow each other easily
      and naturally
Rate 2 if the composition contains the following:
   Ideas which are clear and flow smoothly but lack full development
   because of incomplete treatment of the subject.
Rate 1 if the composition contains the following:
   Limited ideas or stilted and restrained ideas which prevent continuity,
   smooth relationships and associations—
      inadequate details

Chart 7-14 (cont.)

Rate 0 if the composition contains the following:
  Ideas suggested but never carried out—
    no details
    barrenness of expression
    confused impressions
    jumbled and disassociated thoughts

NOTE. From the Teacher's Guide to *New Ways in Composition* (Cambridge, Mass.: The Ealing Corporation, 1968), pp. 34-35. Copyright © 1968. The Ealing Corporation. Used with permission.

For poetry writing, Walter's (1962) list of ten items should be helpful for evaluating and teaching purposes. She calls for

- originality—in thought or phrasing or words
- sincerity—reflects writer's real thoughts
- imagery—simple analogies and picturesque details
- idea—new thought, new image, new phrasing
- feeling—reflects writer's own feelings
- universality—enjoyed by others of their own age
- unity—maintains one point of view throughout
- rhythm—simple, but patterned or cadenced
- accuracy—in use of words
- artistic significance—shows originality, awareness of truth, and sincerity of feeling

The strongest foundation for a poetry-writing program is a planned poetry reading and study program that includes a balance of poems of various characteristics, topics, and forms. Through such a program, children become familiar with what poetry is and its varieties of themes and forms.

Writing centers are a means of encouraging creative writing, particularly if materials and suggested activities are appealing. Assorted colors of notepaper, pens, and stationery are additional attractions.

Some teachers have found commercial sets of material helpful in their composition program. Two such sets are:

The Writing Bug (Creative Writing in Middle Grades) includes activity cards, wall charts, filmstrips, cassettes of sounds, and a teacher's guide.

Aware (A Poetry Learning Unit) includes activity cards, track cards, poetry booklets, tape cassettes, scent samples, braille cards, and a teacher's guide.

Both are published by Random House School Division, 201 East 50th Street, New York, New York 10022. Additional composition programs are cited in chapter 4.

ADDITIONAL CORRECTIVE ACTIVITIES

1. See pages 126–27 in Chapter 6 "Oral Communication" for a discussion of the language-experience approach as a means of producing written expression.

2. Patterned writing helps children to write, imitate, and innovate upon patterns and story forms. Writing success occurs for most children. The procedures for using a poem or story for pattern writing includes close study of the model, discussion about the model, and questions about patterns in the model. Efforts may begin with the whole class, move to small groups and finally to the individual. Here are two books that lend themselves to patterned writing—there are many more: Janina Donamska, *If All the Seas Were One Sea* (New York: Macmillan Co., 1971) and Leland B. Jacobs, *Poetry for Chuckles and Grins* (Champaign, III.: Garrard Publishing Co., 1969).

3. Rhyme arrangements (couplet, triplet, quatrain, and limerick) and syllabic arrangements (haiku, cinquain, lanterne, septolet, tanka) are usually easier for most children than writing free verse poetry.

4. For children having difficulty in composing, several partial sentences could be prepared for completion by the child. For example:

On this April morning . . .
As I look around, I see . . .
As I write, I hear . . .
Now . . .

5. Encourage therapeutic writing (writing of feelings) for youngsters under tensions, such as "How I See Myself", personal experience stories, and the like.
6. The English language relies heavily on word order to convey meaning. Teachers can use the basic sentence patterns as a starting point for those who need it:

The balloon descended. (noun-verb)
The cowboy saddled his horse. (noun-verb-noun)
Dad called Mary a tomboy. (noun-verb-noun-noun)
My boss is an Irishman. (noun-linking verb-noun)

Students may use these basic sentence patterns for writing practice or they may locate examples of the patterns in their reading content material.

7. Experiences with sentences, such as expanding and restructuring them, will increase sentence composition ability. For example, children may enjoy taking a basic noun phrase or verb phrase and expanding it by adding descriptive elements.

Example: Girl sang.
          The tall girl with the long hair sang very softly.

Sentence combining exercises (combining two or more related sentences into one sentence) is a profitable exercise and transformations encourage greater writing flexibility.

Transformation
The girl laughed.
The girl did not laugh.
Is the girl laughing?
Did the girl laugh?
Didn't the girl laugh?

Sentence-combining
The boy hid in the room.
The boy was young.
The young boy hid in the room.

(For more information on this subject, see John C. Mellon, *Transformational Sentence Combining* [Urbana, Ill.: NCTE, 1969] and Frank O'Hare, *Sentence Combining* [Urbana, Ill.: NCTE, 1973].)

REVIEW QUESTIONS AND ACTIVITIES

1. Use the rating scale ideas proposed in this chapter to judge a child's composition. Check vocabulary, elaboration, organization, and structure.
2. Analyze one child's composition using the ideas proposed in this chapter. Prepare a summary chart, providing information about length, syntax, characterization, and plot development.

3. What are some possible causes of low test scores on capitalization skills? For each cause cited, suggest an appropriate remedial treatment.

4. What are some possible causes of low test scores on punctuation skills? For each cause cited, suggest an appropriate remedial treatment.

5. Prepare an analytical test, with follow-up materials, for a particular punctuation or capitalization skill.

6. What are some possible causes of low test scores on sentence sense skills? For each cause cited, suggest an appropriate remedial treatment.

7. Prepare a sample ISP Lesson for development of one particular written communication skill.

8. Prepare an analysis chart for checking one of the following: friendly or business letter; written report; written notice; record keeping; or filling in of forms.

9. Explain how use of rhyming verse or syllabic verse can be utilized as a diagnostic and instructional technique.

10. Use the scale on page 175–77 of this chapter to rate a creative prose writing sample from a child.

11. If feasible, utilize the scales (Carlson's or Yamamato's) to rate strengths and weaknesses in a child's creative story writing.

12. Use Walter's items for evaluating a creative poem sample from a child.

13. Trace the scope and sequence of written expression experiences through the charts provided in the Appendix.

14. Prepare an activity or game for helping a child who needs further experiences in some aspect of written expression.

15. Develop a card file of ideas, games, and language arts books focusing upon strategies and materials for helping a child with written language difficulties.

16. Review articles dealing with the diagnosis and correction of language arts difficulties in the area of written expression.

17. Review sourcebooks, trade books, and multilevel materials that deal specifically with the written expression component of the language arts.

18. Develop a teaching plan related to one of the suggested "Additional Corrective Activities."

19. Read and report on a professional reference dealing with individ-
    ual, expressive writing. Here are two suggested sources:

    Britton, James, et al. *Development of Writing Abilities.* Urbana, Ill.: Na-
    tional Council of Teachers of English, 1975.

    Cramer, Ronald L. *Children's Writing and Language Growth.* Columbus,
    Ohio: Charles E. Merrill Publishing Co., 1979.

20. Use the rating scale ideas proposed on page 149 of this chap-
    ter to check this first grader's written composition. Check vo-
    cabulary, elaboration, organization, and structure.

    One day a little boy was playing with his ball, but a big boy steal his
    ball. The little kid tell on the big kid, so the big kid give the ball back.
    So the big kid and the little kid play a game of ball.

21. Read and report on one of these professional references:

    Cooper, Charles R. and Odell, Lee, eds. *Research on Composing: Points
    of Departure.* Urbana, Ill.: National Council of Teachers of English,
    1978.

    Larson, Richard L. *Children and Writing in the Elementary School.* New
    York: Oxford University Press, 1975.

22. Analyze the following two written stories in terms of T-units, de-
    scriptive words and phrases, and number of words with two or
    more morphemes. See the note and normative data which follow
    the stories.

a. Two Horses

One there was two horses named Blacky. It all started one day in
July. They were having a race to see if his horses could make a race
team. The horses ran faster than any horse. The manager of the two
horses look in the word record to see what the time of the fastest race
was. The manager, Frank, said, "Well, did they make the team? Did
they make the team?"

"Yes. They also broke the word record."

Frank went to downtown. Everybody in town asked them, "Did
they make the team?"

"No."

Everybody look sad.

Frank said, "They broke the world record!"

b. How the Rain Came To Be

One day a bad angel was fighting with a good angel. In heaven God
didn't find out till the next day. They were screaming and holoring

and hitting. God was angry his face turned red and purple. He said fighting in heaven t, t, t. Well he couldn't think of punishment. He thought and thought. He rembered a punishment not to bad and not to tender. He hit them on their bottom. They cried and cried and that's how the rain came to be.

Note: Walter Loban in *Language Development: Kindergarten Through Grade Twelve* (Urbana, Ill.: National Council of Teachers of English, 1976) has suggested some conventions in marking such passages. Brackets are used to enclose mazes, and the number of words per maze are circled in red. A blue slash is at the end of each independent clause with its modifiers (called a T-unit by Hunt and explained in this chapter), with the number of words in that T-unit above the slash. In the case of a compound sentence, "and" is counted with the second T-unit. Contractions of two words into one are counted as two words. The descriptive words and phrases are underlined in green. The words with two or more morphemes can be coded with a red dot over the word.

Some normative data have been provided by Loban:

Average Number of Words Per Communication Unit—
Comparison or Oral and Written Language
(mean)

	High Group		Random Group		Low Group	
Grade	Oral	Written	Oral	Written	Oral	Written
1	7.91	—	6.88	—	5.91	—
2	8.10	—	7.56	—	6.65	—
3	8.38	7.68	7.62	7.60	7.08	5.65
4	9.28	8.83	9.00	8.02	7.55	6.01
5	9.59	9.52	8.82	8.76	7.90	6.29
6	10.32	10.23	9.82	9.04	8.57	6.91
7	11.14	10.83	9.75	8.94	9.01	7.52
8	11.59	11.24	10.71	10.37	9.52	9.49
9	11.79	11.09	10.96	10.05	9.26	8.78
10	12.34	12.59	10.68	11.79	9.41	11.03
11	13.00	11.82	11.17	10.69	10.18	11.21
12	12.84	14.06	11.70	13.27	10.65	11.24

REFERENCES

Carlson, R.K. *An analytical scoring scale for measuring the originality of children's stories.* Hayward, Calif.: California State College, 1964.

Hunt, K.W. *Grammatical structures written at three grade levels,* Research Report No. 3, Champaign, Ill.: National Council of Teachers of English, 1965, p. 23.

Jung, R.K. A new approach to understanding children's language development—analyzing the syntax of compositions, *California English Journal 7* (Dec. 1971) 34–43.

Marcus, M. The Cinquain as a diagnostic and instructional technique, *Elementary English, 51* (Apr. 1974) 561–62, 564.

McKee, P. *Language in the elementary school.* Boston: Houghton-Mifflin, 1934, p. 272

Walter, N.W. Let them write poetry. New York: Holt, Rinehart & Winston, 1962, pp. 144–145. For examples of how such criteria have been used to evaluate poetry-writing, see Gerald Duffy, The construction and validation of an instrument to measure poetry writing performance, *Educational and Psychological Measurement,* 1968, *28,* 1233–1236; Lester S. Golub, stimulating and receiving children's writing: Implications for an elementary writing curriculum, *Elementary English, 48,* 33–49, January 1971, and Phyllis P. Shapiro and Bernard J. Shapiro, Two methods of teaching poetry writing in the fourth grade, *Elementary English,* 1971, *48,* 225–228.

Yamamato, K. *Scoring manuals for evaluating imaginative stories.* Minneapolis: Bureau of Educational Research, College of Education, University of Minnesota, 1961.

8

Spelling

In the diagnostic approach to spelling instruction, the teacher identifies the specific needs of individual children. Four well-established procedures that should be followed in developmental spelling programs are:

- begin a lesson with a pretest.
- teach every child a systematic procedure for learning the spelling of a word.
- have pupils correct their own tests.
- include exercises which cause pupils to practice visual and auditory perception and discrimination.

A good corrective spelling program will maintain the characteristics of any good diagnostic/remedial program by detecting the child's particular errors and successes; by providing frequent instructional periods and relating instruction to other subject areas; by using materials that are interesting and relatively easy at first; by encouraging independent word study; and by devoting attention to motivation and attitude.

TESTS FOR SPELLING

Achievement or language batteries generally include subtests which attempt to measure spelling ability for particular grade levels. While the tests have limitations, they are useful as a general survey to locate the low-achievement pupils and to ascertain the general level of progress for the class as a whole.

For finding the approximate grade level at which a child spells, the Informal Spelling Inventory (ISI) may be utilized. Words on the first-grade list are pronounced once and the pupils write them. Children who spell 70% or more of the first-grade words correctly are tested again, using the second-grade list. Testing continues until the child spells less than 70% of a list correctly. That indicates the approximate level of spelling achievement for instructional purposes.

Below is a listing of words that can be used for an Informal Spelling Inventory. The words are from the *Word Book Spelling Program* (Chicago: Rand McNally Co., 1976).

Grade 1	Grade 2	Grade 3	Grade 4
1. bit	1. ate	1. another	1. bank
2. cane	2. birds	2. before	2. blowing
3. date	3. by	3. called	3. calling
4. egg	4. day	4. city	4. check
5. fog	5. eat	5. cry	5. colored
6. gum	6. for	6. dresses	6. dance
7. home	7. glad	7. feet	7. eaten
8. jam	8. he	8. friend	8. finger
9. joke	9. I	9. great	9. gathered
10. lamp	10. likes	10. heard	10. happened
11. lot	11. me	11. into	11. joke
12. mop	12. not	12. left	12. large
13. nip	13. over	13. merry	13. luck
14. page	14. rabbit	14. never	14. naughty
15. pole	15. second	15. orange	15. pages
16. rid	16. store	16. presents	16. pitcher
17. sad	17. they	17. Santa Claus	17. pushed
18. sore	18. train	18. ship	18. rice
19. tin	19. we	19. skin	19. scared
20. wax	20. would	20. started	20. skated
		21. supper	21. steal
		22. through	22. tail
		23. upon	23. tramp
		24. wear	24. upstairs
		25. woods	25. whose

Grade 5	Grade 6	Grade 7	Grade 8
1. autumn	1. anybody	1. amusing	1. amateur
2. behind	2. bareheaded	2. badly	2. argument

Grade 5	Grade 6	Grade 7	Grade 8
3. button	3. bracelet	3. budget	3. bodies
4. chance	4. carried	4. commercial	4. cashier
5. colony	5. community	5. controversy	5. comfortable
6. dairy	6. dancing	6. definitely	6. controllable
7. drill	7. during	7. disappointed	7. decoration
8. excited	8. expect	8. enable	8. difference
9. follow	9. form	9. envy	9. doubtless
10. giving	10. grapevines	10. familiar	10. equipment
11. inside	11. honey	11. fortune	11. extension
12. leaving	12. jellyfish	12. guardian	12. funeral
13. March	13. let's	13. hygiene	13. hemisphere
14. motor	14. massive	14. interviewed	14. innings
15. nurse	15. mule	15. locate	15. justice
16. perfume	16. office	16. mighty	16. lover
17. possible	17. pioneer	17. notify	17. molecule
18. queen	18. principal	18. peaceable	18. olives
19. route	19. region	19. practicing	19. peculiar
20. scratch	20. seal	20. purchase	20. possibility
21. shower	21. sixth	21. republic	21. pronunciation
22. special	22. spaceship	22. security	22. reception
23. surprise	23. straight	23. sorrow	23. resources
24. umbrella	24. theater	24. submit	24. serviceable
	25. treat	25. through	25. sufficient

Used with permission of Rand McNally Publishing Co.

There are a number of informal assessment procedures that should be utilized prior to more formal testing situations. Some procedures are:

Analyzing written work, including test papers. Are there defects in handwriting that are causing errors? Can the spelling errors be classified as to type? Is there evidence that the student doesn't know important spelling rules?

Analyzing oral spelling. Is pronunciation of the words clear, as well as articulation and enunciation? How does the child spell the word orally (as units, by letter, by digraphs, by syllables)? Is the student able to spell plural forms and derivatives? When the child describes his thought process while studying new words, is it evident that he has a systematic method of study? Does he or she know several different ways to study spelling words?

Interviewing the child. Here questions would be asked regarding knowledge of important spelling rules, his or her attitude towards spelling, and perhaps extent of using the dictionary.

To locate the disabled spellers, objective tests are unnecessary in the primary years and not essential at the intermediate level. However, if there is need for such testing at the intermediate level, the *Test of Written Spelling* (TWS) by S.C. Larsen and D.D. Hammill (Austin, Tex.: Empiric Press, 1976) may be given. This dictated-word test contains words used in 10 commonly employed basal spelling series. It tests the ability of students to spell words that are linguistically consistent as well as those that are not. Three types of normative data are available: spelling ages, grade equivalents, and spelling quotients.

For a rapid method of collecting samples of a pupil's tendencies to spelling errors, *Spelling Errors Tests* by George D. Spache. (Gainesville, Florida: University of Florida.) are recommended. Two separate tests, for use in Grades 2–4 and Grades 5–6, are offered: each test provides opportunities for 12 types of common spelling errors, with ten words devoted to each type. The common types of errors in the Spache lists, along with examples, are

omission of silent letter—bite, bit
omission of sounded letter—and, an
omission of double letter—arrow, arow
addition by doubling—almost, allmost
addition of single letter—dark, darck
transposition or reversal—ankle, ankel
phonetic substitution for vowel—bead, beed
phonetic substitution for consonant—bush, buch
phonetic substitution for syllable—flies, flys
phonetic substitution for word—bare, bear
nonphonetic substitution for vowel—bags, bogs
nonphonetic substitution for consonant—bottom, botton

If a child misspells any word in the way indicated, it is likely that he will make that kind of error on similar words. The teacher can help him by applying the principle, practicing pronunciation, or whatever kind of instruction the error implies. Easily group-administered, scored, recorded, and interpreted, the tests may be recommended as clues to poor spellers.

The Cloze procedure is another instrument which may be used to help appraise specific spelling difficulties; it is particularly useful in the evaluation of a student's knowledge of spelling generalizations. Specific areas of strength and weakness can be pinpointed, and corrective or remedial procedures can be based directly upon the findings. The following items illustrate the procedure.

1. The girl was mak_____ a cake. (ing)
2. Bill was carr_____ a heavy load. (ying)
3. Jane stay_____ all night with Betty. (ed)
4. Jim was enjo_____ himself. (ying)
5. Susan was run_____ down the street. (ning)
6. The teacher said, "Start at the begin_____." (ning)
7. Two pints is the same amount as one q__art. (u)
8. Do you believ__ the story? (e)
9. Go fly a k_____. (ite)
10. My n__ghbor has a new car. (ei)
11. Bill is my best fr__nd. (ie)
12. Don't get t_____ close to the fire. (oo)

A spelling test that yields information about phonic power in spelling is the *Diagnostic Spelling Test* devised by Kottmeyer (1970). The test and norms, along with the phonic and structural elements tested, appear in Chart 8–1.

CHART 8-1. Diagnostic spelling test

Directions:
Give list 1 to any pupil whose placement is second or third grade.
Give list 2 to any pupil whose placement is above Grade 3.
Grade Scoring, List 1:

Below 15 correct:	Below second grade
15-22 correct:	Second grade
23-29 correct:	Third grade

Any pupil who scores above 29 should be given the List 2 Test.
Grade Scoring, List 2:

Below 9 correct:	Below third grade
9-19 correct:	Third grade
20-25 correct:	Fourth grade
26-29 correct:	Fifth grade
Over 29 correct:	Sixth grade or better

Any pupil who scores below 9 should be given the List 1 Test.

LIST 1

Word   *Illustrative Sentence*   *Element Tested*

1. not—He is *not* here.
2. but—Mary is here, *but* Joe is not.
3. get—*Get* the wagon, John.   } short vowels
4. sit—*Sit* down, please.
5. man—Father is a tall *man.*

6. *boat—We sailed our boat* on the lake. }
7. train—Tom has a new toy *train.*   } two vowels together

Chart 8-1 (cont.)

Word	Illustrative Sentence	Element Tested

8. time—It is *time* to come home.
9. like—We *like* ice cream.
} vowel-consonant-e

10. found—We *found* our lost ball.
11. down—Do not fall *down*.
} ow-ou spelling of *ou* sound

12. soon—Our teacher will *soon* be here.
13. good—He is a *good* boy.
} long and short *oo*

14. very—We are *very* glad to be here.
15. happy—Jane is a *happy* girl.
} final *y* as short *i*

16. kept—We *kept* our shoes dry.
17. come—*Come* to our party.
} c and k spellings of the *k* sound

18. what—*What* is your name?
19. those—*Those* are our toys.
20. show—*Show* us the way.
21. much—I feel *much* better.
22. sing—We will *sing* a new song.
} wh, th, sh, ch, and ng spellings and ow spelling of long *o*

23. will—Who *will* help us?
24. doll—Make a dress for the *doll*.
} doubled final consonants

25. after—We play *after* school.
26. sister—My *sister* is older than I.
} er spelling

27. toy—I have a new *toy* train.
} oy spelling of *oi* sound

28. say—*Say* your name clearly.
} ay spelling of long *a* sound

29. little—Tom is a *little* boy.
} le ending

30. one—I have only *one* book.
31. would—*Would* you come with us?
32. pretty—She is a *pretty* girl.
} nonphonetic spellings

LIST 2

Word	Illustrative Sentence	Element Tested

1. flower—A rose is a *flower*.
2. mouth—Open your *mouth*.
} ow-ou spellings of *ou* sound
er ending, th spelling

Chart 8-1 (cont.)

Word	Illustrative Sentence	Element Tested
3. shoot—Joe wants to *shoot* his new gun.		long and short oo, sh
4. stood—We *stood* under the roof.		spelling
5. while—We sang *while* we marched.		wh spelling, vowel-consonant-e
6. third—We are in the *third* grade.		th spelling, vowel before r
7. each—*Each* child has a pencil.		ch spelling, two vowels together.
8. class—Our *class* is reading.		double final consonant, c spelling of k sound

9. jump—We like to *jump* rope.
10. jumps—Mary *jumps* rope.
11. jumped—We *jumped* rope yesterday.
12. jumping—The girls are *jumping* rope now.

addition of s, ed, ing; j spelling of soft g sound

13. hit—*Hit* the ball hard.
14. hitting—John is *hitting* the ball.

doubling final consonant before adding ing

15. bite—Our dog does not *bite*.
16. biting—The dog is *biting* on the bone.

dropping final e before ing

17. study—*Study* your lesson.
18. studies—He *studies* each day.

changing final y to i before ending

19. dark—The sky is *dark* and cloudy.
20. darker—This color is *darker* than that one.
21. darkest—This color is the *darkest* of the three.

er, est endings

22. afternoon—We may play this *afternoon*.
23. grandmother—Our *grandmother* will visit us.

compound words

24. can't—We *can't* go with you.
25. doesn't—Mary *doesn't* like to play.

contractions

Chart 8-1 (cont.)

Word	Illustrative Sentence	Element Tested
26. night—We read to Mother last *night.*		silent gh
27. brought—Joe *brought* his lunch to school.		
28. apple—An *apple* fell from the tree.		le ending
29. again—We must come back *again.*		
30. laugh—Do not *laugh* at other children.		
31. because—We cannot play *because* of the rain.		nonphonetic spelling
32. through—We ran *through* the yard.		

NOTE. Reprinted from *Teacher's Guide to Remedial Reading* by William Kottmeyer. Copyright 1970. Used with permission of Webster/McGraw-Hill.

By supplementing this list with a representative sampling of words in various levels of spellers, the teacher can determine which pupils should be placed in the grade-level speller, and which should work on more fundamental words.

Some writers think that spelling difficulties are severe enough to warrant special treatment if a pupil is behind as much as three-fourths of a year in grade three, and one year in grades four to eight. The *Gates Russell Spelling Diagnostic Tests* (New York: Teacher's College, Columbia Univ., 1937) are the best known standardized individual diagnostic tests. They include the following series of nine tests:

Spelling Words Orally (power test)
Word Pronunciation (reading and speech)
Giving Letters for Sound (oral)
Spelling One Syllable (oral)
Spelling Two Syllables (oral)
Word Reversals (oral)
Spelling Attack (securing evidence as to usual methods of study)
Auditory Discrimination (hearing)
Visual, Auditory, Kinesthetic, and Combined Study Methods (comparison of effectiveness)

Performance on each of the nine tests is evaluated in terms of grade scores. Details of administering and scoring are given in the manual for the test. The comprehensive information compiled by this test leads to the diagnosis of the nature of the spelling disability and to the identification of the causes most likely to be at the root of the difficulty. A corrective and remedial program can then be planned and implemented.

Westerman has presented a modality testing procedure that attempts to discover the kinds of performance produced when varying combinations of learning channels are employed by the child. Figure 8–1 explains the testing procedure.

The specific channels cited at the top of Figure 8–1 have these meanings:

Auditory-vocal channel. The child hears the word spelled aloud, then spells it orally to the teacher. The word is never presented visually.

Auditory-motor channel. The child hears the word spelled aloud, then writes the word on paper.

Visual-vocal channel. In this method, the words are presented on flash cards, identified (i.e., "this word is 'carpet.'"), but are never spelled aloud. The child looks at the word, then spells it orally back to the teacher.

Visual-motor channel. Again, the word is presented visually on a flash card and identified. The child looks at the word, then writes it on paper.

Multi-sensory combination channel. In this method, the child looks at the word on a flash card while it is spelled aloud, then spells it back orally and writes it on paper.

Westerman provides details for the administration of a sensory modality preference test for spelling:[1]

1. Administer a pretest to determine 40 words which are unknown to all children in the group as spelling words. If there is a wide spelling ability range within the class, the teacher may discover that in order to find words which the more able spellers do not know, he must use words which the less able have no hope of learning. In such an instance, there are two alternative solutions:

[1]From G.S. Westerman, *Spelling and Writing* (Sioux Falls, So. Dak., 1975), pp. 42-44, by permission of Adapt Press.

(a) Randomize the words, selecting 40 words of medium difficulty, and hope that a preference pattern can still be seen in the results.

(b) Group the class into two spelling levels to do the testing as originally described. More valid information on each individual pupil can be gathered in this way.

2. Random order the words in five sets containing eight words each, with each set representing a separate modality.

3. Choose two words to teach in each of the five modalities for four consecutive days (i.e., Monday through Thursday). This will total 10 words to be taught each day, two by the auditory-vocal method, two by auditory-motor, and so forth.

4. At the end of each day's instruction, evaluate the teaching and learning by verbally administering the words taught that day and requiring a written response. Tabulate for each child the number of words learned in each modality, thus obtaining a measure of relatively immediate recall.

5. On Friday, verbally administer in randomized order all 40 words taught during the week and record responses in terms of delayed recall. Look for preference patterns for each child by recording the number of correct responses in each modality.

6. Most importantly, draw the children into the experiment. Introduce the procedure as just that, a new way to gain insight into their own most efficient learning style. Most children are amazed to learn that it matters *how* information is processed and are likely to be a partner in this discovery.

7. Give immediate reports to each child on his performance and describe study methods which may correspond to this preference pattern. That is to say, children with a preference for the auditory method might work in pairs, spelling the words aloud if a vocal response seems most effective, or writing the words if they seem to prefer a motor response. Tape recorders could be used effectively with these groups as well. A teacher can devise endless activities which will provide a child with the specific type of practice which he needs. Teaching must then continue on an ongoing, experimental basis, constantly evaluating each method until the best way is found for each child.

CAUSES AND TREATMENT OF SPELLING DEFICIENCIES

The outline shown in Chart 8–2 is a summary of the many causes of spelling deficiency as well as remedial suggestions for the classroom teacher. The reader should refer again to Chapter 1 in thinking about why children have difficulties with spelling. For example, physical factors, particularly general health, vision, and hearing, may be a factor. Intellectual factors such as general immaturity or low mental

FIGURE 8-1. Sensory modality preference testing

	Auditory-Vocal	Auditory-Motor	Visual-Vocal	Visual-Motor	Multisensory
TEACHER	1. Say word ("This is the way to spell chart") 2. Spell word aloud (c-h-a-r-t) 3. Say word again ("chart") 4. "Say the word and spell it for me."	1. Say word. 2. Spell word aloud. 3. Say word again. 4. "Write the word I have just spelled."	1. Show word on card. 2. Name word (do not spell orally) 3. "Look at the word, say it, then spell it for me."	1. Show word on card. 2. Name words. 3. "Look at this word and write it on your paper."	1. Show word on card. 2. Name word. 3. Spell orally. 4. "Look at this word and spell it for me." 5. "Now write it on your paper."
PUPIL	1. Say word ("chart") 2. Spell aloud (c-h-a-r-t)	1. Write word on paper.	1. Say word. 2. Spell orally. 3. Say word again.	1. Copy word from flash card. 2. Cover sample. 3. Write word again—check back and forth until spelled correctly.	1. Say word. 2. Spell orally. 3. Write on paper.
TEACHER	1. If error in student response, say "Almost, Bob—you try it John". Then go back to Bob. 2. After everyone has spelled back word correctly 4 times, say "Now everyone write 'chart'"	1. Repeat spelling orally for correction. 2. After writing word correctly 4 times, say "Turn your paper over and write ___"	1. After each child responds, take word away. 2. Ask each student to spell from memory. 3. After 4 correct responses from each child, say "Everyone write ___"	1. After 4 correct responses, tell children to turn paper over and write word from memory. then write from	1. After each child has responded, cover card. Ask students to spell orally from memory (2 times); then write from memory (2 times). 2. "Now turn your paper over and write ___"

P **U** **P** **I** **L**	1. Write word on paper from memory. 2. Hold paper up for correction. *Do Not Show Flash Card.*	1. Write word on paper from memory. (Correct with flash card.)	1. Write word on paper from memory. (Correct with flash card.)	1. Write word on paper from memory. (Correct with flash card.)

NOTE: From G.S. Westerman, *Spelling and Writing* (Sioux Falls, S. Dak., 1975), p. 40, by permission of Adapt Press, Inc.

CHART 8-2. Diagnostic and remedial chart for spelling

Possible Causes of Low Test Scores	Additional Evidence of Deficiency	Suggested Remedial Treatment
1. Lack of experience with the testing technique	Low score on test contrasted with high score when words are given on dictation test.	Drills on choosing correct spellings from lists of errors on same word; choosing correct forms from long lists, some correct, some incorrect; proofreading own written work.
2. Emphasis on different or wrong vocabulary.	Low scores on test in contrast with good record for daily work.	Check words not taught in your course with lists of known social utility.
3. Failure to develop a critical attitude toward spelling.	Indifference to spelling errors in daily written work.	Emphasize proofreading of own work. Drill on choosing correctly spelled froms in lists. Check pupil's certainty of his judgment of correctness of spelling.
4. Lack of teaching emphasis on individual's own spelling difficulties.	Observation of pupil's misspellings in work.	Have pupils keep lists of misspellings in daily work as basis for individual study. Focus on pupil's own errors. Try for transfer to all written work.
5. Specific learning difficulties;		
a. Faulty pronunciation by the teacher.	Observation of speech habits; informal pronunciation tests based on spelling vocabulary.	Look up the word in dictionary. Pronounce it distinctly for pupil. Have him repeat it while looking at word to associate sight and correct sound.
b. Limited power to visualize or "see" word forms.	Observation test. Have child try to visualize a 3-in. cube painted red. Ask questions: number of faces; number of planes necessary to cut it into 1-in. cubes; number of small cubes; number painted on one side, two sides; three sides, not painted, etc.	Emphasize the practice of looking at the word, closing eyes, and attempting to recall the word, as part of every spelling study period.

c. Difficulties in seeing or in hearing.	Observation; doctor's or nurse's examination.	Refer to nurse or medical service. Move child to front of room near window and blackboard. Stand near him in tests and spelling exercises. Make special effort to speak and write clearly.
d. Failure to associate sounds of letters and syllables with spelling of words.	Individual interview analysis of spelling errors in tests and in daily work.	Go over words with child while he studies them. Teach him to analyze words himself.
e. Tendency to transpose, add, or omit letters.	Analysis of spelling papers; observation of daily work; pronunciation tests.	Emphasize visual recall of words. Have child practice writing the words, exaggerating the formation of the letters. Underline individual hard spots.
f. Tendency to spell unphonetic words phonetically.	Note types of errors made in spelling tests, especially insertion or leaving out letters.	Show that all words are not spelled as they sound. Each word must be learned individually. Emphasize steps in learning to spell. See h below.
g. Difficulties in writing; letter formation.	Observation of daily written work and spelling papers. Check writing with writing scales.	Practice difficult letter formations and combinations. Emphasize need to avoid confusing letter forms, as i, e, r, and t.
h. Failure to master method of learning to spell.	Low scores on daily tests; observe the child's method of study in spelling; test on steps in learning to spell.	Check child's method of learning spelling. Teach steps in learning to spell until he uses them. Steps: (1) look at word, (2) listen as teacher pronounces it, (3) pronounce it by syllables, then say the letters, (4) use it in a sentence, (5) close eyes and visualize it, (6) write it, (7) close eyes and recall, (8) write word. Repeat steps as necessary.

Note: Reproduced from the Manual for Interpreting the *Iowa Language Abilities Test.* Copyright 1948, renewed 1976 by Harcourt Brace Jovanovich, Inc. Reproduced by special permission of the publisher.

age may be evidenced by insufficient memory for sounds and letters, inability to distinguish between words, lack of knowledge of the meanings of words, and similar failings. Environmental factors may be considered in terms of nonstandard language spoken by parents reflected in the speech of the child. Responsibility for other limitations may rest with the school program in matters of specific methods of word study employed and the relationship of spelling to the rest of the school program.

SOME SPECIAL TEACHING STRATEGIES

Children may be grouped for spelling instruction in a manner similar to the grouping for reading instruction, basing the grouping upon results of one of the diagnostic tests previously described. Another way of finding each pupil's instructional level has been proposed by Burrows and associates (1972).

First, a sample list from each grade's speller is needed: 20 to 25 words are selected from each grade list (if there are 250 words in the grade's total list, selecting every tenth word provides an unbiased sample).

Second, the class is tested to determine spelling levels, each child having a sheet of paper on which he can put 20 to 25 words in a column. The first grade list is read first: each word is pronounced once and the pupils write it.

Third, children who spell 70% or more of the first-grade words correctly are tested again, using the second-grade level list. Testing continues (perhaps on following days) until all children spell less than 70% of a list correctly. A likely distribution of levels in a second grade classroom is:

No. of children	Instructional level
5	1
12	2
8	3
5	4

This means there should be four spelling groups, each assigned to the appropriate level.

Fourth, spelling instruction is initiated, using the *test-study* and *corrected test technique* (self-correction). On Monday, each group is given a list of 20 words taken from the master spelling list. The teacher has four lists (grades 1, 2, 3, 4) and reads one word from each list in turn. The children in group one spell the first word; the group two children spell the second word; those in the third group spell the third word; and those in the fourth group, the fourth word.

Fifth, each child is given a typed copy of the words he was asked to spell and checks his own spellings against the list, finding his own mistakes.

Sixth, each misspelled word is studied immediately.

Seventh, on Wednesday the procedure is repeated. All pupils spell the same words again even if they had no misspelled words on Monday. If a child spells all words correctly on both Monday and Wednesday, he is finished for the week. If a child misses the same word on Wednesday that he missed on Monday, he studies it more on Thursday.

Eighth, the test is given again on Friday for those who did not spell all words correctly on Monday and Wednesday.

Ninth, additional delayed-recall checks are made monthly (the words missed in the preceding four weeks are used again in the test-study procedure).

Tenth, instruction is varied by giving the more able spellers enrichment words for spelling, or they can be given a new list on Fridays. For the slowest learners, the number of words per week should be reduced (one-half or fewer of the lesson words).

A first step in corrective spelling is to teach pupils only the most common words—words that they will have occasion to use over and over again. A list of words of highest frequency use is presented in Chart 8–3.

It will be noted that many of these words are "irregular" (lack phoneme-grapheme correspondence). This suggests more regular spellings may be used to stress spelling patterns, along with words that children are interested in using in their writing.

Particular attention should be given to this list. Three little words—*I, the,* and *and*—account for 10% of all words written in English. A child who can spell these three words is automatically a 10% correct speller.

Ten words—*I, the, and, to, a, you, of, in, we,* and *for*—account for 25% of all words in the writing of adults.

Horn's 100 words account for 65% of all words, counting repetitions, written by adults.

The teacher must give careful attention to the pupil's method of study. One specific procedure is outlined in "h" of the "Diagnostic and Remedial Chart for Spelling" on page 197.

CHART 8-3.   Words of highest frequency use

First 100 Words in Order of Frequency				
1. I	21. at	41. do	61. up	81. think
2. the	22. this	42. been	62. day	82. say
3. and	23. with	43. letter	63. much	83. please
4. to	24. but	44. can	64. out	84. him
5. a	25. on	45. would	65. her	85. his
6. you	26. if	46. she	66. order	86. got
7. of	27. all	47. when	67. yours	87. over
8. in	28. so	48. about	68. now	88. make
9. we	29. me	49. they	69. well	89. may
10. for	30. was	50. any	70. an	90. received
11. it	31. very	51. which	71. here	91. before
12. that	32. my	52. some	72. them	92. two
13. is	33. had	53. has	73. see	93. send
14. your	34. our	54. or	74. go	94. after
15. have	35. from	55. there	75. what	95. work
16. will	36. am	56. us	76. come	96. could
17. be	37. one	57. good	77. were	97. dear
18. are	38. time	58. know	78. no	98. made
19. not	39. he	59. just	79. how	99. good
20. as	40. get	60. by	80. did	100. like

NOTE: From *A Basic Writing Vocabulary: 10,000 Words Most Commonly Used in Writing* by Ernest A. Horn. University of Iowa Monographs in Education. First Series, No. 4, Iowa City, Iowa 1926.

Some common spelling patterns may be helpful to some children, but the exceptions must be also noted. After the student has learned the pattern, the exceptions (plus their frequency and significance) can be discussed. No pattern should be presented as foolproof.

Pattern	Example word	Exception
C-V-C (short vowel)	cat, drip	
C-V-C + e (long vowel-silent e)	save	love
C-V-V-C (long first vowel)	leaf	break
C-V (long vowel)	go	to
C-V- (controlled, preceding vowel)	bird	burn

Only spelling rules that apply to a large number of words and have few exceptions should be taught, such as

a. Words ending in silent e usually drop the final e before the addition of suffixes beginning with a vowel, but they keep the e

before the addition of suffixes beginning with a consonant.
Illustration: *make-making; time-timely.*

b. When a word ends in a consonant and *y* change the *y* to *i* before
adding all suffixes except those beginning with *i.* Do not change
y to *i* in adding suffixes to words ending in a vowel and *y* or
when adding a suffix beginning with *i.* Illustration: *baby, babies,
babying; play, played, playing.*

c. Words of one syllable or words accented on the last syllable,
ending in a single consonant preceded by a single vowel,
double the final consonant when adding a suffix beginning with
a vowel. Illustration: *run-running; begin-beginning.*

d. The letter *q* is always followed by u in common English words.
Illustration: *quick, queen, quiet.*

Spelling error charts should be maintained in order to individualize
the work. A sample is Chart 8–4 below.

CHART 8-4. Spelling errors

Name of Child	Plurals	"ie" or "ei"	Double letters	Contrac- tions	Homo- nyms	Silent letters
John						
Carol						
Jerry						
Cathy						

KEY:
I—Needs introduction and teaching
R—Weak; needs review/reinforcement
S—Satisfactory; regular program adequate
M—Has mastered skill; satisfactory at this time

Another checklist for specifying spelling errors might include such
items as the following:

1. Consonant sound used incorrectly (specify letters)
2. Vowel sounds not known
3. Omission of middle sounds
4. Omission of middle syllables
5. Extra letters added
6. Extra syllables added
7. Missequencing of sounds or syllables (transposed)
8. Reversals of parts or whole words
9. Endings omitted
10. Incorrect endings substituted

11. Phonetic spelling
12. Misspelling of nonphonetic words

Other types of errors may be the basis for similar charts, such as the 12 common types of errors suggested by Spache (see page 187); the elements tested by the Cloze procedure (see page 188); or the elements tested in the "Diagnostic Spelling Test (see page 188–91)."

Record charts are best prepared by the observant teacher who studies the pupils' common errors and then classifies them as to type. It is helpful to know that the majority of spelling errors *occur in vowels in mid-syllables of words.* Two-thirds of the errors are in *substitution or omission of letters.* Approximately 20% more of the errors are in *addition, insertion, or transposition of letters.*

Types of errors will likely vary in frequency in different age and grade levels. The most common errors in beginning spelling at the primary levels are:

use of wrong letter for vowel sound (*turm* for *term*)
mispronunciations (*pospone* for *postpone*)
lack of knowledge of phonetic elements (*haw* for *how*)
confusion of words similar in sound (*were* for *where*)
inaccurate formation of derivatives (*stoped* for *stopped*)
omitting or inserting "silent" letters (*stedy* for *steady*)
homonyms (*hole* for *whole*)
transposition of letters (*form* for *from*).

Certain kinds of spelling errors imply different types of correction procedures. When a pupil misspells a phonologically irregular word (such as *again* or *guess*), visual image should be stressed. Incorrect spelling of homonyms (*their, they're, there; your, you're; know, no*) suggests a need to emphasize meanings and perhaps teaching these words in groups. Emphasizing the visual image should help with insertion and omission of "silent" letters (*ofen* for *often, gost* for *ghost,* or *lisen* for *listen*). Knowledge that some letters represent more than one sound (*sertain* for *certain*) may be needed. And the child must be taught that he cannot rely on sound alone (*sum* for *some*).

Nonmastery of important rules appears in the failure to spell such words as *coming, getting, studying,* and *tried.* Accurate speaking and listening should be stressed with words such as *February, lightning, athlete, chimney.* Visualizing and attention to pronunciation may be helpful procedures where transposition of letters occurs in *goes* and *from* written as *gose* and *form. Stars* may appear incorrectly as *stors* due to poor handwriting. Errors involving double consonant letters may be eliminated through stressing visualizing while errors with medial vowel letters suggest a need to emphasize pronunciation and learn about unstressed vowels.

Special attention should be given to structural analysis of words: prefixes, suffixes, and root words; inflectional endings; contractions; compound words; and syllabication and accent. When spelling words through units, more than single graphemes (letters) are considered. Prefixes and suffixes are affixes (groups of letters) added to root words to form new words called derivatives. The result is a change of meaning or a change in the part of speech of the root word.

Prefixes are placed before root words, and suffixes are placed after root words (*un* in *unrelated*; *ful* in *joyful*). Inflectional endings are groups of letters which when added to nouns change the number (*s* in *girls*), case (*'s* of *girl's*) or gender (*ess* in *hostess*); when added to verbs change the tense (*ed* in *walked*) or person (*s* in *walks*); and when added to adjectives change the degree (*est* in *meanest*). They also may change the part of speech of a word (*ly* in *slowly*). The new words that are produced by adding inflectional endings are called variants.

Contractions are words which consist of combinations of two words with one or more letters left out. The missing letters are indicated by an apostrophe (*can't* for *cannot*). Compound words are composed of two words which, when combined, form a new word (*cowboy*). Since many phonics generalizations apply not only to single syllable words, but to syllables within multisyllabic words as well, syllabication and accent are important structural analysis skills.

Special study of certain categories of words (homonyms, homographs, synonyms, antonyms, acronyms, multiple-meaning words, and abbreviations) should also be helpful to the pupil in learning to spell words. Homonyms are words that sound alike, but have different meanings and spellings (*blue-blew*). Homographs are words that are spelled alike, but have different pronunciations and meanings (*bow*—a type of tie; *bow*—to bend at the waist). Synonyms are words that have approximately the same meanings (*beautiful—pretty*). Antonyms are words with nearly opposite meanings (*hot—cold*). Acronyms are words composed of the first letters or syllables of the different words in multiple-word terms (*radar—radio detecting and ranging*). An example of a multiple-meaning word is *run*. *Co.* is an abbreviation for Company.

Individual spelling files or boxes or notebooks (alphabetically organized) may be prepared by the children. These may contain words which have caused the child some difficulty, special vocabulary words from science and social studies, and words which the child wants to learn to spell. Something about word usage, meanings, and formations, may also be included.

Multisensory approaches use several sensory modalities in teaching the language arts. Two of the most well-known approaches of this type are Fernald's VAKT Approach and Gillingham's VAK Approach.

Fernald's VAKT Approach. VAKT stands for Visual, Auditory, Kinesthetic, and Tactile. In this approach the children learn to read and spell by using vision, hearing, muscle movement, and touch.

Fernald's approach is based upon the language experience approach described on page 126 of this volume. The teacher begins by asking the child what words he or she would like to learn. These words are taught individually, and, when the child has an adequate store of words, he composes a story from these words. The teacher types the story for the child to read the next day. Fernald felt that choosing the words and composing the story was important to motivation for learning.

Four developmental phases were utilized by Fernald in teaching words:

1. *Tracing.* When the child requests a word, the teacher writes it in large letters with black crayon on a piece of heavy paper. The child traces the word with his finger and says the word aloud in syllables as he traces. He repeats the tracing process until he can write the word twice without looking at the sample. He says the word as he writes it from memory. Writing from copy is not permitted, nor is erasing to make corrections in an incorrectly written word. These practices hinder learning the word as a unit, according to Fernald. After the lesson, the words are filed alphabetically to provide a bank of the words learned.

   After a word has been successfully written from memory, it is used in a story written by the child. Any words needed for the story which are not already in the child's reading vocabulary are taught by the procedure described above. Therefore, early stories tend to be short. After the story is written, the teacher types it and has the child read the typed version. After the child has reached a point where he consistently achieves success with this phase, he is allowed to drop the tracing phase.

2. *Writing without tracing.* The child learns a new word by following the process described above without the tracing portion. The child looks at the word written by the teacher, says it several times while looking at it, and writes it from memory. Smaller cards with the words typed on one side and written by

the child on the other side may be used during this stage for the word bank. Story writing continues.

3. *Learning from printed words.* The child learns a new word by looking at it in print and saying it to himself. At this stage the word is not written for the child, the teacher merely shows the word to the child and pronounces it. Reading in books is generally begun at this stage.

4. *Generalizing about words.* In this stage, the child recognizes new words by their similarity to words or parts of words already learned.

A detailed description of this method can be found in *Remedial Techniques in Basic School Subjects* by Grace Fernald, (New York: McGraw-Hill, 1943). Research on the Fernald approach has produced mixed results.

Gillingham's VAK Approach. VAK stands for visual, auditory, and kinesthetic. This approach is based upon Samuel Orton's theories about the relationship between cerebral dominance (control of language functions by one of the two hemispheres of the brain) and language arts difficulties. Anna Gillingham and Bessie Stillman have described this approach in their manual *Remedial Teaching for Children with Specific Disability in Reading, Spelling, and Penmanship* (Cambridge, Mass.: Educator's Publishing Service, 1978). Materials which are designed for use with the manual are available from the same publisher. The program cannot be used without careful consultation of the manual. Therefore, this description is only an overview of the approach.

Gillingham and Stillman caution users that the program outlined in the manual must be followed exactly or the procedure may not be successful. They also state that the program is to be used instead of the child's regular language arts instruction. Throughout the duration of the program (a minimum of two years is suggested), the child should not do any reading, writing, or spelling not associated with the program. There is much drill involved in this approach. The learning of letters is followed by blending of the sounds represented by the letters and then combining the blended words (all regularly spelled words) into sentences and stories. An adaptation of the Gillingham method may be found in *A Multi-Sensory Approach to Language Arts for Specific Language Disability Children* by Beth H. Slingerland (Cambridge, Mass.: Educator's Publishing Service, 1974). This method has met with some criticism from a variety of sources for its rigidity and uninteresting materials. However, it has been successful with some remedial students and should be known to language arts specialists.

Games and activities for individuals or small groups can make spelling more interesting to the pupils. One excellent source for spelling games and activities is *Resource Materials for Teachers of Spelling,* 2nd edition, by Paul S. Anderson and Patrick J. Groff (Minneapolis: Burgess Publishing Co., 1968).

Use of selected materials can be very helpful to the teacher who desires to individualize instruction. One representative item, appropriate for spelling, is *Dictionary Skills: A Programmed Learning Series* (a set of 10 color filmstrips and 13 spirit masters), designed so that the individual student may use the materials. The series is available from the International Film Bureau, Inc., 332 South Michigan Ave., Chicago, Illinois, 60605. The lessons (one per filmstrip) concern alphabetical order, letter sections, guide words, syllables, accents, sound symbols, correct spellings, definitions, word forms, and review.

Further ideas about ways to individualize spelling programs in accord with the achievement and ability of children may be gained through close study of spelling textbooks.

Spelling is an essential part of proofreading. Many spelling programs do not give sufficient attention to ways of helping children carry learned skills into functional usage. A sample spelling work sheet that might strengthen proofreading habits and skills is reproduced in Chart 8–5.

THE AFFECTIVE DOMAIN

Questions of the following nature will help the teacher determine children's interest in spelling:
Does the child

enjoy writing?
use a dictionary to look up spellings about which he is unsure?
feel free to request help for spelling of difficult words?
possess a definite and efficient method of learning to spell words?
give eager and prompt attention when the study of new words is begun?
accept spelling errors marked in all written work?
proofread to detect slips and misspellings?
evidence satisfaction with the improvement of spelling?
possess a spirit of pride and cooperation in spelling achievement?

CHART 8-5. A sample spelling worksheet

MORE TRICKY WORDS

1. This is how the teacher marked Lynn's book report.

Lynn
Secret Codes

Want to read and write secret codes? Then read this book! (Its)ˢᵖ codes will boggleᴼᴷ your mind and exciteᴼᴷ your imagination. (Its)ˢᵖ easy to read and (its)ˢᵖ pictures help explain things. (Your)ˢᵖ sure to like it!
9 22 26 23 18 7!
(Read it! — in code)

2. Study the meanings of these homophones.
   your—belonging to you, as in "your desk."
   you're—you are, as in "You're going?"
   its—belonging to it, as in "its leg."
   it's—it is, as in "It's foggy."
3. Correctly complete these sentences using the homophones in #2.
   a. "(It's) gone!" shouted Tony, pointing to (its) empty cage.
   b. If (you're) going out in that storm, (you're) out of (your) mind!

4. Correctly complete these sentences. Study the meanings in #2 when you're unsure of the answer. "I know (its it's) (your you're) coat," said Lou.
   b. If (your you're) late, (its it's) (your you're) own fault.
   c. "(Your You're) sure (its it's) tire is flat?" asked Pat.
   d. "Is (your you're) rabbit in (its it's) cage?" asked Annie.

5. Now help Lynn correctly rewrite his book report spelling the *misspelled* homophones correctly.

Secret Codes
Want to read and write secret codes? Then read this book! (It's) codes will boggle (your) mind and excite (your) imagination. (Its) easy to read and (it's) pictures help explain things. (You're) sure to like it!
---

6. Another set of tricky homophones is:

who's   whose

Use both wrongly in sentences. Ask a friend to find your "errors."

Note. Prepared by Dr. Leo M. Schell, Kansas State University, Manhattan.

Such good attitudes are developed by the teacher who: emphasizes the importance of spelling: uses efficient methods in teaching spelling; insists upon exact work; and provides the opportunity to improve spelling in written work.

ADDITIONAL CORRECTIVE ACTIVITIES

1. Spelling games are very popular with children. (See the source books dealing with spelling for ideas.)
2. Pupils may make themselves a small indexed dictionary by putting words starting with different letters on different pages, indexing them, and arranging them like a dictionary. (Pictures may be used with words.)
3. In addition to a list of words to be learned, a pupil may keep a list of words he can spell—to which he may add from time to time.
4. A typewriter provides motivation and practice.
5. Dictionary activities and games may be useful.
6. Mnemonic devices may be helpful for some children. (There is a *liar* in *familiar*.)
7. Special attention may be given to difficult words such as:

am	and	for
from	my	one
was	we	you
because	children	coming
have	here	know
many	name	our
school	some	building
cousin	friends	guess
haven't	it's	o'clock
Saturday	writing	although
breakfast	countries	everybody
goodby	Halloween	interested
library	minute	sometime
boots	daughter	foreign
forty	freeze	handkerchief
I'd	laid	meeting
pleasant	aisle	buffalo
calendar	carnival	chasing
gymnasium	human	neighbor
separate	sword	

8. Many children have difficulties in spelling common homonyms. The majority of errors made in spelling homonyms occur because the wrong homonym is used. This suggests that while wise use of phonics in spelling can promote spelling power, the correct spell-

ing of homonyms must be associated with the meanings of words and the context in which they are used. Here are some common homonyms introduced in the elementary school years:

no-know	week-weak	hole-whole
one-won	wood-would	sea-see
red-read	our-hour	right-write
too-two	line-lion	its-it's
by-buy	new-knew	your-you're
dear-deer	roll-role	flower-flour
for-four	cent-sent	there-their
here-hear	eight-ate	road-rode

9. Teacher- or student- made crossword puzzles, using the spelling words, or hidden word puzzles are very popular with children.

REVIEW QUESTIONS AND ACTIVITIES

1. Explain how to find the student's approximate grade level in spelling.
2. What are some informal assessment procedures for analyzing difficulties in spelling?
3. What are 12 types of common spelling errors, according to Spache?
4. Prepare a Cloze procedure for checking a student's knowledge of one particular spelling generalization.
5. Administer the Kottmeyer Diagnostic Spelling Test to a child. Write an analysis of the results.
6. Explain a method of checking modality for methods of studying spelling words.
7. Cite some possible causes for low test scores on a spelling test. For each cause, cite at least one remedial treatment.
8. What are five common spelling patterns? Cite example words and exceptions for each.
9. What are some common errors in spelling at the primary level?
10. Why should special attention be provided in the spelling program for (a) structural analysis skills and (b) certain categories of words?
11. Explain the Fernald VAKT approach and the Gillingham VAK approach.

12. How may the extent of a child's interest in spelling be checked informally?
13. Trace the scope and sequence of spelling through the charts provided in the Appendix.
14. Prepare an activity or game for helping a child who needs further experiences in spelling a particular set of words.
15. Develop a card file of ideas, games, and language arts books focusing on strategies and materials for helping a child with spelling difficulties.
16. Review articles dealing with the diagnosis and correction of language arts difficulties in the area of spelling.
17. Review source books, library books, and multilevel materials that deal specifically with spelling.
18. Develop a teaching plan related to one of the "Additional Corrective Activities."
19. Read and report your reactions to several articles dealing with spelling. Try to suggest applications and implications from them for helping children overcome spelling difficulties. Here is one article as a starter: Jerry Zutell, "Some Psycholinguistic Perspectives on Children's Spelling." *Language Arts,* October 1978, *55,* pp. 844–850.
20. Identify (a) the type of error and (b) some remediation ideas for these examples of misspellings:

    a. deda for baby   d. form for from   g. comit for commit
    b. say for stay   e. except for accept h. bushs for bushes
    c. ofen for often   f. days for daze   i. clot for dot

21. Suggest corrective/remedial activities appropriate for spelling-disabled children who have the following characteristics:

    a. general verbal and linguistic retardation
    b. miss words entirely (write "dog" for "radio")
    c. fail to recognize letter-sound relationships
    d. make errors in certain sections of words
    e. use a letter-by-letter method of spelling
    f. use only one (or no) method for word study

REFERENCE

Burrows, A.T., Monson, D., & Stauffer, R.L. *New Horizons in Language Arts.* New York: Harper and Row, 1972, pp. 245–48.

9
Handwriting

A corrective program in handwriting has the characteristics of any good diagnostic and remedial program:

- The importance of handwriting in use situations will be emphasized.
- Only the defects in handwriting evidenced by the child will be attacked and only in as great a "dosage" as can be successfully eliminated.
- Instruction will be managed so as not to classify the pupil in an embarrassing way.
- Improvement should be measured at frequent intervals and the record shown to the child and others involved.
- Materials should be interesting to the pupil and suitably sequenced by difficulty level.
- Teacher attitude will be optimistic and encouraging.
- A variety of exercises and activities will be provided; specific corrective approaches will be used with each child.
- The method used in helping the pupil establish correct handwriting patterns will be subject to experimentation.
- The corrective program will encourage independent, self-instructional procedures.
- Intrinsic, functional practice materials are considered superior to artificial devices unrelated to handwriting uses or purposes.

The handwriting teacher should place prevention above cure. He should check the child's handwriting throughout the day, pay attention to mistakes, and require correction of illegible writing. Emphasis upon handwriting as a means of expression and communication is an additional base for effective handwriting instruction. Careful supervision of the child while he is in the handwriting act is also conducive to prevention of poor handwriting. Good handwriting is developed best through good first teaching.

Diagnosis and remedial instruction are necessary when deficiencies develop in the handwriting practices of a child or a group of children. As in other subject areas, corrective work in handwriting can be applied most effectively on an individual basis, following a careful individual diagnosis.

The presence of desirable psychological conditions is probably as important as any factor in improving handwriting in the classroom. The pupils' attitudes are extremely significant. Better attitude may be developed by helping pupils see that handwriting is important and valuable; by requesting pupils to work on their deficiencies only; by emphasizing individual progress; and by encouraging a spirit of class pride and cooperation in attaining handwriting goals.

One effective plan for beginning appraisal involves explaining handwriting evaluation scales to the pupils, and encouraging pupils to use them in the measurement of their handwriting. Diagnostic charts posted on the bulletin board encourage pupils to identify their own handwriting defects. Further informal analysis by the teacher and pupil may be made of such traits as letter form and size, slant and space, and miscellaneous aspects. Pupils who have attained satisfactory quality and speed may be exempted from handwriting practice for a specific period. This not only encourages the pupils who are able to attain these goals to want to maintain their quality and speed ratings, but equally important, it releases the teacher to devote time to those who are in need of remedial instruction.

ASSESSING READINESS FOR MANUSCRIPT

Such items as the following may provide clues that the child is ready for instruction in manuscript.

The child
1. Exhibits an easy three-finger grasp near the end of the pencil.
2. Maintains a reasonable sitting and writing position.
3. Can copy a model of a triangle with three sharp angles and no openings.

4. Can draw a picture of a person with four body parts: head, body, arms, and legs.
5. Can copy a word, such as his or her own name, from a model card.
6. Proceeds basically from left-to-right sequence in writing.
7. Can copy a common word from the chalkboard.

DETECTING HAND PREFERENCE

One of the first tasks, particularly for the first-grade teacher, is to become aware of pupil hand preference. Ordinarily this is not a difficult job, but for some borderline cases the following ideas listed in Chart 9–1 may be helpful for detecting hand preference.

CHART 9-1. Detecting hand preference

---

1. Place a pencil on a table before the seated child, vertically in front of him, point of pencil midway between right and left hands. Observe the hand with which he or she grasps it.
2. Have the child put a dot in each square of cross-section (1-inch squares may be mimeographed for an entire class) and count the number he can mark in one minute. Is he or she among the best or the poorest in the class? Does he or she shift handedness during this performance?
3. Have the child repeat the performance with his unpreferred hand. Compare speed and quality with the previous record and with the class. Ambidextrous children are often low in the class in the preferred hand test, but high in the unpreferred-hand test. The quality of work of two hands is more similar than those of the majority of children.
4. Note hand used in pretending to throw a ball.
5. Note hand used in pretending to thread a needle.
6. Note hand used in pretending to comb hair.
7. Note hand used in pretending to brush teeth.
8. Note hand used in pretending to eat.
9. Note hand used in pointing to an object across the room.

Note. From *Growing Into Reading* by Marion Monroe. Copyright 1951 by Scott, Foresman and Company. Reprinted by permission.

Hildreth (1950) suggests a more technical approach in proposing that one scheme to determine whether the child is decidedly right- or left-handed or nondominant in handedness is to observe and test the child in a number of different situations and then to compute a handedness index using the formula:

$$\frac{\text{Right minus left}}{\text{Right plus left}} \quad \text{or} \quad \frac{R - L}{R + L}$$

This formula gives the percentage of left or right usage to total observations. The scores will range from –1.00 to 1.00. A score of .00 would mean a condition of ambidexterity or nondominance. High positive scores are obtained by strongly right-handed subjects; low negative scores by strongly left-handed subjects.

Some ideas which have been generally accepted by those engaged in handwriting research and by thoughtful teachers are:

1. If beginning pupils come to school decidedly preferring the left hand, they ought to be helped to become a good left-handed writer. If dominance has been established before the child enters school, there is little justification for attempting to change it.
2. If beginning pupils come to school with unsure handedness, or ambidexterity, they should be encouraged, with their and their parent's full acceptance and willingness, to become a good right-hand writer. It should be remembered that *how* the teacher goes about encouraging handedness may make for positive or negative results.
3. If a child has been in school a few years and has established awkward left-handed habits, changes toward better left-handed habits should be encouraged, again with the full acceptance and willingness of the child and the parent.

MERIT EVALUATION

Standardized Scales

There are a number of general merit scales. The quality of the pupil's handwriting is usually determined by comparing the specimens to be evaluated with samples of established values on grade level scales.

The Evaluation Scales published by Zaner-Bloser, Inc., are the most comprehensive of the general merit scales. Cursive scales for grades 3–9 show specimens classified as excellent, good, average, fair, and poor. Manuscript scales for grades 1 and 2 are also included. Samples of grade 2 and grade 5 scales are provided in Figures 9–1 and 9–2. An explanation of how to use these scales is provided in Chart 9–2.

Using data from merit scales, a scattergram may be prepared which can give some clues to grouping for specific instructional purposes.

For example, the scattergram below for the three fourth-graders indicates that Billy's rate in letters per minute is quite high, but the

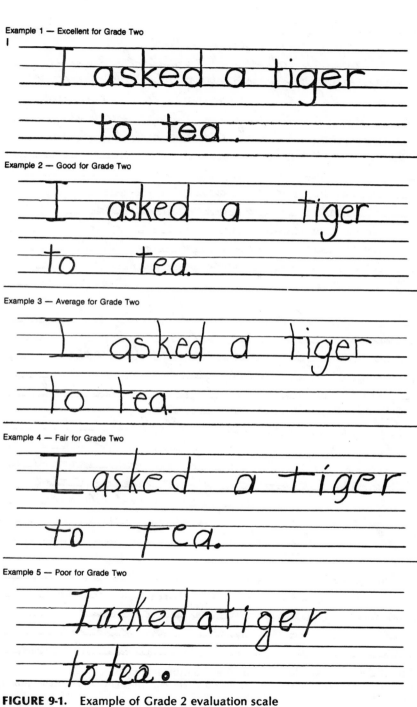

FIGURE 9-1. Example of Grade 2 evaluation scale

Note. From *Creative Growth With Handwriting,* 2nd ed. Copyright © 1979, Zaner-Bloser, Inc., Columbus, Ohio. Used with permission.

Example 1 — Excellent for Grade Five

The jellyfish is jellified --
he could not be brave if he tried:
he shakes, he shivers, and he quakes
from the first moment that he wakes
until he's tucked up tight in bed
with seaweed-sheets around his head.

Example 2 — Good for Grade Five

The jellyfish is jellified --
he could not be brave if he tried:
he shakes, he shivers and he quakes
from the first moment that he wakes
until he's tucked up tight in bed
with seaweed-sheets around his head.

Example 3 — Average for Grade Five

The jellyfish is jellified --
he could not be brave if he tried:
he shakes, he shivers, and he quakes
from the first moment that he wakes
until he's tucked up tight in bed
with seaweed-sheets around his head.

Example 4 — Fair for Grade Five

The jellyfish is jellified -
he could not be brave if he
tried. he shakes, he shivers and he
quakes from the first moment that
he wakes until he's tucked up
tight is bed with seaweed-sheets
around his head.

Example 5 — Poor for Grade Five

The jellyfish is jellified-he could not be
brave if he tried he shakes he shivers
and he quakes from the first moment
that he wakes until he's tucked up tight
in bed with seaweed-sheets around his head.

FIGURE 9-2. Example of Grade 5 evaluation scale
Note. From *Creative Growth With Handwriting*, 2nd ed. Copyright © 1979, Zaner-Bloser,
Inc., Columbus, Ohio. Used with permission.

CHART 9-2.   How to use evaluation scales

I. Writing
 A. The teacher writes the model on a ruled chalkboard.
 B. Students practice writing the model on lined paper.
 C. Using their best handwriting, students then write the model again.

II. Evaluation
Compare the student's writing to the examples on the scale, and if no more than one element needs improvement, the writing is rated *excellent* (Example 1); if no more than two elements need improvement, the writing is rated *good* (Example 2); if no more than three elements need improvement, the writing is rated *average* (Example 3); if no more than four elements need improvement, the writing is rated *fair* (Example 4); and if five elements need improvement, the writing is rated *poor* (Example 5).

Note. Adapted from *Creative Growth With Handwriting,* 2nd ed. Copyright © 1979, Zaner-Bloser, Inc., Columbus, Ohio. Used with permission.

quality is poor. He should be grouped with others who receive instruction in letter formation and other quality features and in reducing speed, until quality is well established. On the other hand, Jane might be in a group where attention is given to increasing rate in letters per minute, without significantly sacrificing quality. Obviously, Joe performs high in both quality and rate and will require only maintenance.

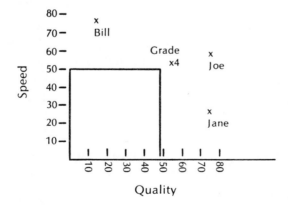

Informal Measures

There are many informal devices which may be used to evaluate aspects of handwriting, such as letter formation, spacing, alignment, slant, and line quality.

Letter Formation. To check letter formation, cut a hole a little larger than a single letter in the center of a small card. Move the card along a line of writing so that the letters are exposed one at a time. Illegible or poorly formed letters stand out clearly and may be noted for further practice.

For manuscript and cursive writing, lines may be drawn along the tops of letters to see if they are of proper and uniform height.

Spacing. In manuscript and cursive, a space of about one letter (small o) between letters—with adjustments according to the series of letters used—is desirable, with a bit more space between words and sentences.

space   space

Alignment. To check alignment, a rule may be used, drawing a line touching the base of as many of the letters as possible.

guess   guess

Slant. Lines of a straight or uniform-slanting nature may be drawn in through the letters. The letters which are off slant are clear to see.

Line Quality. To check line quality, an examination is made of the evenness of the writing pressure.

$$Even \qquad Even$$

These elements, plus a few others, readily lend themselves to a record-keeping chart that reports handwriting progress; Chart 9–3 is an example.

CHART 9-3. Handwriting progress

Pupil Name _____	Oct.	Dec.	Feb.	April
Letter size and form				
Spacing within words				
Spacing between words				
Spacing between sentences				
Alignment				
Slant				
Line quality				
Letter joinings				
Letter endings				
Margins and arrangement				
Neatness				
Position				
Rate of writing				
Key: X-Deficiency noted ✓-Improvement shown O-Satisfactory				

DIAGNOSTIC EVALUATION

There are a few diagnostic scales for handwriting. One of the best is the Zaner-Bloser chart on *Handwriting Faults and How to Correct Them* (This is no longer available from the publisher.) This instrument is recommended for the location of specific faults in handwriting. The chart is helpful since it enables the teacher and the pupil to discover the special handwriting weaknesses that are in need of remedial treatment and gives excellent suggestions for correcting the defects. The chart is large and therefore an excellent visual aid for children. Section 4 of the scale is reproduced in Figure 9–3.

Once children have mastered the basic letter forms and the sequences for producing them, the bulk of instructional time in handwriting should be devoted to helping them to diagnose and remedy their own errors.

DIAGNOSTIC TEACHING STRATEGIES

Diagnostic instruction depends upon analysis of handwriting errors, record-keeping devices, and use of appropriate materials. Two devices that can be used with the pupils for overall analysis of handwriting appear in Charts 9–4 and 9–5.

CHART 9-4. General analysis: manuscript

Write the sentence: The quick brown fox jumps over the lazy dog. Do not try to write more slowly than you do on your daily papers. Then answer these question with Yes or No.

1. Are *a's, o's, d's* and *g's* closed?
2. Do any *o's* look like *a* or *u*?
3. Does *k* look like *h*?
4. Is each letter so plain that it doesn't look like any other letter?
5. Are letters the height of *b* all the same size?
6. Are letters the height of *a* all the same size?
7. Are *d* and *t* the same height?
8. Do *g, f, j, q, p, y,* and *z* come the same distance below the baseline?
9. Do all letters sit on the baseline?
10. Do all letters have a uniform slant?
11. Are letters spaced evenly in words?
12. Do you have room for the letter *o* between words?

SPACING

The spaces between letters and words should be about like this.

This space between words is too wide. Thisistooclose. Thesewordsarehardtoread.

This space between the letters is too — wide. These letters are crowded together too much.

The right spacing is easiest to write and looks best.

Good spacing is necessary to make writing legible. Some writing which is otherwise fairly good may be made very hard to read by too much crowding between letters, lines or between words. Study these copies.

These lines are too close together. The loop letters cross each other or run too close to the letters of the line above and below. Such writing is hard to read.

These lines are far enough apart to be easily read. The words are distinct and the loop letters do not cross each other.

Notice how difficult it is to read crowded lines while the correctly spaced writing is plain and legible.

HOW TO TEST FOR SPACING

correct *spacing* *incorrect* *spacing*

Begin each new word in a sentence directly under the ending stroke of the preceding word.
Place the paper in front of you and mark all letters and words which are unevenly spaced. A good plan to overcome faults in spacing is to increase or decrease the space between all letters and try to keep the space between the letters even.

FIGURE 9-3. Zaner-Bloser handwriting diagnostic scale—Section 4
NOTE. Used with permission of the publisher, Zaner-Bloser, Inc., Columbus, Ohio.

Common Errors and Difficulties

For pupils who do not seem to be ready to write, provide experiences such as construction with tools, drawing on the chalkboard, clay modeling, and paper-cutting. Do much chalkboard work, with lines

CHART 9-5. General analysis: cursive

Write this jingle. Use the questions that follow to check your writing.

> Thirty days hath September,
> April, June, and November;
> All the rest have thirty-one;
> February twenty-eight alone,
> Except in leap year, at which time
> February's days are twenty-nine.

1. Are all the letters correctly made? Are they easy to read?
   a. Are all your a's, o's, and d's fully closed?
   b. Are the i's dotted directly above the letters?
   c. Are your a's written so they do not look like o's or u's?
   d. Is there an open loop in your e's?
   e. Are b's and l's the same height?
   f. Is your n written so it does not look like u?
   g. Are the tips of r's and s's a little taller than letters like u or o?
   h. Are the d's and t's taller than a and shorter than l?
   i. Are the l's, b's, h's, k's, and f's about the same height as the capitals?
   j. Do y and p come the same distance below the baseline?
2. Are your letters the proper size?
3. Did you leave enough spaces between the letters so that your writing is not crowded? Are your words spaced correctly?
4. Do all your letters sit on the baseline?
5. Do your letters have a uniform slant?

---

four inches apart, and begin with words that are meaningful to the child.

The teacher of beginners may be faced with the problem of determining hand preference in an unsure or ambidextrous child. This child should be encouraged to use his right hand for ease in social and work situations.

The most important characteristics of good position for left-handed writers include:

> Place the writing paper clockwise about 30° or more.
> Keep the elbows reasonably close to the body.
> Direct the blunt end of the pencil or pen back over the left shoulder.
> Hold back from the writing point farther than a right-handed writer—at least 1¼ inches (a rubber band or other marker placed around the pencil or pen will serve as a reminder).

Sit at a desk which is adjusted comparatively low so that the writer can look down over the hand and see where the point of the pencil or pen touches the paper.

Lewis and Lewis (1965) analyzed manuscript writing and reported these findings:

- The five most difficult letters (incorrect size) were the descenders; *q, g, p, y,* and *j.*
- The next ten most difficult letters were: *R, d, Y, u, M, S, b, e, r,* and *Z.*
- Letters of the manuscript alphabet rated 21–30 in terms of difficulty were: *n, s, Q, B, t, z, K, W, A,* and *N.*
- Letters of the manuscript alphabet rated 31–47 in order of difficulty were: *C, f, J, w, h, T, x, c, V, F, P, E, x, I, v, i,* and *D.*
- The letters *n, d, q,* and *y* were more susceptible to reversal errors than were most letters.
- The letter *m* was the most difficult of the nondescending letters.
- Incorrect relationship of letter parts was greater in letters *k, R, M,* and *m* than in any other letter.
- The most frequent error in the letter *U* was incorrect relationship of parts (partial omission).
- Errors in the letter *a* were largely due to incorrect size and relationship of the large arc to the vertical line.
- The inversion error occurred in *G.*
- The easiest letters were *l, o, L, O,* and *H.*
- Boys were more prone to error than were girls.

In manuscript, the most common reversal problems involve *d* and *b,* the lower case *s,* and the capital *N.* Most reversals can be avoided by careful initial teaching (and supervised preschool writing attempts.) Instruction calls for emphasizing the correct beginning point, correct direction of motion, and correct sequence of multipart letters. Chalkboard practice is highly recommended for the elimination of reversal errors. In addition, the elimination of confusion with letters such as *d* and *b* is easily accomplished by separating by a week or more the teaching of these two letters. Other teaching suggestions include:

- Associate a strong *b* and *d* sound with words as the letter is taught—as *b* in *boy* and *d* in *dog.*
- Build a close association between *a* and *d.*

- Make the letter *b,* saying "b right."
- Associate lower case *b* with capital *B,* which is seldom reversed.
- Associate lower case *h* (seldom reversed) with *b.*
- Use the kinesthetic approach—tracing of letters.
- Associate capital and lower case *c* and *s.*
- Accompany the *N* with "sharp top always to the left."

Other miscellaneous problems and correction procedures found in manuscript writing are

Writing too large or too small—point out purpose of each line on writing paper
Nonuniform size—check arm-desk and pencil-hand position
Poor spacing—emphasize use of finger or pencil width
Poor alignment—note purpose of base line on writing paper
Too heavy or too light—review hand-pencil position

In cursive writing, Newland (1932) found five types of errors were responsible for most illegible writings:

failure to close letters (*a, b, f, g, j, k, o, p, q, s, y, z*)
closing looped strokes (*l* like *t,* e like *i*)
looping nonlooped strokes (*i* and *e*)
straight up strokes rather than rounded strokes (*n* like *u, c* like *i, h* like *b*)
end stroke difficulty

Four letters—*a, e, r,* and *t*—contribute about 45% of errors. Teachers should give special attention to the proper formation of these letters.
Other common errors noted by teachers include:

making *a* like *u* or *o* or *ci*	*o* like *a* or *r* or *u*
making *b* like *li* or *l* or *k* or *f*	*r* like *i* or *n*
making *d* like *cl* or *i* or *a*	*t* crossed above
i not dotted	*t* like *l*
m like *w*	*w* like *m* or *ur*

Often it is not formation of the individual letter, but its formation with another that causes difficulty. Some difficult combinations are:

be	*ea*	*ng*	*va*
bi	*ei*	*oa*	*ve*

bo	*es*	*oc*	*vi*
br	*fr*	*oi*	*wa*
by	*gr*	*os*	*we*

Some problem numerals, according to Enstrom and Enstrom (1966), are:

0 like 6	7 like 4 or 1 or 9
2 like v	9 like 4 or 1
5 like 3	6 like 0

Some of the most common faulty formations of numerals, according to Newland, are:

making the numeral 1 in such a way that it possesses an ornate short stroke at the top
writing the numeral 2 with an initial short downward stroke
leaving off the horizontal dash on the numeral 5
forgetting to close the loop on the numeral 9, thus confusing it with numeral 4 or making the loop on the 9 so far as to confuse it with 0.

Poor motor coordination may affect a child's ability to write. When this is true, large handwriting should be encouraged; and in severe cases, it may be well for the child to use manuscript only.

Because of the distinctness of the separate letter forms, manuscript style may be advantageous for pupils with defective vision. These pupils should be allowed to use the chalkboard often. For the brain-injured child, cursive writing is generally recommended as the single style by authorities.

One of the most overlooked possible causes of poor handwriting is a lack of interest. The learner needs to realize the value of being able to write rapidly and well and to feel confident in his ability to do so. Interest should be sustained through commending the slightest improvement and by applying handwriting skill to meaningful situations.

Interest may be promoted through such activities as

study of the historical development of handwriting.
opportunities for neat heandwriting in assignments in all content subjects.
use of various media—opaque projector and overhead projector in particular—in handwriting lessons.

charts of "reminders."
bulletin board displays of material related to handwriting.
study of various handwriting tools and various styles of writing.
providing genuine purposes for writing, as letters to parents and
    guests; rewriting papers which will be displayed or put in
    booklets.

Record-Keeping Devices

A study of the common errors and difficulties provides clues for the
development of a chart (see Chart 9–6) which can be used periodically
to check the handwriting of children. From such an analysis, instructional groups may be formed and appropriate lessons can be provided.

Special Materials

Some teachers have found specially prepared work sheets effective
for pupils who have acquired poor handwriting habits. Three such
sheets (see Charts 9–7, 9–8, and 9–9) are reproduced below as illustrations. Similar sheets could be prepared for (a) specific numerals;
(b) manuscript letters, (c) cursive letters; (d) difficulties noted in
letter combination, spacing of letters and words, slant, and alignment; (e) general evaluation of manuscript; and (f) general
evaluation of cursive writing.

In the use of corrective materials, the teacher must give frequent
attention to pupils, getting them started, discussing the materials,
and encouraging them as much as possible by showing an interest in
what they are doing. Some teachers have successfully used the more
able pupils to assist those engaged in corrective work. The pupils are
encouraged to use as many of the special work sheets as they wish or
to redo work sheets several times. Workbooks contain parts that, if
not specifically designed for corrective work, may serve quite well for
some deficiencies.

A few other types of materials suitable for corrective purposes
include the following:

Handwriting with Write and See (Lyon and Carnahan, 407 E. 25th
    Street, Chicago, Illinois 60616). One special feature of this mate-
    rial is that it is programmed. It also uses the learning principle
    of reinforcement and emphasizes the perceptual, as well as the
    motor, aspects of handwriting.
Penskills (An Individualized Handwriting Skills Program). Permits
    pupils to proceed at their own pace and to focus upon their own
    problems.
Alphabet 68 (Numark Educational Systems—Numark Publica-
    tions, 104–20 Queens Boulevard, Forest Hill, New York 11375).

CHART 9-6. Analysis of handwriting difficulties

	Pupils' Names			
Cursive				
Closed letters are closed				
Looped strokes are open				
Nonlooped letters are closed				
Strokes are rounded				
a correctly formed				
e correctly formed				
r correctly formed				
t correctly formed				
n, o, s, t, and v correctly formed				
Combinations are well formed (be, ea, va, wa)				
0 correctly formed				
2 correctly formed				
5 correctly formed				
7 correctly formed				
9 correctly formed				
Manuscript				
q correctly formed				
g correctly formed				
p correctly formed				
y correctly formed				
j correctly formed				
m correctly formed				
b, d, n, s, and y not reversed				

CHART 9-7. Sample work sheet for numerals (Grades 3-6)

---

1. Knowing the correct way to make numerals is important. Look at the numerals below. The arrows show the correct place to begin. Write each numeral.

1 2 3 4 5 6 7 8 9 10

---

2. Here are some telephone numbers. Write them and compare with the models.

V13-4578   456-6283

---

3. Here are some number sentences. Write them and compare with the models.

147 - 38 = 109   576 + 438 = 1014

45 × 36 = 1620

---

4. Write all the even numbers between 0 and 10.

5. Write all the odd numbers between 0 and 10.

6. Write as many three-digit numerals as you can by using only 5, 7, 4.

7. Write the numeral 89. Then by subtracting 3 each time, write the numerals to 62.

8. Think the way you make a "five," then try explaining. (Remember you may not write the numeral or draw in the air.) Try this with another numeral.

9. Use numerals to write the following:
Seven hundred thirty-eight _____
Two tens and nine ones_____

Check points
   a. What numerals do you write best?
   b. Which three numerals do you think you·could improve most?
   c. Why is good numeral writing so important?

This supplementary 68-page booklet is designed as an ungraded approach for use in grade 3 and above, beginning with simplified letters in a stroke-by-stroke sequence.

Improve Your Handwriting for Job Success (Peterson Handwriting System, The MacMillan Company, 866 Third Avenue, New York,

CHART 9-8. Sample work sheet for manuscript "e" (primary grades)

1. Write this word and see how well you make the *e*.

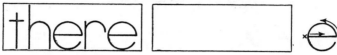

2. Look at how *e* is made.
   a. What part of *e* do you make first?
   b. Where do you begin making the part?
   c. Where does the last stroke of the circle end?
3. Try making *e*'s in these frames. Then work on making *e*'s without using the frames.

4. Look at the word *eat*.
   a. Is *e* as wide as *a*?
   b. Are *e* and *a* the same height?
   c. Write the word *eat*.

5. Try to make good *e*'s as you write these words.

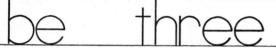

6. Write this sentence and look at the *e*'s. Did you make them correctly?

   Trees are easy to see.

7. Are your *e*'s easier to read now?
   a. Are all your *e*'s round like circles?
   b. Do you remember to make the line in the middle of the letter?
   c. Find some *e*'s you've made on another paper. Are the ones on this page easier to read?

New York 10022). This 64-page booklet is addressed to upper grade children.

Trac-a-bit (Zaner-Bloser, 612 North Park Street, Columbus, Ohio 43215). Charts are plastic coated so they are reusable. Valuable for tracing practice.

Handwriting for Beginners: Manuscript and *Improve Your Handwriting* (Coronet Films, 65 East South Water Street, Chicago, Illinois 60601). These films may prove useful for motivational purposes.

CHART 9-9. Sample work sheet for cursive "a" (Grades 4-6)

1. Write this and see how well you made the a.

road   *a a*

   a. Where does a begin?
   b. Is a closed or open?
   c. Is the up stroke retraced or looped?
   d. Does the concluding stroke set on the base line?
2. Make a row of a's. Make each one look like the one at the first of the row.

a / / / / / / /

3. Look at the letters at the right.
   a. Are a and d the same width?
   b. What is the only difference between the a and d? *a d o*
   c. Write a, d, and o in the space.
4. Write these words. Make good a's.

gray   draw   gave

5. Write this sentence. Make your a's correctly.

I had to read it again.

6. Are you making better a's?
   a. Are you closing all your a's?
   b. Are you retracing, not looping, the upstroke?
   c. Does the connecting stroke sit o the base line?
   d. Do any of your a's look like o's, u's, or i's? they *should not.*

Teachers should keep alert to the increasing number of instructional materials which can be used for diagnostic and corrective purposes.

ADDITIONAL CORRECTIVE ACTIVITIES

1. It is not so much the amount of practice as the correct kind of practice that truly counts in handwriting. Therefore, grouping by need

is appropriate. For some it may be letter formation, others spacing and slant, and still others alignment. At other times such groups might be made on the basis of needs relative to line quality, rate, and other similar aspects.

2. Many children whose cursive is illegible have found it possible to use manuscript successfully. Some left-handed children who write in a "hooked" position have been able to change this position by using manuscript.

3. The child may be unsuccessful with handwriting if he is beset with problems such as too much pressure from home or school, poor teacher-pupil rapport, sibling rivalry, poor relationship with peers, and the like. Provide the best possible environment.

4. Teachers may contribute to handwriting readiness of the pupil with poor small motor coordination by allowing the child to do construction work, drawing and painting, clay modeling, coloring, and other such activities that help in developing eye-hand coordination. Such children may need to trace—in the tactile sense— letters and numerals. Considerable work should be done at the chalkboard.

For children with poor visual-motor coordination (easily detected by teachers as they view children working puzzles, cutting and pasting paper, etc.), there are many letter-formation activities that should be helpful.

a. Letters may be painted on large pieces of drawing paper. Step-by-step verbal instructions should be given the child on the formation of the letter.

b. Component parts of letters may be traced on construction paper. The parts are long, thin rectangles, hollow circles, and parts of hollow circles. Children cut and paste the parts in order to form letters.

c. Letters may be made of rubber, plastic, or cardboard for the child to explore, getting a clearer idea of the form of the letter.

d. A clay pan (or sand pan) can be used, with the child writing in clay with a pencil.

e. Model letters may be made on tag board. Laminate the tagboard so the children can use grease pencils to trace the letters and be erased. Encourage the children to give oral instructions on how they are forming the letter as they practice.

f. Incomplete letters or "dot" letters may be provided for the child to trace.

For practice in correctly holding their pencil, the use of a code system of circles and tape can be used. Colored circles can be put on the fingers that the child should use. Strips of plastic tape that match the colors of the circles can be put on the pencil. The child places the matching finger on the strip of tape with the same color.

The use of a paper with larger-than-normal spaces can be used, with the eventual goal of using standard-sized spaces.

Since writing is a tiresome task for the child with poor visual-motor coordination, the teacher should utilize only short practice periods and offer periods of rest or hand exercise to relieve the tension.

Helping children move to independence in self-evaluation by identifying a sample of handwriting similar to their own involves matching skills, and thus it is also excellent perceptual training.

5. Certain learning disabilities affect writing. Two of these are: a disorder in visual-motor integration known as *dysgraphia* (the person can speak and read but cannot copy or write letters, words, and a deficit in *revisualization* (the person can read but cannot visualize letters or words and cannot write spontaneously nor from dictation). The most useful material for remediation of these disabilities can be found in books and articles dealing with brain-damaged and slow learning children. Some advocate the use of cursive writing for remedial training; others advocate starting with manuscript writing; and still others advocate some form of italic writing, ITA alphabet, or the Distar alphabet. The trend seems to be favoring a modified form of manuscript somewhat close to italic writing. The teacher will have to decide which type of system is most appropriate for the individual child under consideration. (See the article by Irene W. Hanson, "Teaching Remedial Handwriting" *Language Arts* 53 (April 1976), 428–431; 469.)

A reading scheme used in England, called *Breakthrough to Literacy* (published in the United States by Bowmar Publishing Co., Glendale, California 91201) appears to have promise here. It is a version of the language experience approach. Words are printed on cards and the child forms his sentence in a plastic stand with these cards. Next, he copies the sentence directly from this stand into his booklet. The stand can be placed immediately above the line upon which the child is writing. The printing on the cards is very similar to the size the child will use. Since the sentence is the child's own creation, the motivation for writing is high.

6. Pupils can develop their own handwriting scales. Five or more of his own papers, saved over a period of three or four months, furnish the basis of the scale. He will take random cuttings of a few lines from each paper, arrange them in order of the quality of handwriting, and paste them with the best at the top. He should

date each sample to indicate whether his improvement has been erratic or steady. If the child files this scale of his writing in the fall and follows a similar procedure in the spring, he has a good indication of his progress in handwriting during the year.

7. *The Barbe-Lucas Handwriting Skill-guide Check Lists*, 1978, from Zaner-Bloser, Columbus, Ohio, are excellent instruments for pre-testing and posttesting children on the specifics of handwriting. Lists are available for: Readiness, Manuscript—Level One; Manuscript—Level Two; Transition; Cursive Primary Proportion—Level Three; Cursive Primary Proportion—Level Four; and Cursive Adult Proportion. The readiness check list is reproduced on pages 234–35.

REVIEW QUESTIONS AND ACTIVITIES

1. Describe how hand preference may be detected.
2. Describe how a merit handwriting scale may be administered and utilized.
3. What are five features of handwriting that may be checked, using informal devices?
4. What is a diagnostic handwriting evaluation scale?
5. What are some common errors and difficulties in manuscript writing? Illustrate each.
6. What are some common errors and difficulties in cursive handwriting? Illustrate each.
7. Explain features of specially prepared work sheets for children who have acquired poor handwriting habits.
8. What are some commercial materials suitable for corrective handwriting purposes?
9. Trace the scope and sequence of handwriting through the charts provided in the Appendix.
10. Prepare an activity or game for helping a child who needs further experiences in handwriting.
11. Develop a card file of ideas, games, and language concept books focusing upon strategies and materials for helping a child with handwriting difficulties.

Name _____

Age _____ Grade Placement _____ Name of Teacher _____ School _____

	PRE-TEST	POST-TEST

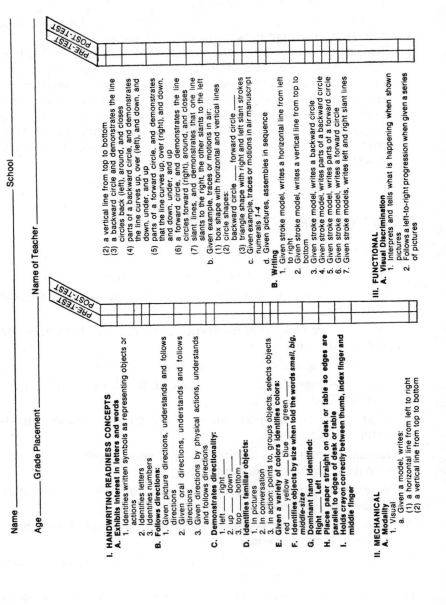

I. HANDWRITING READINESS CONCEPTS

A. Exhibits interest in letters and words
1. Identifies written symbols as representing objects or actions
2. Identifies letters
3. Identifies numbers

B. Follows directions:
1. Given picture directions, understands and follows directions
2. Given oral directions, understands and follows directions
3. Given directions by physical actions, understands and follows directions

C. Demonstrates directionality:
1. left ____ right ____
2. up ____ down ____
3. top ____ bottom ____

D. Identifies familiar objects:
1. In pictures
2. In conversation
3. In action: points to, groups objects, selects objects

E. Given a variety of colors identifies colors:
red ____ yellow ____ blue ____ green ____

F. Identifies objects by size when told the words *small*, *big*, *middle-size*

G. Dominant hand identified:
Right ____ Left ____

H. Places paper straight on desk or table so edges are parallel to edges of desk or table

I. Holds crayon correctly between thumb, index finger and middle finger

II. MECHANICAL

A. Modality
1. Visual
  a. Given a model, writes:
     (1) a horizontal line from left to right
     (2) a vertical line from top to bottom
     (3) a backward circle and demonstrates the line circles back (left), around, and closes
     (4) parts of a backward circle, and demonstrates the line curves up, over (left), and down, and down, under, and up
     (5) parts of a forward circle, and demonstrates that the line curves up, over (right), and down, and down, under, and up
     (6) a forward circle, and demonstrates the line circles forward (right), around, and closes
     (7) slant lines, and demonstrates that one line slants to the right, the other slants to the left
  b. Given example, traces or motions in air:
     (1) box shape with horizontal and vertical lines
     (2) circle shapes:
         backward circle ____ forward circle ____
     (3) triangle shape with right and left slant strokes
  c. Given example, traces or motions in air manuscript numerals *1-4*
  d. Given pictures, assembles in sequence

B. Writing
1. Given stroke model, writes a horizontal line from left to right
2. Given stroke model, writes a vertical line from top to bottom
3. Given stroke model, writes a backward circle
4. Given stroke model, writes parts of a backward circle
5. Given stroke model, writes parts of a forward circle
6. Given stroke model, writes a forward circle
7. Given stroke models, writes left and right slant lines

III. FUNCTIONAL

A. Visual Discrimination
1. Interprets and tells what is happening when shown pictures
2. Follows a left-to-right progression when given a series of pictures

(3) a backward circle and demonstrates that the line circles back (left), around, and closes
(4) parts of a backward circle and demonstrates that the line curves up, over (left), and down, and down, under, and up
(5) parts of a forward circle, and demonstrates that the line curves up, over (right), and down, and down, under, and up
(6) a forward circle, and demonstrates that the line circles forward (right), around, and closes
(7) slant lines, and demonstrates that one line slants to the right, the other slants to the left

b. Given models, draws:
(1) box shape with horizontal lines and vertical lines
(2) circle shapes: backward circles _____ forward circles _____
(3) triangle shapes with right and left slant strokes

c. Given models, writes numerals 1-4
d. Given pictures, recalls sequence

2. Auditory
a. Given oral directions, writes:
(1) a horizontal line from left to right
(2) a vertical line from top to bottom
(3) a backward circle, and demonstrates that the line circles back (left), around, and closes
(4) parts of a backward circle, and demonstrates that the line curves up, over (left), and down, and down, under, and up
(5) parts of a forward circle, and demonstrates that the line curves up, over (right), and down, and down, under, and up
(6) a forward circle, and demonstrates that the line circles forward (right), around, and closes
(7) slant lines, and demonstrates that one line slants to the right, and other to the left

b. Given oral directions, draws:
(1) box shape with horizontal and vertical lines
(2) circle shapes: backward circle _____ forward circle _____
(3) triangle shapes with right and left slant strokes

c. Given oral directions, writes numerals 1-4
d. Given pictures, tells story in sequence

3. Kinesthetic
a. Given example, traces, motions in air or makes body movements:
(1) a horizontal line from left to right

3. Identifies horizontal and vertical lines in common objects
4. Draws picture of himself or herself upon request

B. Oral-Auditory Recognition
1. Uses speaking vocabulary adequate to convey ideas
2. Names common objects
3. Associates pictures to words
4. Recalls and tells a story in sequence after hearing the story read

C. Visual-Motor Skill
1. Writes own first name between headline and baseline when given name model
2. Holds a pair of scissors correctly and cuts paper along a given line

D. Letter Recognition
1. Identifies own name in manuscript
2. Matches upper-case letters to upper-case letter models
3. Matches lower-case letters to lower-case letter models
4. Observes likenesses and differences:
   a. in objects
   b. in letters
   c. in words
   d. in numerals
5. Matches words written in manuscript when given like set of words
6. Matches symbol of number with illustrated number of objects
7. Circles number corresponding to his or her age, given direction and a row of numbers

IV. CREATIVE
A. Creative Thinking
1. Identifies objects which turn forward and backward
2. Appreciates humor visually
3. Appreciates humor auditorially

B. Creative Writing
1. Draws self with identifying characteristic
2. Creates objects with:
   a. straight lines
   b. circles
   c. curves
   d. slant lines
3. Codes by color
4. Colors objects appropriately
5. Writes number of pictured objects

FIGURE 9-4.

SOURCE: *Barbe-Lucas Handwriting Skill Guide Check List: Readiness* (Columbus, Ohio: Zaner-Bloser, Inc., 1978). Reprinted with permission.

235

12. Review articles dealing with the diagnosis and correction of language arts difficulties in the area of handwriting.

13. Review source books, trade books, and multilevel materials that specifically deal with handwriting.

14. Develop a teaching plan related to one of the suggested Additional Corrective Activities.

15. Develop a handwriting attitude scale for (a) teachers and (b) students based on Chart 3–6 in Chapter 3. Administer it to several preservice and inservice teachers and several students. Report your results.

16. Prepare corrective worksheets for these specific handwriting features:

    a. numeral 5
    b. spacing
    c. slant
    d. alignment
    e. manuscript "g"
    f. cursive "r"

17. Suggest additional corrective ideas for improving handwriting.

REFERENCES

Enstrom, E.A. & Enstrom, D. Numerals still count, *Arithmetic Teacher*, February 1966, *13*, pp. 131–134.

Hildreth, G. *Readiness for school beginners*. New York: World Book Co., 1950, pp. 62–63.

Lewis, E.R., & Lewis H.P. An analysis of errors in the formation of manuscript letters by first grade children, *American Educational Research Journal*, 1965, *2*, 25–35.

Newland, T.E. An analytical study of the development of illegibilities in handwriting from lower grades to adulthood, *Journal of Educational Research*, December 1932, *26*, pp. 246–258.

Newland, T.E. *Newland's chart for diagnosis of illegibilities in written arabic numerals*. Bloomington, Illinois: Public School Publishing Co.

10

Case Report Procedures

Careful records must be kept of all observations, interviews, information gleaned from written records, and test results. An individual folder should be kept for each child. The basic data and referral data for a child can be placed on the front of his or her folder. A separate section can be designed inside the folder for test results, health, home background, social, emotional, and personality data, and educational data. A copy of the case report should go into the folder when it is completed, as should reports on corrective and remedial sessions that follow and results of further testing of various types.

Data collection, writing a case report, and an illustrative case report are included in this chapter. The chapter concludes with a discussion of IEP's and the legal responsibility of the language arts teacher.

DATA COLLECTION

Information for a case report may be obtained in several ways: observing the student in different situations, interviewing appropriate people, studying available records, and administering formal and informal tests.

Observation

Observing a child who is having language arts difficulties can yield valuable information. Observation of the child's mental alertness and problem-solving ability, the type of questions asked, and the quality of answers given to questions posed by the teacher provide a basis for a subjective estimate of the child's intellectual ability. This estimate may be useful for supplementing and comparing with standardized intelligence measures.

Observation in the classroom can help the teacher detect attitudes toward language arts. Does the child choose language arts activities during free time? Does the child avoid situations in which language arts are necessary? Does the child complain about language arts assignments?

Observation can also reveal physical problems which may be related to the language arts difficulties.

Home visits permit observation of the child in interaction with some significant people. The amount of linguistic stimulation provided in the home can sometimes be noted, as well as the reaction of other members of the household to the child's problems.

Observation in the classroom and playground settings may reveal language arts strengths and can give insight into the reactions of the child's peers to his or her language arts difficulties.

Perhaps the most useful type of observation is that of the child during language arts instructional periods. The area of language arts is complex; therefore, the diagnosis must proceed from the general to the specific.

The general components of the language arts, as identified in this text, are (a) listening, (b) oral communication, and (c) written composition—with the attendant necessity of spelling and handwriting.

Second, within the general components there are various categories of topics. For example,

Listening
Purposes of listening
Levels of listening
   literal, interpretative
   appreciative
   critical, creative

Oral Communication
Speaking situations
   conversation
   discussion
   description, comparison,
     evaluation
   oral reporting
   storytelling
   drama
   others

Written Communication
Formulating written expression
   topic selection and scope
   ideas
   organization
   details and descriptive
   word choice

   revision and proofreading

Functional Writing
   letter writing
   report writing
   others

Conventions
   capitalization
   punctuation
   sentence sense
   paragraph sense

Usage
  vocabulary
  speech
  dialect

Spelling
Phoneme-grapheme correspondence
Spelling patterns
Structural analysis skills
Special category of words
Rules
Study procedures
Level of spelling
Proofreading
Dictionary habits
Rate

Creative writing
  prose
  poetry

Handwriting
Handedness
Manuscript
Cursive
Quality
  letter form
  spacing
  alignment
  slant
  evenness of pressure

Third, the specifics within the various categories must be identi-fied. One example of a specific for each of the cited categories:

listening—critical and creative listening—recognizing propaganda techniques
oral communication—dialect—phonology (/*d*/ for /*th*/)
written communication—functional (letter writing)—the five parts of a business letter
spelling—rules—making of plural by *s* and *es*
handwriting—quality (letter form)—cursive undercurve begin-nings, as *i, u, w, e, r,* and *s.*

In a functional situation, the student uses language in most of its interrelated aspects. Therefore, a teacher can diagnose more than one aspect of the language arts at one time.

Check lists such as the ones in the preceding chapters are good to use for recording observations systematically. Teachers may develop check lists to meet their own specifications.

Interviews

Interview information may be obtained from the child, classroom teachers, former teachers, parents, and physicians or other special personnel. Interviews may be particularly helpful for obtaining infor-mation on home background, social and emotional adjustment, per-sonality, and health data. The interviewer must treat all information as confidential and use it only to clarify the language arts difficulty of the child.

Interviewers may find it helpful to prepare a list of questions to be answered in each interview. This procedure may assist in keeping the interview focused upon the pertinent data. An interview need not, however, be simply a question-and-answer session limited to the pre-constructed list; the interviewee should be encouraged to elaborate at any time or to supply information not asked for that he or she feels is pertinent.

Interviews with the child who is having difficulties are helpful in developing rapport before beginning any formal testing in gathering information about attitudes and interests. Some home background and information on social and emotional adjustments and personality are also obtainable during these interviews. Also, the teacher can gain information about how the child views the problem and the planned testing and instructional program.

Interviews with current and former teachers may yield information about skills mastery and needs, approaches or materials which succeeded or failed with the child, social and emotional adjustment, personality, and attitudes and interests.

Interviewing of parents should be performed with friendliness and tact and in compliance with the state and federal laws. The teacher should try to find out how the parents perceive the language arts difficulty, when they think the problem started and why, and how they and others have tried to approach the problem. Parents should be informed about the plans for any testing and follow-up corrective/remedial instruction and allowed to ask questions about these procedures. By projecting to parents the message that the interviewer cares about the child, much valuable information will likely be obtained and a foundation for parental support will be established.

Written Records

Some of the information needed for the case report can be obtained from studying written records. The school's cumulative record for a child can be a valuable source of information.

Referral forms for a corrective or remedial language arts program may yield basic data which will not need to be touched upon in an interview. These forms may also raise questions which can be further explored through an interview.

Test Results

Test results are needed for a complete case report analysis. Vision and hearing should be tested if they have not been tested recently; if there are suspicions of health problems, a physical examination may be required.

Many schools have facilities for screening vision and hearing abilities. A telebinocular is generally used for vision screening, although some schools use the Snellen Chart and the AMA Rating Card. The telebinocular test is preferable because it is more thorough. The Snellen Chart alone should not be the screening procedure, for it detects only nearsightedness, not farsightedness which is more frequently a problem. An audiometer is generally used to screen hearing. These devices are screening devices, and any indication of a problem should be referred for an extensive visual or hearing diagnosis by an appropriate professional.

A measure of intelligence can be obtained to help the teacher decide whether the child is a developmental, corrective, or remedial student. The results of group intelligence tests are suspect because they depend upon language ability. Individual intelligence tests are more accurate. Two individual intelligence tests that may be administered by classroom teachers are the *Peabody Picture Vocabulary Test* and the *Slosson Intelligence Test*. The intelligence quotient can be utilized in a formula designed to produce a expectancy grade level which can be compared to the actual performance level to determine if the child's language arts achievement is lagging behind his or her capabilities.

Standardized survey language arts tests suggest the approximate current language arts performance level for a child. These results are valuable, but should be used cautiously and compared to informal test results.

Standardized diagnostic language arts results are needed in order to help pinpoint specific skill strengths and weaknesses of the child. These tests require some expertise for administration. An example of such tests is the *Gates-Russell Diagnostic Spelling Test* (New York: Teacher's College, Columbia Univ., 1937)

Informal tests supply much useful information. The child's dictation of a story from a picture or a written story may be analyzed as explained in an earlier chapter. An informal spelling inventory will provide independent, instructional, and frustration level scores. Teacher-made tests of specific skills are also valuable, as explained in the preceding chapters.

WRITING A CASE REPORT

After data have been collected, the formal case study report may be written. The case report serves as a guide from which the corrective or remedial teacher works. It must be written in such a way that basic data, interpretation of data, and recommendations are easily located and understood. (Care must also be taken to insure compliance with state and federal laws regarding family privacy and inspection of records.)

The case report should include the following topics:

- Basic data—name of child; date of birth; names of parents or guardian; address and phone number; name of school; grade; name of teacher.
- Referral data—who referred the child; reasons for referral.
- Amount of discrepancy between the child's language arts expectancy level and his or her actual language arts performance level.
- Test results—intelligence tests, general achievement tests, diagnostic language arts tests, and other test results which may be available.
- Health data—vision and hearing; speech; and general history, including present status.
- Home background—people living in the home (ages, education, and occupations); child's relationships with these people; socioeconomic level of family; language or languages spoken in the home; amount of reading materials in the home; help received with studies at home and by whom.
- Social, emotional, and personality data—friends (number, ages, sex), activities engaged in with friends, community activities (church, clubs); special interests; employment (reasons for, reactions to); attitudes toward family members, school, teachers, certain subjects, especially the language arts; emotional adjustment; personality characteristics.
- Educational Data—age of starting school; schools attended (grade levels); grades repeated or skipped; grade history in language arts and other school subjects; attendance record; conduct in school, methods of teaching language arts used by the child's teacher or teachers; types of language arts materials used with the child; any previous corrective or remedial instruction offered to child; comparison of language arts progress and achievement to progress and achievement with other subject areas.
- Interpretation of data—consideration of information from all sources in conjunction with each other.
- Recommendations for a corrective or remedial program—specific suggestions in relation to the following areas:
  any need for referral to a specialist (vision, hearing)
  skills which need attention
  level of material that should be used
  possible materials or resources for meeting the child's needs
  Chart 10–1 is a rather fully developed illustrative case study.

CHART 10-1. Illustrative case report

Basic Data
Name of child: John Lee Breen   Date of Birth: March 1, 1969
Name of parents: J. C. Breen (father, deceased)
                 Dixie L. Breen (mother)
Address of Parents: 505 Ocean Street, Central City, TN
Phone Number: 602-3320
Child's School: Central City Elementary
Teacher's Name: Ruth Dixon
Child's Grade Placement: 3rd

Referral Data
Referred by Dixie L. Breen, John's mother
Reason for referral: John spent two years in the first grade, one year in second grade. His teacher thinks that he will have to be retained in the third grade at the end of the year. School reports indicate little progress in the basic language arts skills since the end of the second grade.

Amount of Discrepancy Between Language Arts Expectancy Level and Actual Language Arts Achievement Level

	Grade Equivalent
Language Arts Expectancy Level	4.0
Actual Language Arts Achievement Level	2.7
(Standardized test) Discrepancy	1.3

Summary of Test Results
A. Intelligence Test Scores
    1. *Stanford-Binet Intelligence Scale,* Form L-M (Administered March 15, 1978)
       CA   9 years 0 months
       MA   9 years 0 months
       IQ   100
B. General Achievement Tests   Grade Equivalent
   Stanford Achievement Test
   (Administered April 3, 1978)
   Language Arts
    1. Language (includes letter-writing, capitalization,
       punctuation, usage, and   2.7
       sentence sense)
    2. Spelling   2.8
    Reading
    1. Vocabulary   3.3
    2. Reading Comprehension   3.4
    3. Word Study Skills   3.3

Chart 10-1 (cont)

C. Diagnostic Spelling Test
    1. *Gates-Russell Diagnostic Spelling Test*
        (Administered April 4, 1978)
        a. Spelling words orally   2.4
        b. Word pronunciation   2.6
        c. Giving letters for sound   2.6
        d. Spelling one syllable   2.3
        e. Spelling two syllables   2.8
        f. Word reversals   3.4
        g. Word Attack   Few techniques
                                            (mostly looking at
                                                  words)
        h. Auditory Discrimination   15 out of 15
        i. Study method   Visual
D. Other Test Results
    1. *Oral Dictation of Story* (from Picture)
        a. Number of words—120
        b. Number of Sentences—15
        c. Number of Short Sentences—4
        d. Number of Long Sentences—11
        e. Number of Descriptive Terms—10
    2. *Written Story*
        a. T-unit measures
            Lengths
            5 sentences total
            8 T-units total
            49 words
            6.1 average words per T-unit
            4 words/T-unit minimum
            10 words/T-unit maximum
            5 consecutive sentences on same subject—his pet dog
        b. Syntax
            Compounded T-units: 3/5 sentences (but, so, and)
            Compounded verb phrase: 1/5 sentences
            Clauses: 3/5 sentences
            Pronoun variety (I, he, him, my, it)
            No use of adjectives
        c. Characterization
            Relationship of self with a pet
            Action—play, using a variety of verbs
        d. Plot Development
            Account of play with a pet
    3. *Informal Spelling Inventory*
        Independent Level—Grade 1
        Instructional Level—Middle-high Grade 2
        Frustration Level—Grade 3

Chart 10-1 (cont)

    4. *Kottmeyer Diagnostic Spelling Test*
       (Administered April 6, 1978)
       Correctly spelled 22 of the 32 words, resulting in a grade placement of
       high second grade. Errors occurred on words with these elements:
          vowel-consonant-e (as *time*)
          ow-ou spelling of ou sound (as *found*)
          er-spelling (as *after*)
          le ending (as *little*)
          nonphonetic spellings (as *one*)
    5. *Handwriting Merit Scale*
       (Administered April 6, 1978)
       From the cursive sample, it was judged that John's handwriting is
       average or a little below average. The most obvious needs included:
          closure of letters *d, a*
          nonlooping of *t*
          inconsistent slant
          alignment
       John's speed was 30 letters per minute. John is right-handed.

Health Data
1. Visual Screening Test
   Titus Optical Vision Tester
   (Administered March 22, 1978)
   John scored in the expected column of all tests.
2. Auditory Screening Test
   Beltone Audiometer
   (Administered March 22, 1978)
   The results of the test indicate no hearing difficulties.
3. Speech
   John has a slight stutter when he speaks. He has had two years of speech
   therapy at school. The speech therapist reports little progress. He uses standard English most of the time.
4. General Health
   John appears to be in very good health. He has no previous health history of
   serious illness or injury. He has had most of the childhood diseases, but only
   mild cases.

Home Background
There are five people in John's home (his mother and grandmother and another
brother and sister). John has an older sister who is 11, a fifth grader, and a
younger brother who is 5 and in kindergarten. His mother is in her mid-thirties.
John's grandmother is a high school graduate and his mother is a college
graduate. Standard English is used in the home. His mother is a medical
technologist and his grandmother is the homemaker. The family appears to be
middle class and their economic status to be about average. His father died
when John was 6 years old.

Chart 10-1 (cont)

John has regular chores at home that he performs for an allowance. He does not like to do his chores and tries to escape them whenever he can. His grandmother calls him "lazy."

John gets along with his younger brother, Tom. Tom likes to be around John and imitates him. John argues frequently with his sister, Ruth. She calls John a "dummy." John and his mother seem to get along well.

Both mother and grandmother express concern about John's problems. Neither has offered him any help at home with his language arts assignments. Neither does very much personal reading or writing. They read *Ladies' Home Journal* magazine regularly. They take one local daily newpaper.

Ruth sometimes helps John with his homework, but she often becomes impatient with him and quits before he has finished the task. John does not appreciate her help.

Social, Emotional, and Personality Data

John has three or four friends, all boys, with whom he likes to play. They are all about a year younger than he is. He prefers the company of his younger brother most of the time.

John prefers softball, touch football, or basketball as play activity. John plays on a Little League softball team. He is not a starter, but he thinks he is a "good player." He has a pet dog, Brandy, that he enjoys very much.

John exhibits a positive attitude toward all of the members of the family except his sister. He is somewhat hostile toward her. He states strongly negative attitudes toward school and teachers. Arithmetic is his favorite subject, but he dislikes English, spelling, and handwriting.

John talked freely about himself and his family, school, friends, and other matters, but did not want to talk about English, spelling, and handwriting.

Educational Data

John began school at Central City Elementary when he was 6 years old and repeated the first grade. His grades in language arts have consistently been unsatisfactory; his reading grades have been below average; his grades in mathematics have consistently been satisfactory. His grades for social studies and science have varied.

John has been regular in school attendence. His teachers reported that he is not disruptive in class, but that he does not apply himself. They said at times he appeared nervous and restless. His former teachers and his current teacher claim that his speech impediment makes him impossible to understand. His current teacher lets him sit in the back of the room and do what ever he wants as long as he is quiet. He generally stares out the window.

Language arts instruction in John's classes has been generally whole class instruction, using basal language arts, spelling, and handwriting books. When small group instruction has been provided, John has been assigned the lowest group. He has received no special differentiated instruction, individual or otherwise.

Chart 10-1 (cont)

Interpretation of Data
John's language arts achievement level as determined by the *Stanford Achievement Test* is grade 2.7. John's language arts expectancy level, as computed by formula, is 4.0.

John appears to be about a year and three months behind his capabilities in language arts performance. He needs special individual help to bridge the gap. His consistently higher scores in reading and mathematics suggest room for language arts improvement.

John's speech difficulty seems to have been used as an excuse for failing to offer him instruction. Lack of instruction may be a cause of his problem.

Negative comments at home (being called a "dummy" and "lazy") may have caused a low self-concept and undermined the self-confidence needed for accepting instruction. John's preference for younger playmates may also reflect this lack of self-confidence.

Recommendations for a Corrective and Remedial Program
Corrective and remedial work for John should be given by a language arts specialist. He needs individual assistance to bridge the gap between his achievement level and his expectancy level.

John most particularly needs attention to written composition situations and to development of self-confidence necessary to pursue language arts tasks.

Instructional sessions should include the following activities:
1. As far as possible, alleviate John's personal anxieties by giving him a sense of security and self-respect. Avoid ridicule or neglect; listen attentively and courteously to him.
2. Read aloud to John, providing purposes for listening, and follow-up with literal and interpretative questions to encourage John's active participation in listening. Use tradebooks, listening activities and games based on his sports interests. Move gradually toward use of critical and creative questions. (Use story file, poetry file, listening center materials. Develop listening evaluation scales with John, to be checked by both John and the instructor.)
3. Involve John in varied oral expression activities. Use check lists for different speaking situations. Use systematic instruction where indicated. (Use picture file.)
4. Encourage John to write sentences, and later, stories. Use the language experience approach and activities of high interest. (Use picture file.)
5. After John has produced written samples, analyze by T-units. Check the conventions with basic skill inventories. Use systematic instruction where indicated. Encourage poetry writing, as *cinquain,* and patterned writing. (Use skill files, activity cards, contract cards.)
6. Review functional writing situations presented in second grade language arts textbook. Provide instruction where needed in the functional writing tasks presented by the third grade language textbook.
7. Begin with first and second grade lists of spelling words. Help John to develop a systematic study method for spelling words. Some attention

Chart 10-1 (cont)

should also be given such spelling elements as indicated earlier, as well as structural analysis skills and special category of words (as homonyms).

8. See if the mother or grandmother will help John review spelling words through activities and games you provide for that purpose.
9. In all written work, analyze John's handwriting. Observe common error patterns that need attention. Begin with the most important items. (Use specially prepared work sheets.)
10. Reinforce efforts of the speech therapist, if advisable.
11. Reinforce all of John's successes, no matter how small, with praise.
12. Continue to probe John's interests, attitudes, and self-concepts to provide further instructional clues.

MAINSTREAMED STUDENTS AND INDIVIDUAL EDUCATIONAL PLANS (IEPs)

For children who are "mainstreamed" (the process of integrating children with special needs into a regular educational setting for all or part of the school day), an evaluation report such as the one presented in the preceding case study is prepared. On the basis of the report, an Individual Educational Program (IEP) is prepared. The IEP is a written account of educational objectives, strategies, curriculum modifications, and classroom accommodations for a student with learning problems as required by P.L. 94–142.

The IEP provides a synthesis of all assessment information plus classroom accommodations and instructional plans. The format may include:

I. Summary of Assessment
   A. Areas of strengths
   B. Areas of weaknesses
   C. Approaches that have failed
   D. Learning style(s)
   E. Recommended placement, general program outline, and assignment of personnel responsibility.
II. Classroom Accommodations
   A. General teaching techniques
   B. Language arts modifications (and other subject matter modifications)
III. Instructional Plans
   A. Long range (yearly) objectives, along with materials, strategies, and evidence of mastery
   B. Specific (1–3 months) objectives
   C. Ancillary personnel and services

One reference on the IEP is: Thomas Lovitt, *Writing and Implementing an I.E.P.* (Belmont, Calif.: Fearon-Pitman Publishers, 1979).

LEGAL DEVELOPMENTS

All language arts personnel need to be particularly aware of legal aspects and, in fact, should help initiate programs to bring about legal awareness among school staffs. For example, teachers need to consider such situations as the following:

1. The Buckley Amendment (Educational Aid 464, 1974) prohibits "the release of a student's records without parental consent."
2. P.L. 94–142, 1974, establishes procedural safeguards for fully informing parents or guardians and receiving their permission for evaluation situations. Parents or guardians must "fully understand" all releases that they agree to sign.
3. The Buckley Amendment further provides that all information obtained in a parent interview for background information about a student must be kept confidential. Parental permission must be secured to record the interview through audio- or video-taping, or to have others present at the interview.
4. Parents have the legal right to have an "adequately trained examiner" administer tests (P.L. 94–142). Again, if the testing procedure is to be observed, the parents must be made aware of this fact, as well as if the test procedure is to be recorded or taped for later instructional use.
5. P.L. 94–142 specifically prohibits the use of culturally biased tests.
6. A copy of clinical reports (or at least a summary report) should be sent to the parents or guardians.

Those items suggested above may be of most immediate concern to the language arts teacher. However, the growing legal framework of regulations and laws with regard to reading and other language processes impinge upon all school personnel. One source that considers a broad range of issues is *Reading and the Law,* edited by Robert J. Harper, II, and Gary Kilarr (Newark, Del.: International Reading Association, 1978). Such issues as the following are discussed:

a. minimal literacy standards for graduation
b. educational malpractice suits
c. school systems' classification methods (particularly as they apply to the corrective/remedial student)
d. test bias

Almost all states that have dealt with accountability measures have included reading and other language processes as major criteria for program evaluation. The appendix of the book cited above includes discussion of the laws of each of the states which affect reading or language instruction. Interested persons should supplement this appendix by inquiring of the appropriate state department of education or chief state school officer's headquarters about state regulations and those policies interpreting each regulation.

REVIEW QUESTIONS AND ACTIVITIES

1. What are different methods of collecting data for a case study?
2. What items should be included in a complete case study?
3. Make a list of vocabulary terms that are important to understand in discussing case study procedures.
4. Observe a child who is having difficulties in the language arts for several days in the classroom setting. Record your findings and make recommendations pertinent to language arts.
5. Interview a parent concerning his or her child's language arts problems. Analyze your findings.
6. Interview a teacher about the language arts difficulties of one of his or her students. Analyze your findings.
7. Prepare an illustrative case study for one particular child.
8. Prepare a case study that centers on one particular language arts difficulty, such as oral expression, written expression, spelling, or handwriting.

Selected References

Some Major Sources

Blair, G.M. *Diagnostic and remedial teaching,* rev. edition. New York: Macmillan, 1956. (Chapter 10, Spelling; Chapter 11, Handwriting; and Chapter 12, English).

Bloom, B.S. et al. *Handbook on formative and summative evaluation of student learning.* New York: McGraw-Hill, 1971. (See especially Chapter 15, "Evaluation of Learning in the Language Arts.")

Brueckner, L.J., & Bond, G. *Diagnosis and treatment of learning difficulties.* New York: Appleton-Century Crofts, 1955 (Chapter 10, Language; Chapter 11, Spelling; and Chapter 12, Handwriting).

Marcus, M. *Diagnostic teaching of the language arts.* New York: McGraw-Hill, 1977.

Otto, W. et al. *Corrective and remedial teaching,* 2nd edition. Boston: Houghton-Mifflin, 1973 (Chapter 10, Spelling; Chapter 13, Handwriting; and Chapter 14, Written/Oral Expression).

Other Specialized References

Birch, J.W. *Mainstreaming: Educable retarded children in regular classes.* Reston, Va.: Council for Exceptional Children, 1974.

Coble, C.R. et al. *Mainstreaming language arts and social studies.* Santa Monica, Calif.: Goodyear, 1976.

Cutts, N.E., & Mosely, N. (Eds.). *Providing for individual differences in the elementary school.* Englewood Cliffs, N.J.: Prentice-Hall, 1960.

Drews, R.H. et al. *Practical plans for teaching english in elementary schools.* Dubuque, Iowa: William C. Brown, 1965.

Fagan, W. et al. *Measures for research and evaluation in the English language arts.* Urbana, Ill.: National Council of Teachers of English, 1975.

Gearhart, B.R. *Learning disabilities: Educational strategies.* St. Louis: C.V. Mosby, 1973.

Geyer J.R., & Matanzo, J. *Programmed reading diagnosis for teachers* Columbus, Ohio: Charles E. Merrill, 1977.

Hammill, D.D., & Bartell, N.R. *Teaching children with learning and behavior problems,* 2nd edition. Boston: Allyn and Bacon, 1978.

Henry, Nelson B. (Ed.). *Individualizing instruction.* 61st. Yearbook, Part I. Chicago: National Society for the Study of Education, 1962.

Hewett, F. *Education of exceptional learners.* Boston: Allyn and Bacon, 1974.

Joyce, W.W., & Banks, J.A. *Teaching the language arts to culturally different children.* Reading, Mass.: Addison-Wesley, 1971.

Kirk, S.A. *Educating Exceptional Children,* 2nd edition. New York: Houghton-Mifflin, 1972.

Knight, L.N. *Language arts for the exceptional: The gifted and linguistically different,* Itasca, Ill.: Peacock Publishers, 1974.

Markoff, A.M., *Teaching low-achieving children reading, spelling, and handwriting.* Springfield, Ill.: Charles C Thomas, 1977.

Schattner, R. *Creative dramatics for handicapped children.* New York: John Day, 1967.

Thomas, J.K. *How to teach and administer classes for mentally retarded children.* Minneapolis: T.S. Denison, 1968.

Thomas, J.K. *Teaching language arts to mentally retarded children.* Minneapolis: T.S. Denison, 1971.

Additional Articles on Corrective and Remedial Language Arts

Allen, E.G. and Wright, J. Personalizing handwriting instruction, *Elementary School Journal* 74 (Apr. 1974): 424–29.

Ames, L. True and pseudo slow learners. *The Exceptional Child* 17 (July 1970): 112–18.

Arthur, K. Diagnosis and treatment in remedial education: A review paper. *The Exceptional Child* 21 (July 1974): 114–34.

Backrach, B. Paper fingers. *Instructor* 77 (Feb. 1968): 100.

Banks, E.M. The identification of children with potential learning disabilities, *The Exceptional Child* 17 (Mar. 1970): 27–38.

Beers, et al. The logic behind children's spelling. *The Elementary School Journal* 77 (Jan. 1977): 238–42.

Bordie, J.G. Language tests and linguistically different learners. *Elementary English* 47 (Oct. 1970): 814–21.

Brown, M.E. A practical approach to analyzing children's talk in the classroom. *Language Arts* 54 (May, 1977): 506–10.

Cadenhead, K.; Ashwander, B.; Ussery, M. Helping children with spelling. *Elementary English* 52 (May, 1975): 679–80.

Carter, J.L. and Synolds, D. Effects of relaxation training upon handwriting quality. *Journal of Learning Disabilities* 7 (Apr. 1974): 236–38.

Chalfant, J.C. and Foster, G.E. Identifying learning disabilities in the classroom. *The Exceptional Child* 21 (Mar. 1974): 3–14.

Cochrane, K.J. Common sense and remedial teaching. *The Exceptional Child* 17 (Nov. 1970): 144–48.

Corman, C. Bibliotherapy: Insight for the learning handicapped. *Language Arts* 52 (Oct. 1975): 935–37.

Cramer, R.L. Diagnosing skills by analyzing chlidren's writing. *Reading Teacher* 30 (Dec. 1976): 276–79.

Cramer, R.L. The write way to teach spelling. *Elementary School Journal* 76 (May 1976): 464–67.

Denhoff, E. "Precursive factors to early and identified learning disabilities. *The Exceptional Child* 19 (July 1972): 79–80.

Dixon, C.N. Language experience stories as a diagnostic tool. *Language Arts* 54 (May 1977): 501–05.

Dubois, B. Cultural and social factors in the assessment of language capabilities. *Elementary English* 51 (Feb. 1974): 257–61.

Early, G.H. The case for cursive writing. *Academic Therapy* 9 (Fall 1973): 105–08.

Ediger, M. Diagnosing spelling deficiencies. *School and Community* 63 (Dec. 1976): 10.

Enstrom, E.A. and Enstrom, D.C. In print handwriting: Preventing and solving reversal problems. *Elementary English* 46 (Oct. 1969): 759–64.

Fauke, J. Improvement of handwriting and letter recognition skills: A behavior modification. *Journal of Learning Disabilities* 6 (May 1973): 296–300.

Fehm, S.J. Search for solutions to the problem of educating slow learners in American public schools. *The Exceptional Child* 22 (Mar. 1975): 32–7.

Foerster, L.M. Sinistral power! Help for left-handed children. *Elementary English* 52 (Feb. 1975): 213–15.

Freischlag, J. Motor activities to teach handwriting to the poorly coordinated. *School and Community* 59 (May 1973): 28–9.

Gantt, W.N. Language and learning styles of the educationally disadvantaged. *Elementary School Journal* 73 (Dec. 1972): 138–42.

Genishi, C. and Chambers, R. Informal assessment of the bilingual child. *Language Arts* 54 (May 1977): 496–500.

Golladay, W.M. The teaching of spelling to low ability students. *Elementary English* 48 (Mar. 1971): 366–71.

Golub, L. Stimulating and receiving children's writing: Implications for an elementary writing curriculum. *Elementary English* 48 (Jan. 1971): 33–46.

Gould, S.M. Spelling isn't reading backwards. *Journal of Reading,* Dec. 1976, 220–25.

Graves, D.H. Handwriting is for writing. *Language Arts* 55 (Mar. 1978): 393–99.

Hanson, I.W. Teaching remedial handwriting. *Language Arts* 53 (Apr. 1976): 428–31.

Horton, L.W. Illegibilities in the cursive handwriting of sixth-graders. *Elementary School Journal* 70 (May 1970): 446–50.

Hunt, K. Recent measures in syntactic development. *Elementary English* 43 (Nov. 1966): 732–39.

Johnson, H.W. Flow chart for spelling a word correctly. *Elementary English* 49 (Mar. 1972): 416–17.

Jones, D.M. All children have language problems—Which ones are special? *Elementary English* 49 (May/Dec. 1972): 836–41.

Jung, R.K. A new approach to understanding children's language development. *California English Journal* 7 (Dec. 1971): 32–43.

Katula, R.A., Anonymous jingles and why Johnny can't spell. *Language Arts* 54 (Mar. 1977): 297–300.

Leburn, Y., and Van De Craen, P. Developmental writing disorders and their prevention. *Journal of Special Education* 9 (Summer 1975): 201–07.

Linz, C. Visual education and the slow learner. *The Exceptional Child* 17 (Mar. 1970): 52–57.

McElrary, A. Handwriting and the slow learner. *Elementary English* 41 (Dec. 1964): 865–68.

McLeod J. Research into learning disability. *The Exceptional Child* 17 (Nov. 1970): 130–43.

Marcus, M. The cinquain as a diagnostic and instructional technique. *Elementary English* 41 (Apr. 1974): 561–66, 564.

Melear, J.D. An informal language inventory. *Elementary English* 41 (Apr. 1974): 508–11.

Mendoza, M.; Holt, W.J.; and Jackson, D. Circles and tape. *Teaching exceptional children* 10 (Winter 1978): 48–50.

Morelesion, J.P. NCTE/ERIC report. The slow learner, a winner at last? *Elementary English* 48 (Nov. 1971): 896–901.

Moreney, A.S.; Wepman, J.M.; and Hass, S.K. Developmental speech inaccuracy and speech therapy in the early school years. *Elementary School Journal* 70 (Jan. 1970): 219–24.

Mullins, J. A handwriting model for children with learning disabilities. *Journal of Learning Disabilities* 5 (May 1972): 306–11.

Nemanich, D. Passive verbs in children's writing. *Elementary English* 40 (Nov. 1972): 1064–66.

Plessas, G. Children's errors in spelling homonyms. *Elementary School Journal* 64 (Dec. 1963): 163–68.

Rivers, C. Spelling: It's time to do something. *Learning: The Magazine of Creative Teaching* 3 (Nov. 1974): 72–5.

Rowell, C.G. Don't throw away those spelling test papers . . . yet! *Elementary English* 52 (Feb. 1975): 239–42, 257.

Rudman, M. Informal spelling in the classroom: A more effective approach. *The Reading Teacher* 26 (Mar. 1973): 602–04.

Schell, L.M. B+ in composition; C– in spelling. *Elementary English* 52 (Feb. 1975): 239–42, 257.

Stauffer, R.G. and Pikulski, J.J. A comparison and measure of oral language growth. *Elementary English* 51 (Nov./Dec. 1974): 1151–55.

Tutolo, D.J. A cognitive approach to teaching listening. *Language Arts* 54 (Mar. 1971): 262–65.

Watts, B.H. Special education in the seventies: Promises and problems. *The Exceptional Child* 22 (July 1975): 67–8.

Weaver, S.W. and Rutherford, W.L. A hierarchy of listening skills. *Elementary English* 51 (Nov./Dec. 1974): 1146–50.

Westbrooks, L.K. More prescriptions for ailing penmanship. *Teacher* 94 (Mar. 1977): 59–62.

Zutell, J. Some psycholinguistic perspectives on children's spelling. *Language Arts* 55 (Oct. 1978): 844–50.

Some Professional Journals

Academic Therapy. 1539 Fourth Street, San Rafael, Calif., 94901

Bulletin of the Orton Society. 8415 Bellona Lane, Towson, Md. 21204

Exceptional Children. The Council for Exceptional Children, 1920 Association Drive, Reston, Virginia 22091.

Journal of Learning Disabilities. 101 East Ontario St., Chicago, Ill. 60611

Journal of Special Education. Buttonwood Farms, 3515 Woodhaven Rd., Philadelphia, Pa. 19154

Language Arts (formerly *Elementary English*), National Council of Teachers of English, 1111 Kenyon Road, Urbana, Ill. 61801.

Reading Clinic. The Center for Applied Research in Education, 521 Fifth Ave., New York, N.Y. 10017.

Reading Newsreport. Multimedia Education, 11 West 42nd. St. New York, N.Y. 10036.

Reading Teacher. International Reading Association, 800 Barksdale Road, Newark, Del. 19711.

Slow Learner Workshop. Parker Publishing Company, West Nyack, N.Y. 10994.

Appendix

Scope and Sequence Lists

LANGUAGE SCOPE AND SEQUENCE

K

Listening and Speaking
Developing good oral communication skills
    Listening to directions
    Listening to follow sequence of acts
    Listening to recall details of a story
    Listening to form associations
    Spontaneous speaking during sharing time
    Giving oral definitions of words for familiar objects

Creative Writing
Developing sensitivity to language and ability to use it creatively
    Literature: background for creative writing
    Organizing ideas: learning to tell a story in sequence
    Vocabulary building: discussing pairs of words with opposite meanings; words for telling about size, shape, color; learning to use a dictionary

Language Growth and Change
Developing awareness of the history and changing nature of language
    Nature of language development: from larger units to individual words
    Language development through social contacts
    Uses of language: to exchange ideas with classmates; identify and describe objects in environment; tell a story; give information
    Dialects: different words and expressions used in different neighborhoods

257

Grammar
Developing understanding of English grammar and how it works
  Word order: its function in language
  Sentences: children analyze sentences in stories read to them for correct word order; cause effect relationships
  Nouns: discussing words for singular objects; persons or animals; words for more than one object of person or animal
  Verbs: recognizing present, past, future in oral sentences; using past tense of irregular verbs in sentences
  Punctuation: capitalizing first letter of name

Usage
Developing ability to use language that is always appropriate
  Usage concept: appropriate forms of language
  Verbs: auditory recognition of correct past-tense forms of *buy, give, eat, go, get, run, tell, fall,* and *do*

BOOK 1

Listening and Speaking
Listening and speaking as related activities
Recognizing and inventing rhymes
Listening to note relationships of word order to meaning
Listening to form clear images
Telling a story from sequence of pictures
Discussing pictured situations
Creative dramatics: improving dialogue

Creative Writing
Literature: models for creative writing
Organizing ideas: arranging story elements in sequence
Vocabulary building: classifying words; associating terms with regions; learning to use a picture dictionary
Understanding story structure: filling in details of story from separate elements in pictured situation
Creative writing: inventing oral endings for stories; writing stories about pictured situation

Language Growth and Change
Nature of communication: development of the realization that through language—spoken and written—people share information and experience
Character of language: building awareness of sentence as unit of thought
Uses of language: to exchange ideas; tell a story; give information
Dialects: different people have different ways of expressing the same thought

Language Scope and Sequence from *Language and How to Use It* by A. Schiller et al. Copyright 1973 by Scott, Foresman and Co. Reprinted by permission.

Grammar
Word order: how it affects meaning
Sentences: recognizing complete and incomplete declarative sentences
Nouns: classifying words for animals, people, things, places
Verbs: practice using past-tense forms of irregular verbs
Punctuation: periods, question marks at end of sentence, commas in personal letters

Usage
Usage concept: appropriate forms of language
Verbs: practice in hearing and using appropriate past-tense forms of *see, blow, find, run, tell, take, go, hold, give, buy, catch, come,* etc.

BOOK 2

Listening and Speaking
Listening to directions
Listening to form images and associations
Evaluating what is heard
Listening to establish time relationships
Listening for turning point in a story
Expressing oral reactions to picture story: making inferences
Creative dramatics: dramatizing folk tales, how and why stories, stories created by children themselves
Creating dialogue for puppet shows

Creative Writing
Literature: model for creative writing
Organizing ideas: sorting out words in mixed order; perceiving relationship of word order and meaning: describing a process in orderly sequence
Vocabulary building: using synonyms and antonyms; using a picture dictionary
Creative writing: reviewing story sequence; writing story endings using personification based on observation of real animals; inventing stories about pictured situations

Language Growth and Change
Nature of communication: looking at the variety of ways people get their ideas across to others
Character of language: increase of flexibility in putting words together
Uses of language: to express ideas; tell a story; give information; create word pictures

Grammar
Word order: relationships of word to meaning
Sentences: concepts of subjects; predicates
Nouns: collective nouns and generic words
Verbs: past participles; verbs that describe variety of actions; verbs that describe sounds

Punctuation: exclamation marks; quotation marks and commas in direct address

Usage

Usage concept: appropriate forms of language
Verbs: practice in using past tense forms of irregular verbs: *read, run, slide, fall, dive, tell, swim, shake, dig, find*

BOOK 3

Listening and Speaking

Listening and speaking as related activities; learning to participate in a discussion
Listening for place relationships (text and records)
Listening for details (text and records)
Sensory images from listening (text and records)
Onomatipoeia in poetry
Improvising dialogue in dramatizations

Creative Writing

Literature: models for creative writing
Organizing ideas: paragraphs; paragraphs in dialogue; story beginnings
Vocabulary building: synonyms and antonyms, idioms, similes, metaphors; learning to use dictionary and beginning thesaurus; keeping a personal vocabulary list
Creative writing: story, mystery, fable, myth, fantasy, personal account, book review, experimenting with imagery and mood

Language Growth and Change

Nature of communication: exploration of animal communication, nonverbal and verbal communication
Character of language: developing concept that language puts sounds together in system
Use of language: to tell a story, give information, make word pictures
Origins of words in English (borrowings)
Dialects: different words in different places

Grammar

Word order: how it functions in language
Sentences: subjects and predicates
Nouns: distinguished by noun markers, singular and plural forms, possessives
Pronouns: personal pronouns in subject, object and possessive forms
Verbs: location in predicate: present and past tense, the verb *be*

Usage

Usage concept: appropriate forms of language
Verbs: *go, see, come, give, eat, take, write,* with auxiliaries *have, has, had* (text and records)
Personal pronouns: in subject and object forms (text and records)

BOOK 4

Listening and Speaking
Listening and speaking as related activities
Listening for place relationships (text and records)
Listening to increase vocabulary (text and records)
Dialects: listening to American stories to hear dialectical differences
  (records)
Improvising dialogue in dramatics
Relevance: relation to good speaking

Creative Writing
Literature: models for creative writing
Organizing ideas: paragraphs, arranging paragraphs, development of begin-
  ning, middle, and end in composition
Vocabulary building: synonyms and antonyms; similes, metaphors, idioms,
  maintaining use of dictionary and thesaurus
Creative writing: description, dialogue, character sketch, personified report,
  letter writing, cinquains, rhymed and unrhymed verse; avoiding cliches

Language Growth and Change
History of English: origins in Anglo-Saxon, influences of Norse and Norman
  invasions, developments in America
Etymologies of words: word histories demonstrating influences of other
  languages on English
Dialects: regional differences in accent, stress, and vocabulary (text and
  records)
Literature: demonstrating folklore of Old English, Middle English, and Early
  America

Grammar
Review of Book 3 grammar
Noun phrases: unmarked with noun markers, personal pronouns, indefinite
  pronouns
Verbs and verb markers
Verb Groups: *be + ing, have + en, be + en,* modal + base
Adjectives: inflections of adjectives
Modifiers: adverbs of place, time, manner, nouns and verbs as modifiers

Usage
Usage concept: appropriate forms of language
Personal pronouns: in subject and object forms (text and records)
Verbs: *have + en +* the verbs *buy, bring, teach, catch, begin, run, drink, ring*
  (text and records)

BOOK 5

Listening and Speaking
Listening and speaking as related activities
Listening: maintaining and extending earlier skills under conditions of in-
  creased difficulty—background noise, interference (text and records)

Dialects: listening to hear dialectical differences (records)
Creative dramatics: improvising dialogues

Creative Writing
Literature: models for creative writing
Organizing ideas: basic principles of selection and organization of material; well-formed paragraphs
Vocabulary building: introduction of junior thesarus; synonyms and antonyms; idioms; figurative language
Creative writing: punctuation review; report writing from interviews; completing open-ended stories and playlets; letter writing; word imagery, writing a "book"

Language Growth and Change
Evolution of written language: early cave drawings, Phoenician alphabet, Greek alphabet and its use in parts of the world today, Roman alphabet (records)
Dialects: language changes from place to place (text and records)
Literature: Egyptian and Greek legends augmenting historical narrative

Grammar
Review, maintenance, and extension of subject, predicate, nouns, pronouns, verbs, adjectives, adverbs
Noun phrases: subject; object of preposition; object of verb; predicate complement
Predicates: determined by kind of verb—intransitive (V1), transitive (Vt), the verb *be*, linking
Sentence patterns: four basic sentence patterns built on preceding predicates
Morphology: inflection, derivation, functional shift

Usage
Usage concept: appropriate forms of language
Personal pronouns: understandings about and practice on subject and object forms (text and records)
Verbs: understandings about and practice on common verb forms (text and records)
Subject-verb agreement: understandings and practice (text and records)

BOOK 6

Listening and Speaking
Listening to directions
Listening to discriminate between facts and unfounded claims
Appreciation of literature through listening to recordings

Creative Writing
Literature: models for creative writing; showing dialect in literature
Organizing ideas: note taking, organizing notes; outlining relating ideas in paragraphs

Vocabulary building: maintaining and extending use of resource materials; figurative language

Creative writing: report writing from interviews; developing point of view; describing; revising—drawing on knowledge of grammar, literature, vocabulary, dialect, usage

Language Growth and Change
Uses of language: for self-expression; to show point of view, to show story and paragraph structure; to describe

Dialects: regional idioms that add color and authenticity to writing (text and records)

Literature: demonstrating uses of dialect in writing

Grammar
Review, maintenance, and extension of subject, predicate, nouns, pronouns, verbs, adjectives, adverbs; prepositional phrases and morphology

Coordination: conjunctions

Subordination: imbeddedness

Transformations: interrogative, negative, passive

Usage
Usage concept: appropriate forms in language

Personal pronouns: understandings about and practice on subject and object forms (text and records)

Verbs: understandings and practice on common verb forms (text and records)

Adjectives, Adverbs: understandings and practice (text and records)

SPELLING SCOPE AND SEQUENCE

LEVEL 1

LEVEL 1 introduces students to the sounds and symbols of the alphabet. It also familiarized them with the skills that are basic to spelling mastery. Ample opportunity is provided for developing skills in manuscript writing as individual letter forms are introduced and then used to form words. Even at this early level, children become acquainted with the dictionary in its most elementary form. Charming illustrations help depict the principles being taught.

Phoneme-Grapheme Correspondence
Initial consonant sounds
/l/,/t/,/d/,/h/,/k/,/g/,/f/,/k/,/c/,/b/,/n/,/p/,/m/,/r/,/j/,/s/,/v/,/w/,/y/
Final consonant sounds
/d/, /t/, /g/, /n/, /r/, /p/, /l/, /s/
Vowels
short vowel sounds /a/, /e/, /i/, /o/, /u/

Spelling Scope and Sequence from *The Word Book Spelling Program* by Lorrene L. Ort and Eunice E. Wallace. Developed by Lyons and Carnahan. Reprinted by permission of Rand McNally and Co.

Grouping words by their sounds
   initial consonant sounds
   final consonant sounds

Word-Building Skills
Rhyming words patterns
   -an, -at, -ake, -ine, -et, -ide, -it, -ate
Nonrhyming word patterns
   bu-, ma-, di-, ca-

Developing Language Skills
Introducing study words
Using spelling words in context
Informal letter writing
Sentence completion
Open-ended writing activities

Dictionary Skills
Using a picture dictionary
Alphabetizing
Locating words

Writing Conventions
Improving handwriting skills
   introducing lowercase letter forms
   introducing capital letter forms
     writing capital letters in order
     using in sentences
   writing words and sentences

LEVEL 2

LEVEL 2 leads the students to discover some of the most basic spelling patterns and to learn to form new words through initial and final letter substitution. The core word lists help students to perceive spelling regularities. Spelling vocabularies are increased by "Builder Words" which extend spelling patterns to new words. Games, puzzles, and stories provide opportunities to use the words in meaningful contexts.

Phoneme-Grapheme Correspondence
Consonants
   initial consonant sounds
     /l/, /t/, /n/, /b/, /k/, /d/, /f/, /s/, /h/, /m/, /p/, /g/, /j/, /r/, /v/, /w/, /y/, /z/
   final consonant sounds
     /d/, /p/, /n/, /r/, /m/, /g/, /t/, /l/, /b/
   consonant cluster sounds
     /fl/, /dr/, /sl/, /br/, /st/, /tr/, /pl/, /gr/, /kl/, /gl/, /bl/, /kr/, /hw/, /sw/, /spr/, /str/
   /k/ sound spelled c or k

/z/ sound spelled z or s
double consonant letters *ll, ss*
consonant digraph *th*
Vowels
   short vowel sounds /a/, /e/, /i/, /o/, /u/
   long vowel sounds /ā/, /ē/, /ī/, /ō/
   sounds *oo* represents
   sounds *ou* represents
   vowel digraphs *ay, ai, ee, ea, oa*
   vowel sounds *y* represents

Word-Building Skills
Rhyming word patterns
Nonrhyming word patterns
Vowel-changing patterns
Initial consonant substitution
Plurals
   identifying plurals
   forming plurals
      by changing the root word
      by adding *-s*
      by changing *y* to *i* and adding *-es*
Root words
   identifying root words
   changing roots to form the irregular past tense
Suffixes
   plural-forming (*-s, -es*)
   tense-changing (*-ed, -ing*)
Syllabication
   identifying word parts
   recognizing one-, two-, and three-syllable words
   word ending *-er* in two syllable words

Word Meaning
Words with multiple meanings
Antonyms
   identifying and writing opposites
Synonyms

Developing Language Skills
Using spelling words
   study steps for learning to spell
   using words in context
Story building
Open-ended writing activities
   sentence completion
   riddle completion

Parts of speech
 pronouns (they, my)
 verbs (am, are)
Writing words and sentences

Dictionary Skills
Alphabetizing
Using the dictionary spelling
 to locate words
 to determine vowel sounds

Writing Conventions
Letter forms
Guide to letter formation
Capitalization
Punctuation

LEVEL 3

LEVEL 3 encourages students to extend their knowledge by expanding their spelling skills and by learning some important characteristics of language. They further develop skills by adding endings to root words, in forming commonly used contractions and compound words, and in understanding basic principles of syllabication. Opportunities to use spelling words in context allow students to discover the different functions one word may have.

Phoneme-Grapheme Correspondence
Consonants
 initial consonant sounds
  /j/, /y/, /v/, /n/, /z/, /k/, /l/, /s/, /m/, /p/, /n/, /g/, /f/, /b/, /r/
 final consonant sounds
  /d/, /t/, /m/, /g/, /l/, /n/, /r/, /b/, /p/
 initial consonant clusters
  /br/, /sl/, /dr/, /pl/, /tr/, /sw/, /gl/, /kl/, /hw/, /gr/, /st/, /fr/, /bl/, /sn/, /str/, /kr/, /sp/, /thr/
 final consonant clusters
  /st/, /nd/, /mp/
 initial consonant digraphs
  /sh/, /ch/, /th/, /TH/
 /k/ sound spelled c, k, or ck
 (s) sound spelled ss, s, or c
 double consonant letters ll, ss, ff
Vowels
 short vowel sounds /a/, /e/, /i/, /o/, /u/
 long vowel sounds
  /ā/ vowel patterns ay, ai, a-consonant-e
  /ē/ vowel patterns e, ea, ee, ie
  /ī/ vowel patterns i-consonant-e, i, y, igh, ie
  /ō/ vowel patterns oa, ow, o-consonant-e, o

/ū/ vowel pattern u-consonant-e
vowel sound /ər/
vowel sounds y represents

Word Building Skills
Rhyming word patterns
Nonrhyming word patterns
Vowel-changing patterns
Initial and final consonant substitution
Plurals
  forming plurals
    by adding -s, or -es
    by changing the root word
    by changing y to i and adding -es
Root words
  identifying root words
  adding suffixes to root words
    root word unchanged
    dropping final e
    doubling the final consonant
  changing root words to form irregular past tense
Suffixes
  plural-forming (-s, -es)
  tense-changing (-ed, -ing)
Syllabication
  identifying and writing one-, two-, and three-syllable words
  word ending -er in two-syllable words
Compound words
  identifying compound words
  forming compound words
Contractions
  identifying and writing contractions

Word Meaning
Words with multiple meanings
Word families
Classifying words
Word definition
  using context clues
  word substitution
Antonyms
Synonyms
Homonyms

Developing Language Skills
Using spelling words
  using words in context
  developing spelling vocabularies

Story building
Open-ended writing activities
  riddle completion
  sentence completion
  puzzle completion
  rhyme completion

Dictionary Skills
Alphabetizing
  by first, second, and third letters
Locating words in the dictionary
Discerning multiple meanings of words
Using the dictionary to add prefixes to words
Using the dictionary to determine syllabication
Using the dictionary to determine accent
Using the dictionary to locate compound words

Writing Conventions
Improving handwriting skills
  manuscript letter forms
  cursive letter forms
Capitalization
Punctuation

LEVEL 4

LEVEL 4 introduces some of the less common spelling patterns and some of the variant sound-symbol associations appropriate to words of this level. Students extend their study of previously introduced concepts, further develop knowledge of syllabication and accent, and explore techniques for expanding vocabularies by developing skill in adding suffixes to known root words. An introduction to word origins increases language development.

Phoneme-Grapheme Correspondence
Consonants
  initial and final consonant sounds
  initial and final consonant cluster sounds
  /k/ sound spelled c, k, or ck
  consonant digraphs /ch/, /sh/, /th/, /TH/, /ng/
  double consonant letters ll, ss, ff
  variant spellings

/f/ spelled *gh*	/t/ spelled *ed*
/v/ spelled *lv*	/s/ spelled *st*
/m/ spelled *mb*	/h/ spelled *wh*
/kw/ spelled *qu*	/n/ spelled *kn*
/z/ spelled *s*	

Vowels
   short vowel sounds
   long vowel sounds
      /ā/ patterns a-consonant-e, ay, ai
      /ē/ patterns e, ee, ea
      /ī/ patterns i-consonant-e, igh, y, i, ie
      /ō/ patterns o-consonant-e, oa, ow, o
   sounds oo represents
   /ər/ sound spelled er, ar, or
   variant spellings
      /ā/ spelled ie   /ô/ spelled augh, ough
      /u/ spelled ou, o   /ō/ spelled ou
      /ē/ spelled i   /i/ spelled ie

Word-Building Skills
Word patterns
   -CVC, -VVC, -CVCe, -CC
   rhyming patterns
   consonant substitution
   consonant cluster substitution
   consonant digraph substitution
   vowel substitution
Plurals
   forming plurals
      by changing the root word
      by adding -s, or -es
Suffixes
   identifying suffixes
   meanings of suffixes
   plural-forming (-s, -es)
   tense-changing (-ed, -ing)
   comparative (-er, -est)
   adding suffixes to root words
      -ly, -ness, -er, -ance, -able, -ish, -age, -y, -ful, -less
   generalizations for adding suffixes
      dropping the final consonant
      dropping final e
      changing y to i
   root word unchanged
Root words
   identifying root words
   adding affixes to root words
Syllabication
   identifying syllables
   accented syllables

Word Meaning
Determining meanings of words through—
   context clues
   structural analysis
   synonym-antonym relationships
   inductive and deductive reasoning
Determining similar or opposite meaning
Synonyms
Antonyms
Homonyms
Multiple meanings
Comparing and contrasting
Classification of words into categories
Compound words
   fused
   unjoined
   hyphenated
Words from content areas
   mathematics
   social studies
   language arts
   health

Developing Language Skills
Using spelled words
   sentence completion
   paragraph completion
Open-ended writing activities
   story writing
   sentence completion
   puzzle completion
   limericks
   using similes and metaphors
Understanding verb tense
   regular and irregular past tense
Expressing ideas

Dictionary Skills
Alphabetizing
Locating word meanings
Using entry words
Using guide words
Dictionary pronunciations

Writing Conventions
Improving handwriting skills
   cursive letter forms

Capitalization
Abbreviation

Etymology
Origin and meaning of word parts
Old English derivations
French, Latin derivations
Origin of the names of the days of the week

LEVEL 5

LEVEL 5 emphasizes word derivations, prefixes and suffixes, and irregular verb forms. Word meaning is explored through working with word classifications, analogies, similes, homographs, homophones, antonyms, and synonyms. Games, puzzles, and stories continue to provide interesting context for newly learned spelling words. Students are encouraged to develop spelling skills using words from other content areas. Dictionary skills also become increasingly sophisticated.

Phoneme-Grapheme Correspondence
initial, medial and final consonant cluster sounds
/k/ spelled c, k, ck, or ck
/s/ spelled s, ss, or c
consonant digraphs /ch/, /sh/, /th/, /TH/
variant spellings

/z/ spelled s	/j/ spelled g, ge, or dge
/zh/ spelled ge, s, or z	/m/ spelled mb or mn
/r/ spelled wr	/h/ spelled wh
/n/ spelled kn	/k/ spelled lk
/f/ spelled lf	/sh/ spelled c or s

Vowels
short and long vowel sounds
/ā/ patterns a-consonant-e, ay, ai, a
/ē/ patterns e-consonant-e, e, ee, ea
/ī/ patterns i-consonant-e, igh, y, i
/ō/ patterns o-consonant-e, oa, ou, o
/u/ spelled ew, oo, o, ui, ou
/əl/ spelled le, el, al, ul
/ər/ spelled er, ar, ir, or, ure
/ə/ spelled a, e, i, o, u
variant spellings
/i/ spelled u, e, a,
/u/ spelled o
/ā/ spelled eigh
/ē/ spelled ie, ei, ae, eo, ey, ay, oe
/ō/ spelled ough, ou, oo
/o/ spelled a, augh, o, au

Word-Building Skills
Word patterns
   -VCC, -CVCe, -VCe, -VVC, -CC, -VC
   rhyming and nonrhyming patterns
   consonant cluster substitution
   consonant digraph substitution
   vowel substitution
Plurals
   forming plurals
   by changing the root word
   by adding -s or -es
   by changing y to i and adding -es
Suffixes
   meanings of suffixes
   plural-forming (-s, -es)
   tense changing (-ed, -ing)
   comparative (-er, -est)
   adding suffixes to root words
     -ness, -ly, -er, -ous, -ich, -y
     -able, -ation, -en, -ery, -ion
   word analogies with suffixes
   generalizations for adding suffixes
     doubling the final consonant
     dropping the final e
     changing y to i
     multisyllabic words with -VC endings,
       stressed and unstressed final syllable
Prefixes
   identifying prefixes: re-, dis-, un-, mis-, ex-, out-
   meanings of prefixes: forming opposites with un-
   adding prefixes to root words
Syllabication
   identifying multisyllabic words
   dividing words into syllables
   recognizing suffixes as syllables
   accented syllables
   words with double consonants
   roots ending in double consonants with suffixes
Root words
   root word patterns -VVC, -CC, -VC
   identifying derived Latin roots
Contractions
   identifying contractions
   writing contractions
   use of the apostrophe

Compound words
　identifying and writing fused, unjoined and hyphenated compound words
Irregular verbs
　identifying and writing irregular verbs

Word Meaning
Word relationships
　cause and effect
　fact and opinion
Determining word meaning
　through context clues
　by word use and purpose
　by definition
　by word parts
　by structural analysis
Completing word analogies
Word classification
Verbal equations
Determining similar or opposite meaning
Multiple meanings
Word associations
Synonyms
Antonyms
Homonyms
Homographs
Contrasting word pairs
　direct opposites (antonyms)
　opposites displaying a degree of difference
　intangible or relative contrasts
Comparisons
　similes
　word associations
　comparisons in sentence and paragraph context
　comparisons to establish perspective
Words from content areas
　science
　mathematics
　social studies
　language arts
　health

Developing Language Skills
Using spelling words
　sentence completion
　paragraph completion

Open-ended writing activities
  story writing
  sentence completion
  invitation writing
  riddle completion
  rhyme completion
  puzzle completion

Dictionary Skills
Alphabetizing
Using entry words
Dictionary pronunciation
Locating and using word meanings
Syllabication
Comparative dictionary study

Writing Conventions
Improving handwriting skills
Capitalization
Punctuation
Abbreviation

Etymology
Origin and meaning of word parts
Old English derivations
Latin, Spanish, Mexican Indian, French, Greek and Arabic derivations

LEVEL 6

LEVEL 6 exposes students to an increasing number of words and guides them in applying their knowledge of common root word patterns and spelling generalizations. The students explore the spelling system and basic morphemic principles, learn to make important generalizations about word-building and to become proficient in adding prefixes and suffixes to any root word which they have learned to spell. Their exploration of the use of language includes examination of a haiku poem.

Phoneme-Grapheme Correspondence
Consonants
  initial and final consonant sounds
  initial, medial and final consonant cluster sounds
  /k/ spelled c, k, or ck
  /j/ spelled g
  /s/ spelled c, s, ss, or sc
  consonant digraphs /ch/, /sh/, /th/, /TH/
  digraph endings /shan/, spelled tion, /chər/ spelled ture
  variant spellings
  /n/ spelled kn   /m/ spelled mb

/r/ spelled *wr*   /s/ spelled *st*
/z/ spelled *s*   /g/ spelled *gh*
Vowels
  short vowel sounds
  long vowel sounds
  /ā/ patterns *a*-consonant-*e, ai, ay*
  /ē/ patterns *e, ee, ea*
  /ī/ patterns *i*-consonant-*e, ie, i*
  /ō/ patterns *o*-consonant-*e, oa, ow, o*
  /ū/ patterns *u*-consonant-*e, u*
  /ər/ spelled *er, ar, or*
  vowel digraphs
  vowel sounds *oo* represents: /u/, /u/
  vowel sounds *y* represents
  vowel diphthongs /ou/, /oi/
  variant spellings
  /i/ spelled *e, o*
  /u/ spelled *o*
  /ā/ spelled *au, ey, eigh*
  /ē/ spelled *eo, oe, ie, ey*
  /ī/ spelled *is, igh*

Word Building Skills
Word patterns
  rhyming patterns
Compound words
Root words
  identifying root words
  determining the effect of prefixes and suffixes on root words
Plurals
  forming plurals
    by changing the root word
    by adding *-s* or *-es*
    by changing *y* to *i* and adding *-es*
Prefixes
  identifying prefixes: *en-, un-, dis-, re-*
  adding prefixes to root words
  meanings of prefixes
Suffixes
  identifying suffixes: *-ward, -ure, -ation, -ion, -al, -able, -ive*
  meanings of suffixes
  plural-forming (*-s, -es*)
  tense-changing (*ed, -ing*)
  noun-forming (*-er, -dom, -ist, -ness, -ment*)
  adjective-forming (*-ous, -ful, -less*)
  adverb-forming (*-y, -ly*)
  comparative (*-er, -est*)

for number words (-*ty*, -*th*)
adding suffixes to root words
generalizations for adding suffixes
  doubling the final consonant
  dropping the final *e*
  changing *y* to *i*
  root word unchanged
Syllabication
  identifying syllables
  adding syllables
  dividing words into syllables
  accented syllables
  generalizations for syllabication
Phonemes, graphemes and morphemes
  identifying
  defining
  usage in pronunciation and spelling patterns
  use of the linguistic symbol / /
Contractions
  writing contractions
  meanings of contractions

Word Meaning

Antonyms
  using prefixes to form antonyms
Homonyms
Homographs
Synonyms
Classification of words into groups
Expressing relationships
  using analogies
  casual relationships
Determining word meanings
  using synonyms
  classifying words
  root words
  using sentence definitions
  using contextual analysis
Contrasting word pairs
  direct opposites
  idea contrasts
Comparisons
  through classification
  using similes
  to describe items
  using synonyms

Multiple meanings of words
  denotation and connotation
Words from content areas
  mathematics
  social studies
  language arts
  health

Developing Language Skills
Using spelling words
  sentence completion
  paragraph completion
Open-ended writing activities
  story completion
  sentence completion
  Haiku
  puzzle completion
  rhyme completion
Understanding proverbs, idioms, clichés
Parts of speech
  nouns
  verbs and verb tenses
  adjectives
  adverbs

Dictionary Skills
Alphabetizing
Cross reference
Determining stress or accent
Dictionary respellings
Entry words (double entries)
Locating and using word meanings
Syllabication
Comparative dictionary study

Writing Conventions
Writing number words
Hyphenation
Capitalization
Punctuation
Handwriting
  cursive letter forms

Etymology
Old English derivations
Middle English derivations
Latin, Greek, Old French and Scandinavian derivations

LEVEL 7

LEVEL 7 provides the students with interesting subjects for creative writing and encourages them to use newly learned words in their compositions. The students examine language more closely by looking into word origins and varying forms of written communication. They learn to derive adjectives, adverbs, nouns, verb, and negatives from root words. Students are helped to discover and apply basic morphemic principles, the key to word-building and vocabulary development.

Phoneme-Grapheme Correspondence
Consonants and vowels

/f/ spelled f and ph	/r/ spelled r and wr
/kw/ spelled qu	/r/ spelled k and c
/n/ spelled n and kn	/j/ spelled j, g, dge and ge
/ik/ spelled ic	/ij/ spelled age
/ər/ spelled er, or, ar	/s/ spelled ce

Word Building Skills
Understanding morphology; building words from morphemes
    terms: morphemes (bound and free), roots, prefixes, suffixes
    analyzing word structure
Word patterns
    -VCE, -Ce, -CVC, -VVC, -Vy, -Cy
Suffixes
    identifying and writing suffixes
    inflectional
    derivational
      verb-forming (-en, -ize, -ate)
      adjective forming (-ful, -less, -y, -al, -igh, -ous, -ive)
      adverb-forming (-ly, -ward)
      noun-forming (-ment, -ness, -ity, -ion)
    generalizations for adding suffixes
      doubling the final consonant
      dropping the final e
      changing y to i
      root word unchanged
      words ending with ic
      words ending with ce
      words ending with /ər/
Prefixes
    negative (un-, dis-, in-)
    verb-forming (en-)
    forming words with prefixes
      (ad-, com-, de-, in-, inter-, out-, over-, pre-, per-, pro-, re-, sub-, un-, under-)
Root words
    identifying root word patterns
      -VCC, -Ce, -Cy, -VVC, -Vy, -CVC

forming derivatives by adding suffixes
adding suffixes to polysyllabic words
   stressed and unstressed final syllables
Compound words
  forming fused, unjoined and hyphenated compound words
  checking compound forms in the dictionary
Syllabication
  identifying monosyllabic words
  dividing polysyllabic words
  using the dictionary as a guide
  implications for spelling

Word Meanings

Determining word meaning from word structure (morphemes)
Determining word relationships
  through context clues
  using synonyms
  using homophones
  using analogies
  using antonyms
  using sequence to determine degree of difference
Comparisons and contrasts
  using comparisons to be specific
  using synonyms for precise expression
  using antonyms for precise contrasts
  using negatives
  word analogies contrasting word meaning
Understanding figurative and literal meanings
Understanding idiomatic expressions and phrases
Malapropisms

Developing Language Skills

Using spelling words
  sentence completion
  story completion
  riddle completion
  puzzle completion
Creative writing activities
  essay
  story
  limerick
  pun
  riddle
Developing composition skills
  knowledge of subject matter
  organizing events and details
  proofreading and rewriting

Dictionary Skills
Alphabetizing
Entry words
Dictionary spellings
Dictionary pronunciations
Finding meanings and derivatives
Locating synonyms and antonyms

Writing Conventions
Proofreading
Paragraphing
  narratives with conversation
Punctuation
Handwriting
  improving handwriting skills
  practicing letter forms

Etymology
Understanding etymological symbols and entries
Historical alphabet comparisons
  Runic alphabet
  pictograph writing
  cuneiform writing
Understanding word development
Word families
Doublets
Old and Middle English derivations
American Indian, French, Greek and Latin derivations

LEVEL 8

LEVEL 8 continues to provide meaningful and natural contexts in which students can effectively use spelling words, review and survey words, and challenge words. Students also learn English words derived from Greek, Latin, and French and examine elements that influenced the development of our language. They continue to study the derivation of adverbs, adjectives, nouns, verbs, and negatives. Practical application of words from other content areas is maintained.

Phoneme-Grapheme Correspondence
Consonants
  /s/ spelled ce
  /j/ spelled *dge, ge*
  double consonants and stressed syllables
    affected by short vowel sound
    affected by long vowel sound
  words ending in consonant + *le*

Vowels
/i/, /e/, /ə/ spelled *ie*
/ā/ spelled *ei*
w an ending vowel letter
Variant spellings in words of Greek origin
/f/ spelled *ph*
/r/ spelled *rh*
/s/ spelled *ps*
/i/, /ī/ spelled *y*

Word Building Skills
Word Patterns
-VCC, -Ce, -CVC, -CV, -VVC, -Cy, -Vy, -CVV
Suffixes
identifying and writing
inflectional
plural-forming (*-s, -es*)
verb-forming (*-ing, -ed, -s*)
derivational
verb-forming (*-en, -ize, -ate*)
adjective-forming (*-ous, -ible, -able, -ful, -less, -y, -ive*)
adverb-forming (*-ly, -ally*)
noun-forming (*-us, -ism, -ist, -ity, -ion, -ness, -ment*)
pronunciation-changing
changing in vowel and consonant sounds
shifts in syllable stress
generalizations for adding suffixes
doubling the final consonant
dropping the final *e*
changing *y* to *i*
root word unchanged
words ending with consonant + e
words ending with /ər/
words ending with /əs/
words ending with /əbəl/
adding *-able* to free roots
adding *-ible* to bound roots
words ending with /ənt/, /əns/
words ending with /iz/
words ending with /ər/, /ē/
Prefixes
negative prefixes *un-, mis-, non-, anti-, dis-, in-*
forms of prefix *in-: il-, im-, ir-*
Root words
identifying free and bound roots
adding suffixes to free and bound roots

identify common root word patterns
  -VCC, -Ce, -Cy, -CV, -VVC, -Vy, -CVC, -CVV
adding suffixes to common root word patterns
  forming derivatives
  -CVC monosyllabic words
  words with vowel endings
    roots ending in *o*
    roots ending in vowel plus *w*
  polysyllabic words, stressed and unstressed final syllables
derivations of root words
Compound words
  fused, hyphenated and unjoined compound words
  compound word families
  variant spellings
Syllabication
  polysyllabic words
  words with affixes
Building morphemic analogies, analogous comparison of word structure

Word Meaning
Determining meaning from word structure
  morphemes: roots, suffixes, prefixes
Homophones
Homographs
Synonyms
Antonyms
Comparisons and contrasts
Allomorphs
Assimilation
Word analogies
Malapropisms
Words from content areas
  science
  mathematics
  business
  social studies
  literature
  health
  language study

Developing Language Skills
Using spelling words
  sentence completion
  story completion
  riddle completion
  puzzle completion

Creative writing activities
  essay
  story
  legend/myth
  fable
  limerick
  riddle
Investigating literature
  American Indian tales
  Greek adventure
  Latin epic
  Old English narrative poem
  French legend

Dictionary Skills
Alphabetizing
Dictionary spellings
Dictionary pronunciations
Findings meanings, derivatives
Locating plural forms
Locating antonyms and synonyms

Writing Conventions
Capitalization
Proofreading
Handwriting
  improving handwriting skills
  practicing letter forms

Etymology
Old and Middle English derivations
  changes in spelling and pronunciation
American Indian, French, Italian, Greek and Latin derivations
Borrowed words
  from American Indian, Dutch and Spanish influence

HANDWRITING SCOPE AND SEQUENCE

PRE WRITING

Kind of Writing
Readiness for Manuscript.
Basic strokes for manuscript.
Jeff and Joy introduced.
Left-to-right progression, encouraging free and easy motion.

Handwriting Scope and Sequence from Zaner-Bloser, Inc. © 1975. Reprinted with permission of the publisher, Zaner-Bloser, Inc., Columbus, Ohio.

Vertical and slant lines introduced. New concepts of horizontal and vertical. Counterclockwise circles introduced. Further practice in placing objects, made from the basic strokes, on a baseline.

Basic Habits
Establish correct habits of body, arms, hands, crayon, and paper position for paper work; teach how to hold the chalk and how to stand for chalkboard writing

Paper Rulings
Unruled newsprint and paper with two-inch ruling.

Writing Tools
Large-in-diameter crayons for paper and large-in-diameter chalk for chalkboard.

Elements of Legibility
Left-to-right, and top-down directions; slant lines from top-down; clockwise and counterclockwise circles.

Letter Forms
To illustrate how letters are formed by putting together the basic strokes already learned. Children should be taught to visualize the letter as a whole and then to see the component parts of the letter. Complete alphabet shown on last page of Recorder.

Rhythm-Fluency
A free, full-arm movement when doing shapes and forms.

Applies Uses
To draw familiar objects using the basic strokes of manuscript writing.

Refinement Skills
Effective practice depends upon how well the needs are understood. Without a clear visual concept of what is to be practiced, much time can be uselessly spent. It is important that a child see a correct picture of the element to be studied, be able to recall what he has seen, and retain that visual concept.

Evaluation
Visualization of forms in Recorders and pupil evaluation of results in terms of these forms.

GRADE 1

Kind of Writing
Manuscript writing introduced and developed.
All of the capital and lower-case letters of the manuscript alphabet are introduced and developed. The letters are made up of simple and easily made strokes such as horizontal lines, vertical lines, slant lines, circles, and parts of circles.

Basic Habits

Reteach basic habits as outlined in Teacher's Edition to establish habits that will contribute to ease and legibility of writing, and healthful posture.

Paper Rulings

Progress from unruled newsprint to paper with 2-inch ruling, then to two spaces of 1-inch ruling, and finally to 1-inch with a guide line at mid-space.

Writing Tools

Large crayon for preliminary practice. Introduced primary pencil with a large, coarse lead.

Elements of Legibility

Reinforce basic directions for lines and circles emphasizing firm vertical and slant lines and roundness of circles and parts of circles. All letters of the alphabet are presented with attention to spacing between letters, between words, and between sentences.

Letter Forms

Lower-case, manuscript letters presented three times: individually for form; again in pairs or groups to study like and unlike parts; then in larger groups for similarities in shape and basic strokes.

All upper-case manuscript letters are presented twice. Numerals are presented three times for study and reinforcement.

Rhythm-Fluency

Full-arm movement for ease of writing and fluency.

Applied Uses

Words, sentences, short paragraphs, poetry arrangement, and short courtesy notes are presented.

Refinement Skills

Margins, paragraph arrangement.

Evaluation

Visualization of correct forms in Recorders; daily evaluation with these forms to develop an awareness of errors or irregularities in the practice efforts; comparison with pupils' own earlier recordings to note improvement; measurement of the quality by the Evaluation Scale for Grade 1. There are three Countdown pages for testing the degree of learning of the elements of legible handwriting.

GRADE 2

Kind of Writing

Manuscript writing mastered. Cursive handwriting introduced in last half of year unless this step is made in Grade 3.

Basic Habits
Special attention to the maintenance and reinforcement of the correct habits of position for both right and left handers.

Paper Rulings
Unruled newsprint for developing the kinesthetic and motor images, then two spaces of 1-inch ruled paper for preliminary practice followed by ¾-inch ruled paper with a mid-line for size relationship.

Writing Tools
Same as in Grade 1.

Elements of Legibility
Firm strokes; verticality of the writing; roundness of circles and parts of circles; spacing between letters, between words and between sentences.
Mastery of the manuscript alphabet for ease and fluency in independent writing.

Letter Forms
Upper- and lower-case letters are presented for restudy in groups according to similarity of basic forms. Most of the letters are emphasized a second time for reinforcement. Numerals are presented twice for review and reinforcement.

Rhythm-Fluency
Use jingles that emphasize fluency and rhythm as in Grade One.

Applied Uses
As in Grade 1, plus uses, for punctuation, book reviews, letter writing, addressing envelopes, writing titles, writing abbreviations, and math problems.

Refinement Skills
Neatness, pleasing arrangement of work on the page, margins, paragraph indentations and poetry arrangement. Extended activities and creative expression are encouraged to develop independence in the use of manuscript writing.

Evaluation
As in Grade 1.
Use Evaluation Scale for Grade 2.

TRANSITION—GRADE 2 AND 3

Kind of Writing
Readiness for cursive.
Introductory steps to cursive handwriting.
Manuscript writing retained for day-by-day uses until the individual child feels secure in the use of cursive.

Basic Habits
Reinforce correct working habits.
Note that paper position changes for cursive writing. See Teacher's Edition.
Position
1. Body, Arms, and Hands.
2. Holding the Crayon, Pencil, and Pen.
3. Paper Position for Right-handed Writers.
4. Paper Position for Left-handed Writers.

Paper Rulings
Unruled newsprint for early steps to establish paper position and concept of
slant. Use 1-inch ruled paper, then ¾-inch ruled paper with guide line.

Writing Tools
Same as in Grades 1 and 2.

Elements of Legibility
Slant of cursive writing; lower-case letters in groups according to beginning
strokes; connecting strokes; ease and fluency; and spacing between letters,
words and sentences.

Letter Forms
Cursive form of all lower-case letters. Upper-case letters introduced by similarity of shapes.

Rhythm-Fluency
The rhythmic pattern of each letter is emphasized when presented to establish
the correct form and to develop fluency. Large-size writing encourages a
freer use of the hand and arm in writing.

Applied Uses
Same as for Grades 1 and 2.

Refinement Skills
Applied uses for cursive
All of the elements of good handwriting re-emphasized and taught.

Evaluation
Continue as in Grade 1. Use the Evaluation Scale for Grade 2 Cursive or Grade
3 Cursive—whichever applies. Use Scale for Manuscript Writing for Grade 2
or 3 as a check on the mastery of manuscript to determine readiness for beginning cursive.

GRADE 3

Kind of Writing
All of the steps of cursive handwriting are carefully reviewed and further developed.

Basic Habits
Special attention and checkup to correct faulty habits of position for good results.

Paper Rulings
Continue as for readiness for cursive writing, use two spaces of 1-inch ruled paper to study form and rhythmic pattern in preliminary practice, then to ½-inch ruling, with guide line, for application.

Writing Tools
Primary ballpoint pen or standard-size lead pencil when paper ruling is reduced to ½-inch with the guide line at the ¼-inch mark.

Elements of Legibility
Form and rhythm of all letters of the alphabet; uniform slant and how to get it; minimum letters one-half the size of maximum letters; beginning and ending strokes of all letters; joinings of letters in word writing; and spacing of letters, words, and sentences.

Letter Forms
All lower-case cursive letters presented in three ways: first, by similarity of ending strokes; then with each one's upper-case counterpart; and finally in groups by similarities in form. Upper-case letters presented with their lower-case counterparts.
Numerals receive emphasis twice for reinforcement.

Rhythm-Fluency
Concept of rhythmic patterns if restudied for correct letter forms and fluency. Correct body, arm hand, pen, and paper positions are emphasized as an aid to fluency.

Applied Uses
Basic elements of cursive handwriting presented for use in life situation.

Refinement Skills
As for Grade 2 but as they apply to cursive writing. Proofreading is recommended after writing creatively to correct any errors pertaining to legibility as well as good expression.

Evaluation
Use Evaluation Scale for Grade 3 Cursive.
Check frequently to be sure that no one is practicing an error and to determine who needs more practice, and on what specific point.

GRADE 4

Kind of Writing
Grades 4 through 8 — Refine the cursive style; review and keep manuscript for special needs.

Basic Habits
Body, Arms, and Hands.
Sit well back in the chair so that the hips touch the back of the chair. Face the
    desk squarely.
The chair should be of comfortable height so that the feet rest on the floor.
Incline the body forward, bending from the hips so that both forearms rest on
    the desk. and are at an equal distance from the body.

Paper Rulings
For preliminary practice to study and establish form and rhythm use three-
    quarter inch ruled paper. For final practice and application use three-eighths
    inch ruling with a guide line for size relationship.

Writing Tools
A good ballpoint pen or standard lead pencil.

Elements of Legibility
Reinforce the form and rhythmic pattern of each letter of the alphabet; con-
    tinue size relationship as for Grade 3; good spacing for ease of reading; and
    connecting strokes together with a restudy of beginning and ending strokes.

Letter Forms
All lower-case letters emphasized twice: first, in groups by general characteris-
    tics with attention to rhythmic pattern form, size, slant, and spacing; then for
    reinforcement of form, size, slant, and joinings to other letters in word.
Upper-case letters presented once with emphasis on form, rhythmic pattern,
    and slant.
Numerals are given attention for use in two ways.
Manuscript writing reviewed in three suggested uses for it.

Rhythm-Fluency
As for Grade 3. An average rate of writing for this grade is about 50 letters per
    minute.

Applied Uses
Studied improvement of page arrangement as in previous grades plus arrange-
    ment of an outline.

Refinement Skills
Continue as in Grade 3.

Evaluation
Check practice results often by having children place their work under the
    master samples to see if they are achieving a good letter form. Encourage
    verbalization so that there is understanding of what is wrong and where
    there needs to be correction.

GRADE 5

Kind of Writing
Reinforcement of cursive handwriting. Review of Manuscript forms.

Basic Habits

Holding the crayon, pencil and pen—The writing instrument is held between the thumb and first two fingers about an inch above the point. The first finger rests on the top of the crayon, pencil or pen. The end of the thumb is placed against the writing instrument to hold it high in the hand and near the large knuckle.

Paper Rulings

Use 3/8-inch ruled paper. Introduce "adult" proportion of letters. Use two spaces of the paper for preliminary practice on form, and rhythm.

Writing Tools

Same as for Grade 4.

Elements of Legibility

Same as for Grade 4. Change to "adult" size relationship. Include study of line quality and alignment.

Letter Forms

All letters, both upper- and lower-case reinforced at least once in content related to the many uses for handwriting at this level. Manuscript forms are reviewed with emphasis on size adjustment to fit uses for it.

Numerals are reviewed twice.

Rhythm-Fluency

Same as in Grade 3.

An average rate for this grade is about 60 letters per minute.

Applied Uses

Continue letter analysis, arrangement, proportion, and use for school assignments.

Refinement Skills

Each pupil will list, in the recording area of his Recorder, the "faults" or elements of legible handwriting which he will want to correct this year. The recording will be a point of reference as the year's work progresses.

Evaluation

As for previous grades. Use Evaluation Scale for Grade 5.

GRADE 6

Kind of Writing

Re-emphasis and mastery of cursive handwriting.

Manuscript reinforced for special needs.

Basic Habits

Continue working for correct habits of position.

Paper rulings

Use 3/8-inch ruled paper as for Grade 5.

Writing Tools

Same as for Grade 4.

Elements of Legibility
Emphasize all elements of legibility to round out the legibility of each pupil's writing.

Letter Forms
All lower-case letters receive restudy at least once. Upper-case letters are presented three times for study and practice.
· Manuscript writing is reviewed with emphasis on size adjustment to fit uses for it.
Numerals receive re-emphasis twice.

Rhythm-Fluency
Same as in Grades 3, 4, and 5. Fluency is given special attention. Average rate for this grade is about 65 to 70 letters per minute.

Applied Uses
Cursive handwriting that is uniform in slant, size, spacing, that may be easily read.

Refinement Skills
Same as for Grade 5.

Evaluation
Use Evaluation Scale for Grade 6. Use of the Diagnostic Ruler is helpful to check the forms of the numerals. The practice papers may also be folded at the line above the writing to be checked, placed underneath the models in the book, and compared.

GRADE 7

Kind of Writing
Mastery and refinement of cursive handwriting.
Manuscript reviewed for special uses.

Basic Habits
Same as for Grades 4, 5, and 6.

Paper Rulings
The same 3/8-inch ruled paper as in Grade 6.
Refine concept of "adult" proportion. Continue as in Grades 5 and 6 for practice policies.

Writing Tools
Same as for Grade 4.

Elements of Legibility
Same as for Grades 5 and 6.

Letter Forms
All lower-case letters are restudied in four groupings; upper-case letters are reinforced at least once; numerals are restudied in two presentations; manuscript writing is reviewed in two different situations where that form of writing is recommended.

Rhythm-Fluency
Same as in previous grades. Average rate is about 70-75 letters per minute.

Applied Uses
To help students stimulate a discussion on the merits of legible handwriting before having the paragraph written on practice paper.

Refinement Skills
Same as in previous grades plus practice in writing on unruled paper with pleasing results.

Evaluation
Use Evaluation Scale for Grade 7.

GRADE 8

Kind of Writing
Additional refinement of cursive handwriting.
Refinement of manuscript writing for special uses.

Basic Habits
Good posture, paper correctly placed on desk. Good arm and hand position.

Paper Rulings
Use 3/8-inch ruled paper.
Same as for Grade 7.

Writing Tools
Same as for Grade 4.

Elements of Legibility
Same as for Grades 5 and 6.

Letter Forms
All lower-case letters are restudied in two ways: once in groups according to similar beginning strokes; and then in groups by similar ending strokes.
Upper-case letters are restudied in groups by similarities in form.
Numerals are restudied twice; manuscript is reviewed twice.

Rhythm-Fluency
Same as in previous grades with extra attention to fluency to develop a rate of from 75 to 80 letters per minute, commensurate with needs for writing in High School and beyond.

Applied Uses
To refine all handwriting activities and perfect them.

Refinement Skills
Same as in previous grades plus practice in writing on unruled paper, and adjusting size of writing to the varying spaces in which it may need to be done.

Evaluation
Use Evaluation Scale for Grade 8.

Index